# FIVE DECADES OF PLANNING AND TRIBAL DEVELOPMENT

# FIVE DECADES OF PLANNING AND TRIBAL DEVELOPMENT

## Jharkhand and Uttaranchal

Dr. M. Shakeel Ahmad

GYAN

GYAN PUBLISHING HOUSE

NEW DELHI-110002

Five Decades of Planning and Tribal Development
*(Tribal Studies)*

Rs. 590

ISBN: 81-212-0840-8



Published in 2004 in India by
Gyan Publishing House
5, Ansari Road, Darya Ganj, New Delhi-110002
Phones : 23282060, 23261060, Fax : (011) 23285914
E-mail : gyanbook@vsnl.com
Website : http://www.gyanbooks.com

*Laser Typesetting at* : Shree Vaishnavi Creations, Delhi
*Printed at* : Mehra Offset Press, Delhi

# Contents

# List of Tables

## Table 1 to 8 - Uttaranchal

# List of Tables

## Table 1 to 8 - Jharkhand



# List of Maps

# Foreword

The term "Development" is a loose one, and seeks to reconcilc the economic, political and social aspects, which can, at times, be mutually exclusive. It is an arrangement by which economic, social and political power is redistributed and readjusted.

While economc growth and social justice appear at times to be mutually exclusive, the former is increasingly becoming a sine-qua-non for the letter. After all, how can we distribute poverty?

After five decades of planned development, the Scheduled Tribes, who constitute 8.08 per cent of the country's population, still remain 'under-served.' The human development indices of the Scheduled Tribes are still at a much lower level as compared to the general population.

Our planned development is an ongoing process, requiring constant attention adn motivation on both sides, and accepatability of the programmes. There is no optimum limit of development. Tribal development will be a reality if the desire for change is felt as the need of the entire community, by the community.

In this scenario, a critical analysis of the arious programmes and schemes implemented so far for the welfare and development of the Scheduled Tribes assumes greater relevance. It is necessary to understand how far these programmes have reached the grassroot levels. Very few attempts have been made in this direction and research projects often tend to ignore ground realities. The book authored by Dr. M. shakeel Ahmad, a 'practitioner' with experience in the field as well as being the 'nodal' officer for

Schedued Tribe welfare at the national level is, therefore, a welcome addition. This in depth research and study of various aspects of tribal development in the States of Jharkahnd and Uttaranchal would certainly be of immense help for the policy makers and the implementation machinery at the district level. The suggestions and recommendations given at the end would be of utmost help in ensuring timely corrective action for some of the schemes.

With the Tenth Five Year Plan in operation, it would be possible to accomplish an all round development of the Scheduled Tribes, with inputs both from the government and non-governmental organizations, as the approach to empowerment has to be holistic in nature. The period is one of transition, where dependence on the State has to be gradually reduced.

**Dr. B. S. Baswan**

# Preface

The Imperial Gazetteer of India, 1911 defines a Tribe as a "Collection of families bearing a common name, speaking a common dialect, occupying or professing to occupy a common territory and is not usually endogamous though originally it might have been so". Prof. D.N. Majumdar has defined a tribe as "a collection of families or group of families bearing a common name, members of which occupy the same territories, speak the same language and observe certain taboos regarding marriage, profession or occupation and have developed a well-assessed system of reciprocity and mutuality of obligations".

India is one of the few nations of the world with a thriving tribal population in different parts of the country. There are at present, 582 Tribal Communities spread all over India. About 82 per cent of the Scheduled Tribes population is concentrated in Central and Western parts of the country, whereas 11 per cent is dispresed in various parts of Southern India and the rest in the North-Eastern parts and the Islands.

The lists of Scheduled Tribes were notified, for the first time, under the Constitution (Scheduled Tribes) order, 1950. This list has been modified, amended or supplemented from time to time. For example, in Uttar Pradesh, the Scheduled Tribes were notified for the first time in 1967 vide the Constitution (Scheduled Tribes) (Uttar Pradesh) order, 1967.

The statutory lists of Scheduled Tribes for States and Union Territory's are notified in pursuance of Article 342 of the Constitution. Scheduled Tribes may belong to any religion unlike Scheduled Castes who can only be Hindu, Sikh or Buddhist.

The tribal people generally live in forest areas, though with the spread of education many now live in towns and cities as well, with less powerful tribes being forced to occupy the farthest hills like the Paharias, the Birhors, the Jarawas, the Buxas, the Chenchus and other primitive tribes which now number seventy five. Each tribe has its own system of coping with the problems relating to their environment, customs and practices.

On a cursory glance, the tribal society appears to be primitive and not worthy of a sustained study. Previous studies have concentrated on sociological aspects and on tribal cultures and traditions. But a closer look will reveal that the tribal society is environment friendly, self-sustaining and not a wasteful one. Their lifestyle is attuned to their environment and the economy is essentially forest based with dependence on terrace cultivation and collection of minor forest produce.

Gunnar Myrdal, the celebrated Swedish economist has stated that economic development depends on two factors, attitudinal change and institutional change. An awareness about their rights, their duties and responsibilities and their involvement in the process of development has to be created through the tribal elders and the Gram Sabhas. New leadership among the tribals has been slowly emerging due to better educational facilities. Since independence, efforts have been made through five year plans to bring about qualitative changes in tribal life.

Pandit Jawaharlal Nehru, the first Prime Minister of India wrote on 9th October 1958 a foreword to Dr. Verrier Elwin's book 'A Philosophy for NEFA', where he outlined the Government of India's approach to tribal development. He said, "We cannot allow matters to drift in tribal areas or just not take interest in them in the world of today; that is not possible or desirable. At the same time, we should avoid over-administering these areas and in particular send too many outsiders into tribal territory. It is between these two extreme positions that we have to function. Development has to be ensured in various areas, such as communications, medical facilities, education and better agriculture."

After five decades of planned development, the Scheduled Tribes still remain under developed. The human development indices of the ST population are still at a much lower level as compared to the general population of the country. Fast and accelerated developmental efforts are required in a more holistic manner if our tribal population has to compete in this era of liberalisation and globalisation.

The working group's report for the Ninth Five Year Plan (1997-2002) made the significant observation that the "Tribals continue to form the poorest, most backward and most vulnerable section of Indian society despite all developmental strategies, programmes and schemes including Tribal Sub-Plan strategy. As globalisation and liberalisation usher in fierce economic competition, only the fittest can survive and the weakest, particularly the tribals, may be driven to the wall unless protective measures are taken for safeguarding the tribals from the onslaught and urgent steps are taken to develop their skill and competitive ability."

There is very little data on tribal households and their quality of life, based on human development aspects. The National Council of Applied Economic Research (NCAER) had conducted a nation-wide sample survey in 1994 of over 33,000 rural households spread over 1,765 villages in 195 districts of 16 States with the sample size of tribal people being 4,220. It showed that 92.6 per cent of tribals lived in rural areas but urbanisation of tribals had increased from 2.7 per cent in 1961 to 7.4 in 1991, due to spread of education and diversification of occupations.

In this backdrop, a critical analysis of the various welfare and development programmes implemented so far vis-à-vis their reach to the grass root level, using the policy research as a tool for analyzing various social and economic issues affecting the STs, assumes importance. Efforts made in this direction are few and far between. This study is a small step in that direction.

**Dr. M. S. Ahmad**

# Acknowledgements

This study would not have been possible without the encouragement and support of the Ministry of Tribal Affairs who very graciously sanctioned me study leave and the pobublication grant. The Director, Indian Institute of Public Adminstration, New Delhi very kindly allowed me to do research work at the Institute and Dr. R.K. Barik of the I.I.P.A. was designated as the guide of this study. My sincere thanks are due to them. The Director, Lal Bahadur Shastri National Academy of Administration (LBSNAA), and Executive Director, National Institute of Administrative Research (NIAR), Mussoorie provided me an opportunity for field study in the Jaunsar-Bawar area and other tribal pockets of Dehradun district in Uttaranchal. Prof. H.C. Pokhriyal, Senior Consultant, NIAR, Mussoorie was of immense help in finalising the Research Methodology while Mr. R.K. Bharadwaj, Research Associate, NIAR helped in the analysis of the filled up questionnaires of the field study.

In the field study in Jharkhand, Shri P. C. Oraon Director, Tribal Research Institute, Ranchi provided all assistance. I am thankful to him and his staff.

Finally, the full support of my wife, Yasmin was a big contributing factor in te successful completion of the study. My daughters Hena and Saba cheerfully took up the task of typing the draft of the present book.

I am thankful to them and appreciate their active cooperation in this endeavour.

**Dr. M. S. Ahmad**

# Introduction

Tribal population constitutes a sizeable proportion (8.08 percent) of the country's total population, but they have not been able to derive benefits from the national development programs proportionate to their numbers. The first plan document (1951) elaborated this concern and observed that "the conditions are now generally such that there has to be a positive policy of assisting the tribal people to develop their natural resources and to evolve a productive economic life wherein they will enjoy the fruits of their labor and will not be exploited by more organized forces from outside". In the light of these observations, a number of Government sponsored programs were initiated to ameliorate the status and standard of living of the tribal population. Greater thrust came in the fifth five-year plan when the Government adopted the tribal sub-plan strategy. But even after five decades of planned development, there is a general feeling that the benefits of such programs have not reached the targeted group in a substantial way.

## Need and Scope of the Study

Since the beginning of the planned development, a number of well meaning programs have been taken up by the State, yet we have been experiencing restlessness in the tribal regions of the country. Many of these agitations have found expression in violence. There is a growing feeling among the tribal population that they have been drained of their natural resources and outnumbered by outsiders in their own land. The common legal and business laws have further alienated them and have resulted in the decline of their traditional socio-economic institutions. The alienation and agitations are, however more on the ground that economic benefit has not accrued to them in the same way as it has been in the case of non-tribal regions which dominate the socio-politico-economic life of the country.

It therefore, becomes important to examine the design and implementation process of the government sponsored programs with special reference to the benefits that have accrued to the tribal population. The suitability and scope of participation of tribal population must also be examined closely. Presently, the Government at the Central level are running through the State governments, the following schemes/programs for the development of the Scheduled Tribes:-

1. Special Central Assistance to tribal Sub-plan;
2. Grants under first proviso to Article 275(1) of the Constitution;
3. Residential schools including Ashram Schools;
4. Girls Hostels;
5. Boys Hostels;
6. Vocational Training programs;
7. Educational Complexes in Low Literacy Pockets;
8. Grant-in-aid to State Tribal Development Cooperative Corporation and others for Minor Forest Produce operations;
9. Price Support to Operations of Tribal Cooperative Marketing Development Federation of India Ltd. (TRIFED);
10. Investment in share capital of TRIFED;
11. Village Grain Bank Scheme;
12. Grants-in-aid to Voluntary Organizations working for the welfare of Scheduled Tribes;
13. Upgradation of Merit of Scheduled Tribe students;
14. Post Matric Scholarships;
15. Book Banks;
16. Overseas Scholarships;

17. Coaching and Allied Scheme for Scheduled Tribes
18. Research and Training;

**Objective of the Study**

The main purpose of present study is to examine the various Central and Centrally sponsored programs for the welfare and development of the tribal population of the country. Due to constraints of time, the study has been confined to the two newly created sates and the two important programs of tribal development viz. Special Central assistance under the Tribal Sub-plan and Grants under Article 275(1) of the Constitution.

The present study starts with the general examination of the government programs and it is followed by a detailed study of the program strategy, design, funding methods, implementation and monitoring procedures of the two important programmes, namely Special Central Assistance to tribal sub-plan and Grants under Article 275(1) of the constitution. The study tries to find out the suitability of these schemes/programs from the point of view of the development needs of the tribal region. It further assesses the socio-economic impact of these programs. On the basis of collected data and information, the study attempts to find out its impact and the rate of success.

**Over-view of Literature**

Very few studies have been done to find out the impact of development programs earlier and their scope has been limited and the problem of region has mainly been examined from the sociological point of view. The present study tries to place greater emphasis on the economic variables, such as the design of the programs, funding procedures, organizational structure, scope of people's participation and benefits accruing to the targeted groups.

Some of the important books relating to the study of the area and the tribal development programmes are briefly mentioned.

"Himalayan Polyandry" is a major anthropological study of Jaunsar-Bawar done by Dr. D.N. Majumdar, Professor of

Lucknow University and published in 1962. The study is Anthropology, a painstaking one, done over a long period of twenty two years, in which the author spent almost five years in the Jaunsar-Bawar area visiting every village. This study was done at the behest of the Programme Evaluation organization of the Planning Commission to evaluate the working of community development project in the Chakrata area which was taken up in the year 1954 and completed in three years. The book is in three parts. Part I of the book gives the past and present history as well the detailed geography of Jaunsar Bawar. It also gives the details of the castes, the Scheduled castes and the Scheduled tribes in Jaunsar Bawar. The cultural pattern, the administrative system and the Community Development Programmes have also been discussed. He mentions that the people of this area are polyandrous. Thereafter selection of villages for field study have been explained in detail. Part II discusses the social stratification and caste hierarchy, village organisation, occupations and economy, education and religion of the people of Jaunsar Bawar. Part III gives the impact of Community Development Programmes and the changes it has brought about.

"Hindus of the Himalayas" by Gerald D. Berreman (1972) is based on ethnographic research done in the late fifties by the author in and around Sirkanda, a village in the Dehradun district and located in the lower Himalayas. The book faithfully delineates the caste structure of the hills and describes the relatively isolated village, Sirkanda which consisted of 384 persons during the year 1957-58 when the research was conducted. The society as today was divided into the higher castes which consisted of Rajputs and Brahmins and the lower castes who were artisans and menials.

The author mentions the limitations of the study in his introduction but asserts that the village can serve as a useful focus for research as it is a manageable unit for ethnological research. Although no village is representative of rural India as a whole, any village properly understood represents in a general way, villages of a particular type and area. He quotes

Prof. S.C. Dube that "what we need today is a series of studies of village communities from different parts of the country covering the many divergent patterns of organization and ethos. Until this is done, our picture of social systems in rural India will remain vague and inadequate".

In the Epilogue, the author mentions his return to Sirkanda, a decade later when he found the caste hierarchy intact, the women still unlettered and there being little material change in the village.

A study was made by IAS probationers in the year 1973 as part of their village study programme in the blocks of Chakrata and Kalsi which forms the Jaunsar-Bawar region of Dehradun district. It was published in the spring 1975 issue of 'The Administrator', LBSNAA, Mussoorie.

This team of probationers was led by Shri S.C. Khairwal and it describes the scenario in Jaunsar Bawar as it existed in the early seventies. They found the area to be predominantly agricultural with animal husbandry as the second occupation. They found the Rajputs to be the land owning class and Koltas being agricultural labourers. The traditional village Panchayat was known as 'Khumri' which was dominated by the upper castes namely Brahmins and Rajputs. People were indifferent towards school education.

Another team of probationers visited Kalsi Block which together with Chakrata Block forms the Chakrata tehsil. Here also the predominant occupation was agriculture. The lower castes namely Koltas, Doms and Bajgis were found to be highly indebted. Polyandry was practised in general by all castes. Some Rajput families also indulged in polygamy.

The book 'Bonded for ever' by Nadeem Hasnain (1982) is about the life of the Koltas – a menial caste group living in abject poverty in the Jaunsar – Bawar area. They are still at the mercy of the landlords who exploit them and sometimes keep them in bondage. This book brings out in graphic detail the misery of the lives of the Koltas. The book is divided in two parts. The first part gives the introduction and the history of the area and the people. The second part discusses in detail the economic and social condition of the Koltas.

The author has highlighted the pitiable condition in which Koltas live, which in his words is a form of virtual slavery and semi-starvation. They are treated as untouchables in the region. Brahmins and Rajputs of the area, who are usually the landlords, belong to a different racial stock. Koltas and Doms are at the lower rung of the caste order and are poor and mostly landless. This book presents various facets of poverty among the Koltas in all its dimensions and is a valuable addition to the study of this impovrished caste who are also Scheduled tribes by virtue of their being residents of Jaunsar Bawar.

"Central Himalayan Panorama" edited by Shri S.K. Biswas (1993) is a collection of articles dealing with the issue of development in the hills. The studies of tribal life cast in an anthropological framework, bring out the problem of these people in facing the onslaught of the development programmes without polluting their distinctive modes of life. The book is in two volumes – the first volume deals with nature, people and legends while the second volume examines the various facets of development and ecology of the region. Its conclusion is that the general feature of hill life is marked by unscientific exploitation, wasteful competition and a struggle for growth.

There are also serious limitations in such an anthology. The chapters are disconnected and disjointed. The book presents the Central Himalayan Panorama and not a picture of life there in its entirety.

This book is a product of contributions from people of various disciplines – Economics, Sociology, Geology, Geography, Botany, Zoology, Agriculture, Horticulture, Engineering, Histroy, Mountaineering, Anthropology and Tourism etc. but is not a specialised study in any subject. However, it gives the reader many unknown facts of life in the hills.

"Economy of Uttaranchal" edited by P.C. Pandey and others (2001) is a collection of 31 papers categorized under three sections: Policy Planning, Resolution and

Development, Philosophy, Natural Resource Management and Human Resource Development. This collection throws open issues relevant for the new State. All these articles were contributed at a national seminar on "The economy of Uttarakhand in the context of an independent state organised by the Kumaon University, Nainital in March 1999.

The issues which are central to the proposed model of economic growth for the new state are the relationship between the public and the private sector and the enterpreneurial activity led development. It has also to learn lessons from the sweet and sour experiences of the fifty years of planning. The book also indicates the key sectors of economic growth. In the case of Uttaranchal, it is horticulture, tourism and social forestry. Watershed development is another important area as it is central to maintaining the basic needs of the people i.e. water, food, fodder and fuel in a particular catchment.

The report on "Integrated Area Development Plan" for Chakrata Block (1995) done by the Centre for Micro-Planning, LBSNAA, Mussoorie has been done with the objective to prepare an integrated area development plan for the Chakrata Block which is a backward area in the State of Uttaranchal.

Integrated Area Development Planning is a methodology for decentralized development. After the 73rd and 74th Amendments, the need for a participatory planning approach is self-evident. The concept of decentralized planning originates from the approach of participatory development.

For preparation of this report, a comprehensive village and household survey has been conducted in Chakrata Block which is a tribal block in Dehradun district.

On the basis of the survey, education, health and infrastructure sectors have been identified as the priority areas with various economic packages for participatory development and poverty eradication. Education is the core of the minimum needs programme and has to be taken up as a mass literacy campaign in Chakrata Block.

This plan basically incorporates the economic sector, the social sector specially education and health and the infrastructure sector and will be of use in future planning.

Dr. R. P. Dhyani's book 'A new approach to economic planning' for the rural poor of Uttaranchal (2001) is based on empirical knowledge. Dr. Dhyani is of the view that people are bypassed by market mechanism under conditions where they lack education, suffer from health problems and are faced with poverty. For this micro-level planning, model should be developed for the different geo-climatic regions of Uttaranchal. Bottom up planning should guide development plans.

This study has primarily focussed on the people of rural hills who consist of the greater part of the population of Uttaranchal. One of the features of this study is evolution of natural region wise methodology of economic planning for extension services of rural development.

A team of IAS probationers visited the districts of Ranchi, Giridih and Dumka in Jharkhand (Bihar) during 1989-90 and presented three case studies on tribal development and other issues relating to land and forests in the tribal areas. They took the help of the Household Schedule to collect the minimum basic information from all the households in the village and they mainly pertain to land-holding distribution, occupational and educational background and the composition of the households. The probationers also collected data relating to district profile and the village profile.

This report on 'Tribal and Forest Question in Bihar' issued by the Land Reform Unit of Lal Bahadur Shastri National Academy of Administration, Mussoorie analyses the macro studies on the tribal land and forest rights in Jharkhand followed by the micro-studies which are the case studies of the individual probationers.

'Tribal Society in India' by A.K. Pandey (1977) is a study which tries to investigate the problem of underdevelopment, the culture of powerlessness and poverty among tribals vis-à-vis the Indian Society. The author contends that kinship in a tribal society is inherently ideological in that it reproduces class and so perpetuates the established patterns of social inequality and social order of the contemporary tribal India.

Dr. A.K. Pandey's study of tribal society in India, drawing strength and insights from his understanding of tribes in India, in general, and of the Oraons in particular, raises issues that get reflected in a general survey of the tribal situation in India and the tribes in Bihar (now Jharkhand).

Jharkhand movement – ethinicity and culture of silence by Sajal Basu (1994) covers a wide range of issues relating to movement for a separate state of Jharkhand. It also covers other aspects of the region viz. people and the economy, myths, language and script, ethnicity, nationality etc. the book is a study of the gradual transformation of the movement into a broad based ethnic movement involving economic and cultural issues affecting the indigenous groups.

Development of Bihar and Jharkhand: Problems and Prospects (2001) edited by Sharat Kumar and Praveen Jha is a collection of contributions from some of the well known observers of Bihar's economy. The papers grouped under five thematic heads, explore the problems and prospects associated with the different areas and sectors of the economy. It calls for a new beginning in the light of the creation of a separate state of Jharkhand. The book contains chapters on forestry, tribal development, agricultural labour, land development and land reforms.

'Jharkhand movement-origin and evolution' by S.Narayan (ed. 1992) highlights the problems of the tribes of the area and presents an authentic picture of the ground reality as it existed in the Jharkhand region a decade earlier.

The District Gazetteer of Jharkhand by S.C. Bhatt (2002) gives us information about the districts of the new state, its mines and minerals, places of tourist interest and the development scenario. It gives accurate information about the history and geography of the area, agriculture, irrigation, Industries, Trade and Commerce etc.

The book by Victor Das entitled 'Jharkhand-Castle over

the Graves' and published by Inter-India Publications, New Delhi (1992) gives a backgroud of the Jharkhand movement.

Jharkhand, rightly referred to as 'the Rurh of India' produces almost all kinds of minerals and forest wealth is in abundance. This book was published when the movement for the creation of a separate state of Jharkhand had developed schisms and had divided itself into two unequal sections-the larger section led by redoubtable tribal leaders without any substantial programme and the smaller section which sought to motivate people to stand up by emphasising the basic anomaly of the situation-alienation of tribal lands, commercialisation of forests, the unscrupulous money lenders and the exploitation of tribal women.

The question which this book poses is: If Jharkhand materialises, who will benefit from it – the poor tribal caught between these two pincer like sections or the leaders of the larger section. Now when the State has been formed two years ago, the doubts of the author have come true in that it is the tribal leaders who have benefitted and not the poor tribals who still toil in their lands without irrigation and power and are being exploited on all sides.

**Research Methodology**

The two newly created states namely Uttaranchal and Jharkhand were taken up for field survey on the suggestion of the Director, Indian Institute of Public Administration, New Delhi as they represent historically and geographically the diverese tribal population of our country. While the Chakrata-Kalsi area of Dehradun district is remote and hilly, the Ormanjhi and Murhu Blocks lie in Chotanagpur Plateau and are closer to Ranchi, the capital of Jharkhand. Their study also gives an idea of the problems and failures of the tribal development administration as well as the noted successes wherever local tribal leaders have taken up the schemes for tribal development and made it familiar to their area of habitation as was found in Guttigarha village in Murhu Block.

Chakrata and Kalsi blocks forming the Jaunsar-Bawar area are predominantly tribal and the acccessibility to the block and its officers is one of the major constraints of its residents. The accessibility to transport facilities, schools, medical facilities and communication network are other major constraints for the people living in the area.

The reason for choosing the Jaunsar-Bawar area was that the ITDP for Chakrata-Kalsi was started in the Sixth Five year plan period and had been functioning till the end of the Ninth Five year plan. Another reason was that the Chakrata and Kalsi Blocks had a high percentage of ST population (65%) and were relatively underdeveloped among the other blocks of Dehradun District. The other two Blocks, Vikasnagar and Doiwala were taken up as they had pockets of Buxa tribals who are categorised as a primitive tribal group.

The real challenge of tribal development is to improve the infrastructure and initiate income generating programmes without disrupting their socio-cultural and ecological systems. This study tries to have a look on the existing arrangements of the development infrastructure and the constraints in development and planning. In order to make a fruitful study; data has been collected from both primary and secondary sources in order to understand the issues involved. Data and information has been collected from the Government Departments at the Central and State level as well as interviews with the beneficiaries and administrators in the field and evaluation studies done by the Ministry and the Planning Commission. Survey schedule has been designed to obtain information regarding the outflow of funds under the Tribal Sub-plan and Article 275(1) of the Constitution as well as the pattern and extent of benefit flowing from the government sponsored programs, status of beneficiaries, implementational framework and their impact on the economic status of the tribals. For assessing the status of beneficiaries and the benefits resulting from such programs, one district of Uttaranchal state viz. Dehradun has been taken up. Further among the chosen district, the tribal blocks of Chakrata and Kalsi have been taken up for assessing the impact of the programs on the beneficiaries. To look into the specific problems of

Primitive Tribal groups, the blocks of Vikasnagar and Doiwala have also been added for study.

In Jharkhand, the two Blocks, Murhu in Khunti sub-division and Ormanjhi in Ranchi Sadar sub-division of Ranchi district were chosen as they had a concentration of Munda and Oraon tribes respectively. These two tribes are predominant in Chotanagpur area of Jharkhand.

## SELECTION OF VILLAGES FOR FIELD STUDY

The selection of villages for field study was done after detailed discussions with the officers of the State government and the district administration of Dehradun and Ranchi. The selection was made on the consideration that the villages must have a representative character and should be predominantly tribal and must contain the beneficiaries of the Tribal Development programmes.

In all seven villages were selected for field study in Dehradun district – Sujau and Oli in Chakrata Block, Lakhwar, Haripur Bias and Kalsi Bazar in Kalsi Block, Shahpur in Vikas Nagar Block and Nagal Bulandawala in Doiwala Block. While Oli village in Chakrata was a Kolta habitation, the last two villages had a concentration of Buxas, a primitive tribal group. Further, while the two villages of Chakrata Block namely Sujau and Oli were remote, Lakhwar, Haripur Bias and Kalsi Bazar falling in Kalsi Block had seen a lot of contact with the outsiders.

In Jharkhand, the district of Ranchi was chosen for field study as it is the hub of the newly formed state and tribal movement has been more assertive in this area. Since the district has two sub-divisions namely Sadar sub-division and Khunti, one Block from each sub-division was chosen – namely Murhu in Khunti sub-division and Ormanjhi in Ranchi Sadar sub-division. This was done after discussion with the Director, Tribal Research Institute Ranchi who has done extensive research in the field of tribal development in Jharkhand.

### Pre-field Survey

Before going for field work, a trip was made to the above

mentioned blocks to have a tentative assessment of the physiographic condition of the region and to get an idea of the economy ,culture and society of the tribals residing there. Thereafter, detailed discussions were held with the district development officials of Ranchi and Dehradun districts and the Subdivisional Officer, Tehsildar and BDO's of Chakrata, Kalsi, Vikasnagar and Murhu Blocks.

Another round of discussion was held with the Secretary Department of Welfare, Uttaranchal, the Additional Secretary and the Joint Director of Tribal welfare at Dehradun.

Similar exercise was done in the case of the study in Jharkhand also. Before going for field work, discussions were held with the officers who are engaged in the tribal development administration both at Ranchi and in the two Blocks covered and the research officers in the Tribal Research Institute, Ranchi who have been frequent visitiors to these areas. Thereafter, Rukka village along with its adjoining tolas were selected in Ormanjhi Block and Guttigarha village along with its tolas was selected in the Murhu Block. Here it may be mentioned that Guttigarha village is inhabited exclusively by Mundas, who are an important tribal group in Ranchi district and Rukka village had a predominantly Oraon popultion who are the other important tribe in this district.

**Survey Schedule**

Survey schedule was prepared on the basis of the inputs received from the field and feedbacks received from the state government and the Ministry of Tribal Affairs. The survey schedule is at Annexure.

**Limitations of the Study**

Present study which is an individual effort, has been conducted and completed within a short period of time. Moreover, the study has been confined to the Dehradun district of the state of Uttaranchal and Ranchi district of Jharkhand as these districts represent the diverse tribal population of the country. Dehradun contains the tribal blocks of Chakrata and Kalsi as well as being the habitat of

Buxas who are a primitive tribal group and who live in Vikasnagar and Doiwala blocks. Thus, this district represents the problems of the tribals living both in the highlands and the plains of India. Similiarly Ranchi district has been the centre of activity of tribal leaders and has been in the forefront of Jharkhand movement and represents the hopes and aspirations of the tribals.

The field study has been spread over a period of nine months. The various chapters have been designed to give a comprehensive account of the ongoing tribal development programmes, working of the Panchayati Raj in Scheduled Areas, forest policies and their impact on the tribals living in the four blocks chosen for study. For this purpose, a large amount of primary and secondary data has been collected and studied and used. Review of the government programmes and the working of the Panchayati Raj institutions has been done on the basis of secondary data obtained from the Ministry of Tribal Affairs, Planning Commission, National Commission of SCs and STs and published works available in the libraries of the Indian Institute of Public Administration, New Delhi, the Registrar-General of India, the National Archives of India, the Central Secretariat Library, New Delhi, the Tribal Research Institute Ranchi and the libraries of the LBSNAA and NIAR, Mussoorie. Apart from collection of primary data through field study and PRAs (Participatory Rural Appraisal), secondary data has been collected from published documents available in the form of books, journals, seminar reports, previous study reports, plan documents, tribal sub-plan documents, annual reports of the various Ministries of the Government of India, materials in the National Archives of India and the Director-General of Census of India.

This study is limited to the review of the two government programmes mentioned earlier and the benefits accruing through these programmes to the tribal people and the impact of these programmes on the education and economic development of the tribals in the selected blocks.

Lack of availability of any recent impact evaluation study was another serious limitation. The impact study has therefore been done with the help of prepared questionnaires and direct interaction with the tribal people living in Chakrata and Kalsi blocks and primitive tribal group (Buxas) living in Vikasnagar and Doiwala blocks of Dehradun district and Munda and Oraon tribals residing in Guttigarha village and Rukka village alongwith its tolas. Mathematical errors and data inconsistency on the part of the government departments in the form of reports and documents have posed another serious limitation in the processing of data.

# 1

# Profile of the Scheduled Tribes and the Schemes and Programs for the Development of Scheduled Tribes

India has the largest concentration of tribal people anywhere in the world except perhaps in Africa. The tribals are children of nature and their lifestyle is conditioned by the ecosystem. India, with a variety of ecosystems, presents a varied tribal population throughout its length and breadth. They live mostly in villages though a small portion of their population has now settled in small towns as well as cities.

As per the 1991 census, the Scheduled Tribes constitute 8.08 per cent of the total population of the country and occupy 20 per cent of the geographical area. Out of this area, a substantial portion consists of forests which contain natural resources. But the paradox is that while some enclaves within the large tribal areas have burst forth into unprecedented economic activity, the tribal people living in and around them have not been able to get out of the poverty line. Majority of the tribal population is heavily dependent on forests for their livelihood. It has been estimated that 2 per cent of the total tribals resided in forest villages and 5 per cent of them occupied forestland while 12 per cent of the total tribals were shifting cultivators.

As per 1991 census, 42.02 per cent of the Scheduled tribe population were main workers, out of which 54.50 per cent were cultivators and 32.69 per cent were agricultural labourers. Therefore, 87 per cent of the main workers were largely dependent on agriculture. 42.9 per cent of the operational holdings of Scheduled Tribes belong to small farmers category(1 to 2 hectare).

In the field of educational development, the literacy rate of Scheduled Tribes is around 29.60 per cent as against the national average of 52 per cent. More than three-quarter of the Scheduled tribe women are illiterate; the female literacy rate among tribals being only 18.2 per cent.[1]

These disparities are compounded by higher dropout rates(77 per cent among Scheduled Tribes as compared to 52.8 per cent overall) in formal education resulting in their low representation in the higher education. Not surprisingly, the cumulative effect of the neglect has been the large number of Scheduled Tribes living below the poverty line; which is substantially higher than the national average. As per the study made by the Planning Commission in 1993-4, the percentage of Scheduled Tribes living below the poverty line was 51.94 per cent in rural areas and 41.14 per cent in urban areas. This has resulted in increasing unrest among the tribals and has found its manifestation in the extremist activities in the tribal region of the country.

Out of the total Scheduled tribe population of 67.8 million (as per 1991 census) about 80 per cent are found in Central and Western parts of India, 11 per cent in South India and the rest in the North-Eastern States.

There is no definition of Scheduled caste and the Scheduled tribe in the Constitution. But the President is empowered to draw up a list in consultation with the Governor of each state, subject to revision by parliament. The President first issued orders in 1950 specifying the Scheduled Caste and Scheduled Tribe in the different states of India. There are now 582 Tribes (with many overlapping types in more than one state) as per the Schedule notified under Article 342 of the Indian Constitution. Among these notified till now, 75 tribal groups who are still in the primitive stage have been identified as Primitive Tribal Groups (PTGs) by the Ministry of Tribal Affairs, Government of India and a special scheme has been introduced for their development in the year 1998-99. These primitive Tribes continue to live in isolated areas and practise either primitive agriculture or are at food gathering stage. The number of some of these groups has either stagnated or has shown a declining trend. They require protection and special provisions for their development.

According to the census figures, the population of Scheduled Tribes in general has been increasing since the first census of independent India taken in 1951.

**(Figures in millions)**

| *Census Years* | *Total Population* | *Population of Scheduled Tribes* | *Proportion of Scheduled Tribe Population to total Population* |
|---|---|---|---|
| 1951 | 361.1 | 19.1 | 5.29 |
| 1961 | 439.2 | 30.1 | 6.85 |
| 1971 | 548.2 | 38.0 | 6.93 |
| 1981 | 685.2 | 51.6 | 7.53 |
| 1991 | 846.3 | 67.8 | 8.08 |

The decadal population growth between census years 1981-1991 in respect of the tribal population has been much more (31.64 per cent) than the entire population of India (23.51 per cent). The sex ratio among the Scheduled Tribes is also more favourable at 972 females per 1000 males than the rest (929 females per 1000 males).

Even after fifty five years of independence, the per capita income of the tribals continue to be one of the lowest in the country and their alienation from their own land continues. As on 31st January 1999, the tribals were alienated from 9,17,590 acres of land and only 5,37,610 acres of such land had been restored as on date.

The Planning Commission's sub-group on Policies and legislations relating to Protection and Development of Scheduled Tribes (2001) has reported that landlessness among the STs has increased. In 1961, 68.18 per cent of the STs were cultivators. As per the 1991 census report, this came down to 54.5 per cent. The report has pinpointed two causes behind the dispossession of tribal lands. First, the entry of plains men into the interior tribal areas and second, the increasing pace of industrialisation and urbanisation.[2]

After five decades of planning, it is now time to critically review the activities pertaining to tribal development and also provide useful suggestions to correct what has gone wrong. The current development ideology is that you cannot develop other people; you can help them develop and take care of themselves as people develop in their own ways. It is now realized that mistakes have been made in the interpretation of policies and implementation of plans. For example the tribal sub-plan strategy has so far focussed on the individual's elevation above the poverty line; while following the tribal ethos, the emphasis should have been on the elevation of the entire community focussing on their economy, education, health, communications, etc. This would be more lasting as the individual is bound to again sink below the poverty line in the absence of the development of the community's economy, infrastructure and so on.

In the age of globalisation, the danger to the tribal areas is greater as they abound in natural resources and the already ongoing mining and industrial activities by the state and central governments are likely to be enhanced manifold with the coming of multi-national companies. Land and forest are central to the tribals' development and survival and the increasing land alienation and displacement are causes of worry. For reducing global warming, the regeneration of forests is a must and for this, the tribals have to participate in its protection with a sense of ownership. With economic empowerment, political empowerment will also come with the better working of the Scheduled areas (both the Fifth and the Sixth Schedule) in the context of the Panchayat (Extension to the Scheduled areas) Act, 2000.

The area inhabited by the tribals constitutes a significant part of the under-developed areas of the country. The tribals live mostly in isolated villages or hamlets. As per rough estimates, the prominent tribal areas constitute about 20 per cent of the total geographical area of the country.

## Constraints in Tribal Development

There are many constraints that are responsible for the

lower pace of the tribal development. Some of the major constraints are:

*(i)* ***Destruction of Forests:*** The forests are not only the source of livelihood for poor tribals but there also exists a symbiotic relationship between the tribals and the forests. The reducing forest cover is harming and depleting forest resources leading to food insecurity in a large percentage of the tribal population.

According to the State of Forest Report (1997) brought out by the Forest Survey of India, Dehradun excepting Himachal Pradesh, Karnataka, Maharashtra, Tripura, Rajasthan and West Bengal, forests have shown a remarkable decline in almost all tribal areas of the country. The loss of forest cover in the tribal districts of the country is to the tune of 4,899 sq. kms. and 5,937 sq. kms. as compared to 1995 and 1993 reports respectively. Such a declining trend of the forests in the tribal districts of India deeply affects the sustainability of the tribal forest areas.

*(ii)* ***Lack of Awareness:*** Persistent lack of awareness among tribal population about various developmental programs launched by the government of the Union and the states results in pilferation of these resources leading to their exploitation.

*(iii)* ***Protection of Tribal Rights and Concessions:*** Though the government of India and the Indian constitution have provided many rights and concessions to the tribals, but they remain deprived of the benefits arising out of such statutory provisions due to their ignorance and apathy of the implementing agencies.

*(iv)* The tribals live in a wide variety of agro-climatic and geographical conditions spread across the length and breath of the country. Due to the remoteness of their habitation, and the lack of markets in localities nearby, their produce very often does not fetch them fair price and the tribal cultivators and collectors of forest produce are forced to resort to distress sale and thereby they are exploited by traders and other middlemen.

**Present Position:** As per the survey made by the Planning Commission in 1993-94, 51.94 per cent of the

Scheduled Tribes living in rural areas and 41.14 per cent of STs living in the urban areas fell below the poverty line.

**Percentage of Population below Poverty Line**
**States - 1993-94**
**(as per the Official Methodology)**

| S.N. | States | Rural | | Urban | |
|---|---|---|---|---|---|
| | | Scheduled Caste | Scheduled Tribe | Scheduled Caste | Scheduled Tribe |
| 1. | Andhra Pradesh | 26.02 | 25.66 | 43.82 | 46.68 |
| 2. | Assam | 45.38 | 41.44 | 14.34 | 7.11 |
| 3. | Bihar | 70.66 | 69.75 | 55.16 | 35.76 |
| 4. | Gujarat | 32.26 | 31.20 | 44.99 | 35.47 |
| 5. | Haryana | 46.56 | 00.00 | 23.58 | 0.00 |
| 6. | Himachal Pradesh | 36.89 | 63.94 | 18.52 | 0.00 |
| 7. | Karnataka | 46.36 | 37.33 | 61.59 | 62.05 |
| 8. | Kerala | 36.43 | 37.34 | 31.59 | 1.08 |
| 9. | Madhya Pradesh | 45.83 | 56.69 | 65.00 | 65.28 |
| 10. | Maharashtra | 51.64 | 50.58 | 52.56 | 61.28 |
| 11. | Orissa | 48.95 | 71.26 | 47.45 | 64.85 |
| 12. | Punjab | 22.08 | 00.00 | 27.96 | 0.00 |
| 13. | Rajasthan | 38.38 | 46.23 | 48.63 | 13.21 |
| 14. | Tamil Nadu | 44.05 | 44.37 | 61.50 | 30.08 |
| 15. | Uttar Pradesh | 58.99 | 37.11 | 58.02 | 36.88 |
| 16. | West Bengal | 45.29 | 61.95 | 37.73 | 19.41 |
| | All - India | 48.11 | 51.94 | 49.48 | 41.14 |

*Source:* Planning Commission, New Delhi, 2001.

According to another estimate made by the Planning Commission in 1999-2000, the percentage of STs below the

**Percent age of Population below Poverty Line by States for 1999-2000**

| S.N. | States | Rural | | | Urban | | |
|---|---|---|---|---|---|---|---|
| | | *Scheduled Caste* | *Scheduled Tribe* | *All* | *Scheduled Caste* | *Scheduled Tribe* | *All* |
| 1. | Andhra Pradesh | 16.49 | 23.82 | 11.14 | 41.42 | 44.99 | 26.53 |
| 2. | Assam | 44.00 | 38.73 | 40.20 | 19.99 | 2.70 | 7.47 |
| 3. | Bihar | 59.81 | 59.68 | 44.22 | 51.91 | 39.47 | 32.95 |
| 4. | Gujarat | 17.77 | 29.11 | 13.17 | 29.13 | 36.66 | 15.59 |
| 5. | Haryana | 19.03 | 0.00 | 8.27 | 25.38 | 0.00 | 9.99 |
| 6. | Himachal Pradesh | 13.15 | 5.73 | 7.94 | 6.74 | 0.00 | 4.63 |
| 7. | Karnataka | 26.22 | 25.49 | 17.36 | 47.01 | 51.37 | 25.25 |
| 8. | Kerala | 14.64 | 24.20 | 9.38 | 24.15 | 0.00 | 20.27 |
| 9. | Madhya Pradesh | 41.29 | 56.26 | 37.09 | 54.24 | 52.59 | 38.54 |
| 10. | Maharashtra | 33.27 | 43.56 | 23.82 | 39.88 | 42.98 | 26.91 |
| 11. | Orissa | 51.83 | 73.93 | 48.13 | 70.59 | 59.58 | 43.13 |
| 12. | Punjab | 12.39 | 0.00 | 6.44 | 11.30 | 0.00 | 5.80 |
| 13. | Rajasthan | 19.62 | 25.27 | 13.65 | 41.82 | 20.71 | 19.85 |
| 14. | Tamil Nadu | 32.59 | 43.20 | 20.55 | 44.94 | 5.22 | 22.17 |
| 15. | Uttar Pradesh | 43.65 | 34.06 | 31.22 | 43.51 | 13.27 | 30.90 |
| 16. | West Bengal | 35.10 | 50.02 | 31.82 | 28.15 | 31.88 | 14.86 |
| 17. | All India | 36.25 | 45.86 | 27.11 | 38.47 | 34.75 | 23.65 |

*Source:* Planning Commission, New Delhi, 2001.

poverty line has come down to 45.86 per cent in rural areas and in urban areas this percentage comes to 34.75 per cent.

The estimates given above show that in course of 5-6 years, the percentage of STs below poverty line has come down by about 6 per cent, though they are still much below the all-India average of people being below the poverty line which is 26.10 per cent.

**Education**

The State wise ST literacy rates show wide variations among the 22 States and 4 Union Territories. The variation among States is from 17.16 in Andhra Pradesh to 82.73 in Mizoram. Seven States and Union Territories have literacy percentage less than the all India figure of 29.60. Thus, two thirds of the total ST population has been at a literacy level less than the all India ST average and less than half of the literacy level of the total population.

The ST female literacy rates varied from 4.42 per cent in Rajasthan to 78.70 per cent in Mizoram. The average all India literacy rate was 18.19 per cent. The five states which together account for 51.69 per cent of the female ST population in the country continued to remain below the national average of ST female literacy during the decade 1981-1991.

| | | |
|---|---|---|
| Rajasthan | - | 4.42 per cent |
| Andhra Pradesh | - | 8.68 per cent |
| Orissa | - | 10.21 per cent |
| Madhya Pradesh | - | 10.73 per cent |
| Bihar and Jharkhand | - | 14.75 per cent |

It is thus apparent that the bulk of ST female population subsists at a literacy level below 20 per cent.[1]

After the formation of the separate ministry of Tribal Affairs in October 1999, the following actions were taken to provide more focus to tribal welfare and development:

(a) All the state governments were asked to adopt the

Maharashtra pattern of planning and devolution of funds earmarked for tribal sub-plan areas. The pattern followed in Maharashtra is that the funds earmarked for tribal sub-plans are placed with the tribal development department of the state government which releases funds to different line departments for execution of developmental works under the tribal sub-plan. This process ensures that diversion and pilferage is minimised and better utilisation of funds meant for tribal development takes place.

(b) A new central sector scheme exclusively for the development of the primitive tribal groups was introduced.

(c) More NGO's were allotted funds for working in the tribal areas for the upliftment of the tribals. Good and established NGOs having all India character were identified as 'Established voluntary agencies'.

(d) Strict monitoring of the performance of the state governments and the NGOs were made so that the scope of misutilisation of funds was reduced.

## Schemes for the Development of Scheduled Tribes

***1. Special Central Assistance (SCA) for Tribal Sub-plan (TSP):*** This is a major program for the focussed development of tribals and tribal areas. Started in the fifth five-year plan, the special central assistance is provided by the government of India to the tribal sub-plan of States/UTs as an additive to the state plan to fill gaps in the budgetary provisions towards TSP. It is basically meant for family oriented income generation schemes in sectors like agriculture, horticulture, minor irrigation, soil conservation, animal husbandry, forest, education, cooperatives, fisheries, village and small industries, etc; and infrastructural development incidental thereto. The assistance given is hundred percent and it is expected to act as a catalyst for giving a boost to investment by the state governments and financial institutions. The release of fund is broadly on the basis of the Scheduled tribe population, geographical area and inverse proportion of per capita net state domestic product.

The state government in turn releases funds on the basis of certain norms for ITDPs, MADA pockets, clusters, Primitive tribal groups and dispersed tribal groups and about 70 per cent of the SCA fund is spent on family oriented schemes and only 30 per cent on the infrastructure incidental to such schemes. There is a thinking to change this proportion by assigning 80 per cent of the SCA funds to infrastructure development and only 20 per cent for individual/family oriented schemes since individual/family oriented schemes can be taken up under the schemes of the Ministry of Rural development and also funded through the National Scheduled Tribes Finance and Development corporation. The Ministry of Tribal Affairs has also found that there is no check or monitoring of the release of SCA funds by the state governments to the implementing agencies. Moreover there is also unusual delay in the release of SCA funds by the state governments to the implementing agencies. Some states have also not opened separate budget heads for showing the TSP funds.

The following statement will show that after the introduction of TSP concept in the fifth five-year plan, there has been a tremendous increase in the flow of funds for tribal development.

*(Rs. in crores)*

| *Five Year Plan* | *Total plan Outlay* | *Tribal Development Programs/Flow to TSP* | *Percentage* |
|---|---|---|---|
| First plan | 1960 | 19.93 | 1.0 |
| Second plan | 4672 | 42.92 | 0.9 |
| Third plan | 8577 | 50.53 | 0.6 |
| Fourth plan | 15902 | 75.00 | 0.5 |
| Fifth plan | 39322 | 1102.00 | 3.01 |
| Sixth plan | 97500 | 5535.00 | 5.00 |
| Seventh plan | 1,80,000 | 10,500.00 | 5.00 |
| Eight plan | 1,66,756.36 | 15,800.05 | 9.47 |
| Ninth Plan | 2,89,147.14 | 23,375.08 | 8.08 |

*Source*: Annual Report of the Ministry of Tribal Affairs (2001-2002).

***2. Grants under Article 275(1) of the Constitution:*** Every year, funds are released to the state governments to meet the cost of such schemes of development as may be undertaken by them for promoting the welfare of Scheduled Tribes and for raising the level of administration of the Scheduled areas to that of the rest of the state. The objective is to promote the welfare of Scheduled Tribes and better administration of Scheduled areas. The scheme covers all tribal sub-plan and tribal majority states of the country.

This is a central sector scheme and 100 per cent grants are provided by the Ministry of Tribal Affairs to the state governments. The grants are provided on the basis of Scheduled tribe population percentage of the state. The Ministry, which earlier used to release the funds without identifying the projects, has now decided to release funds to the state governments against specific infrastructure development and welfare projects from the year 2000-2001. With a view to provide quality education to Scheduled Tribe students it has been decided to establish 100 residential schools from the grants available under this scheme during the Ninth five year plan. These schools will run classes from VI to XII. Each of the 100 schools will be provided a non-recurring grant of Rs. 2.5 crores.

***3. Boys and Girls' Hostels for Scheduled Tribe Students:*** This is a centrally sponsored scheme launched in the year 1961-62 with central assistance limited to 50 per cent. 50 per cent fund is to be provided by the state governments. This is given for construction of hostel building and extension of existing hostels. In the case of Union territories, the central government releases 100 per cent as assistance. The maintenance of these hostels and their buildings are the responsibility of the state governments/ UTs. This is a useful scheme for enabling the Scheduled tribe students to study in hospitable environments and promoting literacy among tribal girls and boys who have many handicaps due to poor socio-economic condition.

Since the land for the building is to be provided by the state governments free of cost and moreover, 50 per cent of the funds are to be provided by them, there has been poor demand for the construction of the new hostels. The state government has also to bear the recurring and non-recurring cost of the running and the maintenance of these hostels.

***4. Ashram Schools in TSP Areas:*** This is a centrally sponsored scheme launched during 1990-91 with an objective to extend educational facilities like establishing residential schools for Scheduled Tribes in an environment conducive to learning. The funds under the scheme are given to the states on a matching basis i.e. 50-50 while 100 per cent assistance is given to the UTs. The scheme provides funds for the construction of school buildings from the primary standard to the senior secondary stage of education. It also allows for upgradation of existing primary level Ashram schools.

Under this scheme, besides the school buildings, the construction of hostels for students and staff quarters are also undertaken. The state government has to provide land free of cost for such constructions. Grant is provided for other non-recurring items of expenditure like purchase of furniture, equipments, sets of books for school and hostel library. A sum of Rs. 44.86 crores was earmarked for this program in the Ninth five year plan. This scheme suffers from the same ailment namely the failure of the state governments to provide 50 per cent fund out of their own budgets.

***5. Scheme for Educational Complex in low Literacy Pockets for Development of Female Literacy:*** It is known that the literacy level among females in the Scheduled Tribes is abysmally low. This scheme is meant to tackle this problem through identification of 134 districts in the country, which have below 10 per cent literacy rate among Scheduled tribe females. The scheme is implemented through NGOs, cooperative societies and state governments.

The primary objective of the scheme is promotion of education among tribal girls in the identified low-literacy districts of the country. The secondary objective is to improve the socio-economic condition of the poor and illiterate tribal population. It is a central sector scheme and the government of India provides 100 per cent funds. The educational complexes are established in the rural areas of the notified districts and have classes from I to V with provision for upgradation upto XII provided they have sufficient accommodation for class rooms, hostels, kitchen, gardening and for sports. These educational complexes impart not only formal education to tribal girls but also train the students in agriculture, animal husbandry and other vocations and crafts which will make them skilled for leading a better life. The teaching from class I to III is done in the tribal dialects of the area and women teachers having proficiency in tribal dialects are engaged as teachers.

Though the strength of students in each class has been fixed at 30, a maximum of 10 more students, if available in the locality, are admitted as day scholars. The recurring grants provided to run the educational complexes is 9000/- per student per year. This includes expenses on accommodation, food, clothing, payment of salary to teachers etc. The students are provided two sets of uniform ,one set of school books besides free food and medicine. Besides the above, the student's parents are given the incentive of Rs.50/- per month. A sum of Rs.1000 per student is also given as a non-recurring grant for purchase of cots, mattresses, utensils, etc.

Under this scheme ,128 Educational complexes have been established from the year 1995-96 to 2000-01.

***6. Scheme for Vocational Training in Tribal Areas:*** Realising the need for skill upgradation and to equip the tribal youths for self-employment ,this scheme was introduced in 1992-93 and is continuing since then.

The main aim of the scheme is to develop the skill of the tribal youths for a variety of trades and prepare them for new job opportunities as well as self-employment in area close to their villages as well as outside. The secondary aim is to improve the socio-economic condition of tribal youths by enhancing their earnings.

This scheme covers all the states and union territories and 100 per cent grants under the schemes are provided to state/UTs and other organisations implementing the scheme. These organisations can either be set up by the government as autonomous bodies under a statute of state or central government or NGOs registered under the Socities Registration Act, 1960.

Under the program, while no predefined cost heads are stipulated, at the project formation stage, each implementing agency is required to submit a detailed project proposal in the prescribed format clearly bringing out the program modalities and individual expenditure heads. While approving the projects the extent of support to the projects as a whole and to each component of the project against which there is permissible re-appropriation to the extent of 20 per cent of the total grant is indicated.

Each vocational training center under the scheme may cater to light vocational courses in traditional skills depending upon the employment potential of the area. Keeping in view the potential of even skilled persons in interior areas, each tribal boy/girl is trained in two trades of his/her choice. The duration of each course is three months. After the end of six months each trainee is attached to the master craftman in a semi urban/urban area for another period of six months to learn his skill by practical experience.

After the training is over, the agencies running the vocational training centres are required to arrange for loans and subsidies either through ITDP/SGSY or through any other agency for enabling each successful candidate to start his/her job.

Each vocational training centre is provided financial assistance for purchase of training equipments to run the courses of five trades as decided by the agency concerned once in five years at the rate of Rs.2.40 lakhs per VTC.

The recurring grant to run the VTCs is of Rs.13,500 per trainee per year. There is a provision that each VTC should have one chief instructor, four trade instructors, one workshop attendant, one watchman, one peon, one accountant and one part-time sweeper. Each trainee in the centre is paid stipend at the rate of Rs.350 per month and raw material worth Rs.1200 per annum.

The agencies are also given grant-in-aid to run the VTCs either in rented building or in the building owned by the organisation. The rate of rent allowed per month is fixed at a maximum limit of Rs.8000. Maintenance grant in case, the building is owned by the organisation will be @ 10 per cent of the rent allowed per month.

***7. Scheme for Development of Primitive Tribal Groups (PTGs):*** These groups practising primitive agricultural practices and having low level of literacy and stagnant or diminishing population face various problems in their progress and development. To cater to the need of such group, a separate scheme was introduced in the year 1998-99 which mainly focuses on ensuring food security and the protection and development of PTGs.

The objective and purpose of this scheme is that funds under the central sector scheme for the development of PTGs will be available only for those items/activities which though very crucial for the survival, protection and development of PTGs are not specifically catered to by any existing scheme. The activities under the scheme may include measures such as awareness generation and confidence building, training for skill development, improvement in agriculture technology, housing, education and health standards.

The scheme covers 75 PTGs spread over 18 states and one UT. 100 per cent funds are provided by the Ministry of Tribal Affairs for the programs mentioned above. Those activities which focus on helping the beneficiaries to cope up with extreme adverse conditions threatening their survival are taken up on priority basis.

The projects sanctioned, by a selection committee constituted by the ministry, are executed under the supervision of states/UTs. They can be executed either by the agencies under the state government or by NGOs having capability and willingness to work in remote areas.

***8. Centrally Sponsored Scheme of Research and Training:*** These schemes are in operation since the first five year plan. Under this scheme ,grants are given to various Tribal Research institutes on sharing basis of 50:50 between the state and the central government.

Besides the above, research fellowships are awarded for research in various aspects of tribal development on 100 per cent basis. These are to be sponsored by the concerned TRIs/state governments. Funds are also provided to the institutes and organisations for conducting research and evaluation studies, workshops and seminars and publication of books related to tribals and tribal development.

A Research Advisory Committee has been constituted by the ministry to screen and approve the research proposals received from various organisations. There are both official and non-official members in this committee.

The allocation under this scheme has increased substantially from the first five year plan to the ninth five year plan. The allocation in ninth five year plan is Rs.25 crores. There is also a proposal to set up a National Institute for research and training at the central level.

***9. Educational Development of Scheduled Tribes:*** For the promotion of education among the Scheduled Tribes, the following schemes are in operation :

(a) Centrally sponsored scheme of post-matric scholarship.

(b) National overseas scholarship scheme for higher studies abroad.

(c) Book bank scheme.

(d) Scheme of upgradation of merit.

(e) Coaching for competitive examinations.

These schemes are in pursuance of the constitutional directives under Article16 (A) and 16(AA) which makes it obligatory for the state to make reservations in appointments of posts and in matters of promotion to any class of posts and services in favor of the Scheduled Tribes. Due to the low literacy level and high dropout rates among the tribal students, the advantage of the reservation is taken only by a fraction of the people belonging to the Scheduled Tribes. The above schemes are meant to counter these shortcomings and help the tribal students to continue their studies and also get coaching for appearing at the competitive examinations.

The scheme of post-matric scholarship is open to all Scheduled Tribes students studying in India and is awarded by the state government/UTs. The funds for it are provided by the government of India over and above the committed liability of the respective state governments/UT administration. The northeastern states have however been exempted from making their own budgetary provisions towards committed liability from the ninth five-year plan onwards and the entire expenditure for them will be borne by the central ministry.

For pursuing higher education in science and technology in foreign countries, the scheme of national oversees scholarship is in operation since 1954-55. Ten scholarships are awarded each year for pursuing post-graduate, doctoral and post-doctoral studies in engineering, science and technology for a period ranging from one to four years. Five scholars, who are in receipt of a merit scholarship from a foreign university/government where cost of passage is not provided ,are also granted cost of passage (to and fro) by the economy class.

For the use of tribal students engaged in study of medicine, engineering ,business management etc, the book bank scheme is in operation. Under this scheme, textbooks are purchased (upto Rs.7500) and given to students for their use. An amount of Rs.2000 or actual cost which ever is less, is also given for purchase of steel almirah to keep the books. This is a centrally sponsored scheme and the expenses of this program are shared between the central government and the state government on 50:50 basis. However in respect of union territories, cent percent grant is given by the central government.

The performance of this scheme has not been encouraging over the years. The main reason is the inability of the state government to provide 50 per cent of the cost of the scheme and for this reason, the funds released in the earlier years remain unutilized. Although this is a good welfare scheme, yet the implementation is lacking.

The upgradation of merit scheme provides remedial and special classes for Scheduled tribe students in class XI and

XII with the aim of removing deficiency in certain school subjects and also to provide special coaching to prepare students for pre-medical and pre-engineering competitive examinations.

For this purpose, the state governments/UTs select certain schools in different districts/towns having hostel facilities and also showing good results in class X and XII examinations. The coaching starts from class IX in the identified schools and continues till the awardees complete class XII. Coaching is provided in linguistic skills, science ,and mathematics and given special focus on the preparation of competitive examinations. Preference is given to girl students who are meritorious. For this scheme, 100 per cent assistance is provided to the states/UTs.

Together with this, a separate scheme of pre-examination coaching is also in operation. This is meant to enable the students of tribal communities to improve their representation and standard of performance in competitive examinations for various posts and services under the Union and state governments. State government run institutions/universities and private coaching institutes conduct these programs and for that they are paid on per unit basis. These are contractual in nature and are open to Scheduled Tribes candidates whose own and parents' income does not exceed Rs.44,500 per annum.

***10. Protection of Tribals from Exploitation:*** The tribals live in a wide variety of agro-climatic and geographical conditions spread over the length and breath of the country. Majority of them earn their livelihood from forests and agricultural produce. Due to the remoteness of their habitation and lack of markets in localities nearby; their produce often does not fetch them fair price and they are forced to go for distress sale. Thus they are exploited by the traders and the middlemen. To remedy this situation, the Tribal Cooperative Marketing Development Federation of India Ltd. (TRIFED) has been set up. To ensure that the tribals get remunerative prices for their product, the state tribal cooperative federations involved in the procurement of tribal produce and its marketing are provided grants-in-aid by the central government. Under this scheme, the Ministry provides 100 per cent grant for taking up collection of minor forest produce.

***11. Village Grain Bank Scheme:*** In some parts of the country, the tribals face situation of starvation as their economy remains at sub-subsistence level and they are not in a position to face drought and floods. Lack of purchasing power makes them incapable of getting foodgrains from the fair price shops. To meet such a situation, the village grain bank scheme has been started from the Ninth Five year plan.

The main objective of the scheme is to provide some safeguard against non-availability of foodgrains in remote tribal areas. The scheme covers all village having 50 per cent or more tribal population and is presently run in thirteen states namely Andhra Pradesh, Jharkhand, Gujarat, Kerala, Madhya Pradesh, Manipur, Orissa, Rajasthan,Tamilnadu, Uttranchal, West Bengal, Tripura and Maharashtra.

The villages where grain banks are to be established are chosen by the concerned state government. The most populous and poorest of the village is first selected and one quintal of local grain per member family is purchased for which fund is provided by the central government through the TRIFED. The scheme is fully participative and community based with no administrative cost and no recurring expenditure. Any needy family can draw grain at the time of need from the village grain bank in four installments of upto 25 kg. each. It can be returned at the time of the next harvest so as to recoup the stock. The interest on such loan is 5 per cent for the period upto 3 months and beyond that and upto 6 months, it is 10 per cent. In the event of non-payment beyond 6 months, the membership of the individual is liable to lapse but it may be revived after repayment. For the implementation of this program, a working committee of seven members is constituted by the project officer ITDP. Its tenure is generally of three years.

***12. Promotion of Voluntary Efforts:*** It has been widely recognized that the task of the development of Scheduled Tribes cannot be achieved through the efforts of the government alone. The strategy for their rapid development requires thorough understanding of their socio-economic values, their tradition and culture. Sometimes, the developmental programs suffer from the lack of knowledge of the tribal traditions and culture by the government officials, as they are more target-oriented. It is here that the roles of voluntary non-governmental organizations become important as many of them have been rendering yeoman services in the tribal areas by living there and interacting with the tribal communities of the area. For this purpose the Ministry of Tribal Affairs supports many welfare programs especially in the field of education and medical care run by the NGOs through the scheme of grant-in-aid to the voluntary organizations working for the welfare of Scheduled Tribes.

This scheme is in operation since 1953-54 but its scope has been increased from the year 1998-99. The schemes run through NGOs include residential schools, hostels, medical centers, computer training centers, shorthand and typing units, balwadis, libraries and audio-visual units. 90 per cent of the fund for a program is given by the Ministry and 10 per cent is to be contributed by the NGO. From the year 1999-2000, 100 per cent fund is also available to the NGOs working in the Scheduled areas.

The main objective of the scheme is to provide for an over-all improvement and development of the Scheduled Tribes through voluntary efforts in the field of education, health and sanitation, environment, drinking water, legal redressal service and those need-based socio-economic upliftment efforts having direct beneficial impact on the target groups.

Monitoring of the activities of the NGOs receiving fund from the ministry is done through field inspections by the officers of the central government and the state government or by any other agency designated by the Ministry.

Monitoring is also done for the other schemes run by

the central and state government mentioned earlier through evaluation studies conducted by Tribal Research Institutes/ Universities/other institutions or agencies especially designated for this purpose.

***13. Schemes for the Financial Assistance to Scheduled Tribes*** : A new National Finance and Development Corporation meant for the economic development of Scheduled Tribes has been started in the year 2001after bifurcation of the National SC and ST Finance and Development Corporation. This Corporation would provide financial assistance at concessional rates for income generating activities and training in skill development to STs whose annual income is below double the poverty line. This assistance for self-employment purposes would be available upto Rs. 10 lakhs through the State channelising agencies which are in many cases the State Scheduled Tribes Finance and Development Corporation. The projects undertaken under this program should be technically feasible and financially viable. The Corporation would provide term loan, seed capital, bridge loan etc. at concessional rates of interest. The maximum amount available would be 85 per cent of the project cost with 10 per cent coming from the State Corporations and 5 per cent from the beneficiary concerned. It provides finance in the sectors of agriculture, horticulture, animal husbandry and dairy, minor irrigation, small industries, small trade and transport services. This scheme will also help in removing indebtedness among tribals and provide finance at concessional rates which the commercial banks have so far failed to provide.

It has been widely acknowledged that the tribal population in the country lies at the lowest rung of the ladder in terms of economic development. The economic disability caused by poor asset possession has rendered their participation in the developmental process less than average. It is in this context that the finance corporations have come to acquire an increasingly significant role in providing development finance to the tribals for their economic upliftment. In fact, supply of timely and adequate credit to the Scheduled Tribes is a very crucial input for increasing their productivity and production in the field of agriculture and allied activities.

**14. *Monitoring and Evaluation:*** Monitoring and Evaluation is vital to ensure realization of targets. In regard to sectoral programs and schemes of development of tribal communities, policy planning, monitoring and evaluation etc is the responsibility of the concerned central ministries, state governments and UT administrations. Greater attention is also tc be paid to concurrent monitoring and evaluation through existing field agencies on the principles of checks and balances. The monitoring mechanism has to be strong and effective if the Tribal Sub plan concept is to be made a reality. The feedback from the field through regular monitoring and periodical evaluation is needed to provide the necessary material for re-orientation of policy and approach to tribal development.[3]

**15. *Governor's Report:*** For the administration of the Scheduled areas, the Governor of the State has a special responsibility. It is customary for the Governor to send the annual report within six months of the close of the financial year to the President of India. The Governor's report is an objective evaluation of the developmental efforts made by the State government in the Scheduled areas of the state. It also includes assessment of the situation in the Scheduled areas with reference to the administration and implementation of the protective laws.

## Reference

1. Bhupinder Singh and Neeti Mahanti – Tribal Education in India Inter-India publications, New Delhi, 1995, pp. 20-21.
2. Report of the Sub-group on policies and legislations relating to protection and development of ST, (2001), Planning Commission, Government of India, New Delhi.
3. Annual Report 2001-2002 of the Ministry of Tribal Affairs, Government of India, New Delhi, pp. 12-18.

# 2

# India's Tribal Policy

## Tribal Policy before Independence

During the period of British rule, the approach to the development of tribals was at best only ambivalent. Their approach was marked by the desire to leave the tribal areas alone from their administrative interference. The reasons for such a policy were the difficulties in governing an independent, valiant and self-respecting group of people in a hostile area devoid of any modern communication facilities. As a result, these tribal areas received least attention in the scheme of development and they were left to the whims of the local Zamindars and other petty officials, who invariably let no opportunity of exploiting the tribal gullibility escape. This resulted in further isolation of the tribals from the mainstream development activities and increased the opportunities for their exploitation.

The various aspects of administration of the tribal areas were examined in detail for the first time by the Indian Statutory Commission called the Simon Commission. The Commission broadly recommended that the responsibility of the tribal tracts should be entrusted to the Center. Their reasons were:

(i) The simple tribal communities needed protection from economic subjugation of their neighbours, freedom to pursue their traditional methods of livelihood and follow their ancestral customs and traditions.

(ii) It was the responsibility of the administration to assist the people suitably so as to enable them to manage their affairs in the changing situation. This vital task could not be left to the initiative of individuals or societies.

(iii) The Provincial governments would not be in a position to spare the funds required for achieving the above objectives from their revenues.

The Commission recommended that the tribal areas may be classified into two categories viz. 'Excluded' and 'Partially Excluded' Areas. A new scheme was also adopted for the administration of 'Excluded' and 'Partially Excluded' Areas in the Government of India Act, 1935. Sections 91 and 92 of the Government of India Act, 1935 gave extensive powers to the Governor. They were as follows:

(i) No Act of the Federal legislature or the Provincial legislature would apply to these areas except on the direction of the Governor who was empowered to make such exceptions and modifications as he considered necessary.

(ii) The Governor could make regulations for peace and good governance of the said areas. However, such regulations required assent of the Governor General before they could come into effect.

Thus the traditional system of governance of the tribal people remained uninterfaced during the British period.

When India became free and a Constitution was enacted, the task before the framers of the Constitution was to devise a suitable formula which would protect the economic interests of the tribals, safeguard their way of life, and ensure their development so that they might take their legitimate place in the general life of the country.

The Constitutional frame adopted for this purpose broadly followed the two-way classification of the Government of India Act, 1935. The Excluded areas were mostly termed as the 'Tribal Areas' for whose administration special provisions were made in a separate schedule, namely, the Sixth Schedule of the Constitution. The 'Partially Excluded' Areas were named as the 'Scheduled Areas' for which special provisions were made under the Fifth Schedule of the Constitution.

The provisions under these two Schedules envisage sharing of responsibility between the concerned States and the Union government. In this scheme of sharing of the responsibility of the Scheduled Areas in terms of the executive powers of the Union and the States, the final authority vests with the Union while the States are expected to manage their affairs in accordance with law subject to the directions of the Union Government.

The Constitution has devoted more than 20 Articles on the redressal and upliftment of the underprivileged sections of society and affirming the policy of positive discrimination and reservation for Scheduled Tribes. Special attention has also been given to their accelerated development through the planning process since the advent of first five-year plan. The Government has also taken measures to extend Panchayati Raj to Scheduled areas through an Act of Parliament. Another major innovation was the introduction of the Tribal Sub plan concept in all state and central ministry plans for the apportionment of funds to tribal welfare in accordance with their population and genius. For it was Pandit Jawaharlal Nehru, the first Prime Minister of India who called for letting the tribals develop in accordance with their genius.

For the protection, socio-economic and political development of Scheduled Tribes, the Constitution of India makes the following provisions:

**1. Social**

(a) Equality before law (Article 14).

(b) The state to make provisions for the advancement of any socially and educationally backward classes of citizens or for the Scheduled caste and Scheduled Tribes [Article 15(4)].

(c) Equality of opportunities for all citizens in matters relating to employment or appointment to any office under the state (Article 16).

(d) The state to make provisions for reservation in appointment, posts in favor of any backward class citizens which in the opinion of the state is not adequately represented in the Services under the State [Article 16(4)].

(e) The State to make provisions in matters of promotion to any class or classes of posts in the Services in favour of the Scheduled caste and Scheduled tribes [Article 16(4A)].

(f) A National Commission for the Scheduled caste and Scheduled tribes to investigate, monitor and evaluate all matters relating to Constitutional safeguards provided for the Scheduled caste and Scheduled Tribes [Article 338].

(g) Appointment of a Commission to report on the administration of the Scheduled areas and the welfare of the Scheduled tribes in the States [Article 339].

(h) Appointment of a Commission to investigate the conditions of socially and educationally backward classes and the difficulties under which they labour and to make recommendations to remove such difficulties.(Article 340).

(i) To specify the Tribes [Article 342].

**2. Economic**

(a) The state to promote with special care the educational and economic interests of the weaker sections of the people, and in particular of the Scheduled caste and Scheduled tribes, and protect them from social injustice and all forms of exploitation [Article 46].

(b) Grant-in-aid from the Consolidated Fund of India each year for promoting the welfare of the Scheduled tribes and administration of Scheduled areas [Article 275(1)].

(c) The claims of the members of the Scheduled castes and the Scheduled tribes in the appointments to services and posts in connection with the affairs of the Union or of a State to be taken into consideration consistent with the maintenance of efficiency of administration [Article 335].

### 3. Political

(a) Through the Fifth Schedule, the administration and control of in any State, other than the States of Assam, Meghalaya, Tripura and Mizoram by ensuring submission of annual reports by the Governor to the President of India regarding the administration of the Scheduled areas and setting up of a Tribal Advisory Council to advise on such matters pertaining to the welfare and advancement of the Scheduled tribes [Article 244(1)].

(b) Special provision through the Sixth Schedule for the administration of the Tribal areas in the States of Assam, Meghalaya, Tripura and Mizoram by designating certain tribal areas as Autonomous districts and Autonomous Regions and also by constituting District Councils, Autonomous Councils and Regional Councils [Article 244(2)].

(c) Reservation of seats for the Scheduled castes and the Scheduled tribes in the House of the People [Article 330].

(d) Reservation of seats for the Scheduled Castes and the Scheduled Tribes in the Legislative Assemblies of the State [Article 332].

(e) Reservation of seats for the Scheduled Castes and the Scheduled tribes in every Panchayat [Article 243D].

(f) Extension of the 73rd and 74th Amendment to the Constitution to the Scheduled Areas through the Panchayats (Extension to the Scheduled Areas) Act, 1996 to ensure effective participation of the tribals in the process of planning and decision making.

### The Fifth Schedule

The Fifth Schedule of the Constitution imposes a special responsibility on the State for peace and good governance of the tribal areas. The executive powers of the Union extend to giving directions to the States as to the administration of such areas. The regulation making powers conferred by the Fifth Schedule on the Governor is a unique device designed to help imparting flexibility to the Union and State laws applicable to the Scheduled Areas. Purposefully used, the provisions of the Fifth Schedule can be of great help in reinforcing the effectiveness of the Tribal sub-plan mechanism in the tribal areas.

Under the Fifth Schedule of the Constitution, two important provisions have been made:

(i) Constituting the Tribes Advisory Council, and

(ii) Submission of the periodical reports on the administration of the Scheduled Area by the Governor of the State.

**The Tribes Advisory Councils**

According to para 4 of the Fifth Schedule of the Constitution, States having scheduled areas are required to constitute a Tribes Advisory Council consisting of not more than 20 members of whom about three fourths should be representatives of Scheduled Tribes in the Legislative Assemblies of the States. States not having Scheduled Areas but having Scheduled Tribes population may also have a Council.

The Council is expected to advise on matters pertaining to welfare and advancement of Scheduled Tribes in the States. Tribes Advisory Council are in existence in eight states having Scheduled Areas, i.e., Andhra Pradesh, Bihar, Gujarat, Himachal Pradesh, Madhya Pradesh, Maharashtra, Orissa and Rajasthan. Two states not having Scheduled Areas i.e. Tamilnadu and West Bengal have also got the Tribes Advisory Council. State Boards have been constituted in Kerala, Tripura and Uttar Pradesh.

At least two meetings of the Advisory Council should be held each year. In the meeting of the Council, policy matters relating to the development of Scheduled Tribes should be discussed and finalized. As early as 1961, the Dhebar Commission had pointed out that the meetings of the Councils were not being held twice a year as prescribed under the rules. The same trend continues more or less to this day.

**Governor's Report**

Para 5 of the Fifth Schedule of the Constitution requires

the Governor of each State having Scheduled Area to make an annual report to the President regarding administration of such areas in the State. In practice the report which is being sent to the President is the progress report of the development schemes of the Tribal sub-plan areas and not the report of the Scheduled Tribal Area.

The report is thus not in terms of the qualitative assessment of the impact of the development schemes on the tribals and the administration of the Scheduled Area but a collection of statistics pertaining to the financial and physical achievements. Pandit Jawaharlal Nehru, the first Prime Minister of India had said, "the development of the tribal people should be judged not in terms of achievements of the financial and physical targets but in terms of the quality of life of the tribal people involved". But this has been lost sight of.

Mention has been made earlier of the fact that the Governor of a State has been empowered to make regulations for peace and good governance of the Scheduled Areas. Nevertheless, tribal resurgence has been asserting itself against exploitation in land, labour, forest and excise matters.

## Sixth Schedule

In the Sixth Schedule areas, the powers are centralised and vested with the district council. The 'district' itself is a territory inhabited by a tribe. This stands out in sharp contrast to the provision in the Fifth Schedule where the basic unit is the village.

## Evolution of a National Policy of Tribal Development

The question confronting policy makers in independent India was whether the tribals were to be allowed to follow their inclination in accepting or rejecting the cultural and social pattern represented by their neighbours or were they to be compelled or coaxed to abandon their cultural traditional values.

Verrier Elwin, who was a well wisher of tribals, advocated integration of the tribal people in the Indian society. He had concretized this in the following principles enunciated by him:

1. We must help the tribes to come to terms with their own past so that their present and future will not be a denial of it but a natural evolution of it.
2. We must fight the danger of pauperization, the creation of a special class called tribals which will want to be labeled 'backward' in order to seek material benefit from the government.
3. It is essential to avoid creating a sense of inferiority in the tribal people. This means we must not impose our own ideas on them. We must not make them feel ashamed of their own natural way.
4. We should lay much greater stress on the possibility of the tribal people helping us. At present, the emphasis is on our helping them. Let us teach them that their own culture, their own arts are precious things that we respect and need.
5. We must try to ensure that the tribal people do not lose their freedom and their zest for living.[1]

Based on this concept of integration is Pandit Jawaharlal Nehru's Panchsheel of tribal development. They are:

1. People should develop along the lines of their own genius and we should avoid imposing anything on them. We should try to encourage, in every way, their own tribal art and culture.
2. Tribal rights in land and forest should be respected.
3. We should try to train and build up a team of their own people to do the work of administration and development. We should avoid introducing too many outsiders into tribal territory.
4. We should not over-administer these areas or overwhelm them with a multiplicity of schemes. We should work through; and not in rivalry to their own social and cultural institutions.
5. We should judge results not by statistics or the amount

of money spent but the quality of human character that is evolved.'

Nehru's above five principles also broadly represent the Government of India's attitude towards tribal development and administration since the advent of the five year plans.[2] After independence, Government of India has also been appointing Commissions and Ccommittees to help formulate suitable policies and programmes for tribal development. The first such important Commission appointed under Article 339 (1) was the Scheduled Areas and Scheduled Tribe Commission headed by Shri U.N. Dhebar in 1960. It emphasised the need of the protection of the rights and interests of the tribal people in the Scheduled Areas and highlighted the importance of education and health care.

Another expert Committee headed by Prof. S.C. Dube was constituted in 1972 to look into tribal development issues, It pointed out the problems of indebtedness and land-alienation among the tribals and suggested that cooperative credit and institutional finance should be channelised in the tribal areas.

Earlier to that, the National Commission of Labour (1969) had recognised land and forest as the core issues of tribal concern.

Thereafter, working groups constituted for the preparation of successive five year plans have been going in detail into the working of the schemes and programmes for the development of Scheduled Tribes. The latest working group for the Tenth Five Year Plan which submitted its report recently has lamented the fact that mistakes have been made in the interpretation and implementation of Pandit Nehru's Adivasi panchsheel. It says that the current development ideology is that you cannot develop other people, you can only help them develop and take care of themselves as people develop in their own ways. It suggests that following the tribal ethos, the emphasis should be on the elevation of the entire community from all points of view like economy, education, health, communication and so on. The development of individual that may be the aim of the present policy should be changed to the development of the entire community. The word 'empowerment' should not only mean economic empowerment but also include political empowerment.[3]

Another strategy has been developed for the primitive tribal groups. The National Development Council while finalizing the ninth five year plan document observed the following:

"While the all round development of STs in general will be addressed through the continuing programs but with added thrust and support, the primitive tribal groups (PTGs) who are leading an extremely precarious life and some of whom are on the verge of extinction due to hunger, starvation and diseases, will be attended to, on a priority basis in the ninth plan. As the ongoing programs have not been able to alleviate the conditions of the PTGs, an integrated action plan will be launched for them incorporating supply of safe drinking water, nutrition, food security, health coverage, educational facilities etc. The proposed Action Plan for the PTGs will have an in-built flexibility to cater to the specific needs of each tribe and its environment."[4]

Another area, which has been highlighted in the working group report for the Tenth Five Year Plan, is the advent of globalization. It says that the tribal areas abound in natural resources and the already ongoing mining and industrial activities by the States and central governments are likely to be enhanced manifold with the coming of MNCs. It has recommended that the tribals of the concerned area must be a party to the agreement (MOU) along with the external agency and the States and central governments. At no cost, should the tribal be deprived of his ownership on the land. If a village is uprooted or displaced, the whole village should be so resettled that there remains a cultural continuity even after relocation. It has also suggested that the tribals should have 15 to 20% share in the company in addition to having a lead time to prepare himself for employment before the proposed undertaking is in operation.

It has also recommended the protection of the forest and environment in order to reduce global warming, and that there should be a 10-year ban on the commercial felling of trees.[5]

To implement the Constitutional provisions relating to tribals, the Ministry of Home Affairs was earlier given the responsibility of tribal development at the Government of India level. The Dhebar Commission's recommendation to establish a separate department of Tribal Affairs under a separate minister in the Ministry of Home Affairs was not accepted. Ultimately in October 1999, the Government of India constituted a separate Ministry of Tribal Affairs with a separate Cabinet minister. In between, the work of tribal development was entrusted to the Ministry of Welfare, which had been constituted in 1986 and thereafter rechristened as the Ministry of Social Justice and Empowerment in 1998.

Under the Constitutional provisions, tribal welfare ministries were set up in the States of Bihar, Madhya Pradesh and Orissa. Separate departments of tribal welfare were also established in these States. In other States, either combined departments of Scheduled Castes and Scheduled Tribes were set up or the Welfare departments were entrusted with the responsibility of tribal welfare. Usually District Collectors and other district level officers responsible for community development and social welfare were closely associated with the implementation of the tribal welfare programs.

## Integration in the Regional and National Setting

The base of the Indian culture being "unity in diversity", the social reformers, anthropologists and the administrators combined their skills and adopted an integrated approach towards the tribals.

Area development approach to develop the area in its totality found favor in the Fourth Five Year Plan and from the Fifth Five year plan, the drawing up of the tribal sub-plan was a clear reflection of the policy of integration with the regional and national setting.

After independence, the government gave a serious thought to the problems of tribal development and suggested an enlightened approach to develop the tribals along the line of their own genius. The Constituent Assembly appointed a sub-committee under Shri A.V.Thakkar to study the problems of the weaker sections and to suggest necessary measures for their upliftment. The most important finding of this Committee was "to establish the principle that the new democratic state had a responsibility for the welfare of the tribal people living in inaccessible and remote areas and the development of such areas". Shri Thakkar identified the tribal problems as poverty, illiteracy, lack of communication, ill health, defects in administration and lack of leadership. The Constituent Assembly accepted the recommendations of the sub-committee and thereafter the tribal development became an integral part of India's development.[6]

## References

1. Verrier Elwin – Nehru's Forward in 'A Philosophy for NEFA', Shillong, 1964, pp.(xi).
2. *Ibid.*
3. Report of the Working Group for the Tenth Five-year Plan, Planning Commission, New Delhi, 2002.
4. *Ibid.*
5. *Ibid.*
6. Amir Hassan- Tribal Administration in India, B.R. Publishing Corporation, Delhi, 1988, pp. 54-55.

# 3

# Approach to Tribal Development

As mentioned in the earlier chapter, the Indian Constitution had provided several safeguards for the Scheduled tribes. These safeguards were in the nature of special facilities for the spread of education among the tribes such as scholarships, freeships and grants, reservation of seats in government services and elected bodies such as the Parliament, the State legislatures, local bodies and the Gram Panchayats and specified funds for organizing tribal welfare in the States and Union Territories.

The national policy of tribal development rests largely on the statement made by Pundit Nehru in his note on 'A philosophy for NEFA', which is as follows:

"We cannot allow matters to drift in the tribal area or just not take interest in them. In the world of today, that is not possible or desirable. At the same time, we should avoid over-administering these areas and, in particular, sending too many outsiders into tribal territory... It is between these two extreme positions that we have to function. Development in various ways there has to be, such as communications, medical facilities, education and better agriculture. These avenues of development, should, however, be pursued within the broad framework of the five fundamental principles."[1]

The action, for development of tribals has, infact, emerged from India's struggle for independence. The ethos of tribal development that has emerged from the nation's history of struggle for independence, the constitutional safegards and the five year plans make it clear that we want to improve the socio-economic condition of the tribals. Our approach is that the tribal development should move forward along the line acceptable to the tribal genius. The genius consists of the tribal structures, which have provided stability and strength to the tribal society. What is important about the genius is that its continuity gives social and cultural identity to the people. And, therefore, at any stage if that genius is threatened, the inevitable consequence is the failure of development.

After the attainment of independence, Government was faced immediately with three tasks:

(a) Removing the communication gap between tribals and the regional community in the framework of national integration

(b) Protecting the resource base and the cultural apparatus which can provide the collective efforts for meeting national challenges

(c) Initiating measures for meeting the immediate needs of the tribal population and facilitating the process of participatory development.

In the Constitution, three strategies were adopted to deal with the tribal problem:

(1) The Fifth Schedule enumerated measures for the administration of tribal areas in those states that had a substantial population of the tribals. In such areas, the Union Government could give directions to the state and the Governor was given special powers for overseeing the administration of Scheduled areas.

(2) The Sixth Schedule was meant for tribal majority states in which provision was made for the establishment of autonomous district councils which could make laws for the management of land and forests, shifting cultivation, appointment of chiefs and Headmen, inheritance of property, marriage and divorce, social customs and anything relating to village administration.

(3) Article 275 of the Constitution provided for grant-in-aid to the states for promoting the welfare of the Scheduled

tribes in raising the level of administration of Scheduled areas.

In view of the above strategy, the emphasis on the development of Scheduled tribes was focused on the following in the post-independence period:

(a) Provision of immediate relief in terms of amenities and building up the productive infrastructure for future growth;

(b) Emphasis on resource mobilization and provision of social service infrastructure;

(c) Reduction of disparity and growth with justice. Efforts were also made for enlargement and commercialization of the resource base;

(d) Participatory development with focus on self-management, harnessing of productive forces for meeting the basic needs as well as to contribute to self-reliant growth.[2]

Immediately afterwards, the First Plan prepared in 1951 laid down the principle that 'the general development programs should be so designed as to cater adequately to the backward classes and the special provision should be used for securing additional and more intensified development'[3]

Pandit Jawaharlal Nehru, the first Prime Minister of India had set the right approach to tribal development when he said that by evolving of human character, he meant the bestowing of the boon of education on the tribal people which is the key to further development.

In pursuance of the special responsibilities given to the Indian State for the development of the tribals, the First Plan document observed that " the conditions are now generally such that there has to be positive policy of assisting the tribal population to develop their natural resources and to evolve a productive economic life wherein they will enjoy the fruits of their labour and will not be exploited by more organized economic forces from outside."[4]

The Second Five Year plan (1956-61) promised to ensure

that "the benefits of economic development accrue more and more to the relatively less privileged classes of society in order to reduce inequalities".[5] As for the Scheduled Tribes, "Welfare programs have to be based on respect and understanding of their culture and traditions and an appreciation of the social, psychological and economic problems with which they are faced". An important landmark during the second plan was the opening of 43 special multi-purpose Tribal Blocks (TDBs). Each was planned for about 25,000 people as against 65,000 in a normal Block. The Committee set up under the chairmanship of Mr. Verrier Elwin (1959) studied the working of these Blocks and found that they were providing very useful services.

The Third Five-year plan document describes the basic features of the socialist pattern of society, which also reflects the philosophy behind the framework of the Fifth and Sixth Schedules of the Constitution. It says that "Essentially, this means that the basic criterion for determining lines of advance must not be private profit, but social gain, and the pattern of development and the Structure of socio-economic relations should be so planned that they result not only in appreciable increase in national income and employment but also in greater equality in incomes and wealth... The benefits of economic development must accrue more and more to the really less privileged classes of society, and there should be progressive reduction of the concentration of incomes, wealth and economic power. The accent on the socialist pattern of society is on attainment of positive goals, the raising of living standards, the enlargement of opportunities for all, the promotion of enterprise among the disadvantaged classes and the creation of a sense of partnership among all sections of the community. The positive goals provide the criteria for basic decisions. The Directive Principles of State Policy in the Constitution have indicated the approach in broad terms; the socialistic pattern of society is a more concretized expression of this approach. Economic policy and institutional changes have to be planned in a manner that would secure economic advancement along democratic and egalitarian lines..."[6]

The Fourth Five-Year plan (1969-74) proclaimed that the

'basic goal was to realize rapid increase in the standard of the living of the people though measures which also promote equality and social justice'.[7] An important step during this period was setting up of six pilot projects in Andhra Pradesh, Bihar, Madhya Pradesh and Orissa in the year 1971-72 as central sector scheme with the primary objective of combating political unrest and left wing extremism. A separate Tribal Development Agency was established for each project. These agencies were later merged with Integrated Tribal Development Projects during the Fifth Plan.

The Fifth Five-Year plan (1974-78) marks a shift in approach reflected in the launching of Tribal Sub-Plan (TSP) for the direct benefit and development of tribals. The TSP stipulated that the funds of the State and Center should be quantified on population proportion basis, with budgetary mechanisms to ensure accountability, non-divertability and utilization for the welfare and development of STs. The TSP strategy is being implemented in 194 Integrated Tribal Development Projects, 252 pockets of Tribal concentration under Modified Area Development Approach (MADA); 78 clusters, and habitations of 75 Primitive Tribal Groups. There has been substantial increase in the flow of funds for the development of ST's under this arrangement, resulting in expansion of infrastructure facilities and enlargement of the coverage of the target groups in beneficiary oriented programs.

Since the beginning of the Fifth Five-year plan, the Tribal Sub-Plan approach and the Special Central Assistance to Tribal Sub-Plan has been instrumental in speeding up the allocation of funds for the development of Scheduled Tribes. As a result of this approach, various Central Ministries and the State Governments have to earmark a certain percentage of their funds in proportion to population of Scheduled Tribes in each State/ UT for the specific development of Scheduled Tribes.

However one of the major problems in this approach is that although TSP has been defined to mean schemes meant primarily for the benefit of STs, this has never been fully brought out. Consequently the Central Ministries have not taken the matter of TSP seriously and most of them have not earmarked funds for TSP on one pretext or another. Similarly though the state governments have indicated the flow to TSP, there has been no systematic monitoring and the inflow to TSP has been far much lower than that indicated in the plan budget.

The TSP approach was the result of reports of various committees like the Task Force on Development of Tribal Areas headed by Shri L.P.Vidyarthi in 1972 and the Working Group on personnel policy for the Tribal Areas under Shri R.N.Haldipur. Several other groups and committees also went into problems of tribal areas like cooperatives, rural indebtedness, land alienation, excise policy etc. The result of these deliberations was the birth of new strategy of tribal sub-plan within the broad framework of state and the Central plans. The tribal sub-plan was implemented through ITDPs which served as units of planning and implementation. At the project level, the Project officer was responsible for coordinating, monitoring and evaluating the programs, implemented by the various departments. It was however, observed that there was a lack of functional integration at the project level and the performance of tribal development administration was far from satisfactory. The Project officer neither monitored the expenditure effectively, nor exercised supervision over the schemes under the Sub-plan. Schemes were delayed and for that justification were offered by the officials concerned.

The emphasis in the Sub-plan strategy was not merely area-based, but with focus on the Scheduled Tribe population. The STs numbering over 250 tribes and speaking over 100 languages have their own distinct socio-cultural and ecological milieu. To treat their problem with efficiency, they were divided into three categories, namely (a) tribes residing in areas of traditional tribal concentration; (b) dispersed tribal population and (c) primitive tribes wherever they resided whether in areas of tribal concentration or outside. In areas of tribal concentration, an element of area development planning was incorporated in the development schemes.

The broad approach of the TSP strategy was continued during the Sixth Plan period with greater emphasis on specific objectives, namely;

(a) Raising of productivity levels of tribal activities with a view to enabling a targeted number of families to rise above the poverty line;

(b) Development of human resources and upgradation of education;

(c) Elimination of exploitation of tribals in the field of land alienation, money lending, trade, excise and forest ;

(d) Development of adequate infrastructure.

By the end of this plan period, dividends of the new Tribal Sub-plan strategy were reaped in the shape of a more integrated approach to planning and implementation, large financial allocation both by the Center and the States and considerably larger physical achievement in amelioration of poverty of the targeted groups as also in the general and social service sectors. Among the important contributions of the Tribal Sub-plan strategy over a period of years has been the gradual evaluation of the concept of family-oriented programs for eradication of poverty. The emphasis on family-oriented and beneficiary-oriented schemes during the Sixth plan had a perceptible impact in substantially boosting up the number of tribal families economically assisted. The long-term objective of the TSP approach was to narrow the gap between the levels of development of the tribal areas and other areas while improving the quality of life of the tribal communities.

The strategy for the Sixth plan emphasized the consolidation of the gains of protective measures, employment programs, education and health services. It also sought to ensure a higher degree of devolution of funds so that atleast 50% of the tribal families were provided assistance to cross the poverty line. In this plan, the emphasis was on family oriented economic activities rather than infrastructure development schemes.

The Seventh five year plan (1985-90) was committed to growth with equity, social justice, self-reliance, improved efficiency and productivity and called for a strategy built around agricultural growth, creation of jobs and all-round technological upgradation, specialized industry and measures to improve the quality of life.

Tribal development is based on the twin approach namely, protection of their interests through legislative and administrative support and promotion of developmental efforts through plan schemes. In the Eighth five-year plan (1992-97), efforts were intensified to bridge the gap between the levels of development of the Scheduled Tribes and those of the other sections of the society so that by the turn of the century these disadvantaged sections could be brought-at-par with the rest of the society. The allotment for the development of STs was increased during the plan period along with emphasis on the elimination of their exploitation.

The Ninth five year plan (1997-2002) envisaged advancement of STs through a process of empowerment wherein efforts are to be made to create an enabling environment conducive for the exercise of their rights freely, enjoyment of their privileges and leading a life of self-confidence and dignity at par with other citizens of the country. This encompasses three vital components namely;

(i) social empowerment,

(ii) economic empowerment and

(iii) social justice.

The approach paper to the tenth five-year plan (2002-2007) makes a strong case for a tribal policy. It says , " From the viewpoint of the policy, it is important to understand that tribal communities are vulnerable not only because they are poor, assetless and illiterate compared to the general population; often their distinct vulnerability arises from their inability to negotiate and cope with the process of integration with the mainstream economy, society, cultural and political system, from which they were historically protected as a result of their relative isolation. Post independence, the requirements of planned development brought with them the scepter of dams, mines, industries and roads on tribal lands. With these came the concomitant processes of displacement, both literal and metaphorical –as tribal institutions and practices were forced into uneasy existence with or gave way to market or formal state institutions (most significantly in the legal sphere), tribals found themselves at a profound disadvantage with respect to the influx of better equipped outsiders into tribal areas. The repercussions for the already fragile socio-economic livelihood base of the tribals were devastating- ranging from the loss of livelihoods, land alienation on a vast scale, to hereditary bondage."[7]

The following persistent problems have proved to bc intractible and continue to plague the planners and administrators:[8]

i. Land alienation and their restoration

ii. Indebtedness

iii. Tribal Forest Rights, Development of forest villages and shifting cultivation

iv. To give effect to the provisions of Panchayats (extension to the Scheduled (Areas) Act of 1996 through required legislation at the State level

v. Involuntary displacement due to development projects and lack of proper rehabilitation.

vi. Survival, protection and development of the Primitive Tribal Groups (PTGs)

vii. Effective and meaningful implementation of the strategy of Tribal Sub-Plan.

To tackle the above problems of the tribals, the working group for the empowrment of Scheduled Tribes in the Tenth Five year plan has advocated a comprehensive national policy for the empowerment of the tribals which will lay down the responsibilities of the different wings of the government with appropriate accountability.

The Working Group for the Tenth Five-year plan has obscrvcd that the schemes that are being implemented at present are mostly straitjacketed schemes with little flexibility or maneuverability. These schemes need to be more flexible and need-based. The tendency so far has been to spread the resources uniformly in the entire tribal area in accordance with the availability of funds. This thin spread makes the schemes ineffective and no tangible results are available on the ground despite substantial amount being spent in the last fifty years. This has to change and area specific programs in accordance with availability of funds have to be adopted.[9]

Planning is not an end in itself. It is a means to an end and the end is the achievement of pre-determined goals. These goals in aggregate terms are to increase gross national production and per capita income, to facilitate distribution of the gross national product in a more equitable manner and to enhance the provision of full employment opportunities. These aggregate goals are to be sorted out sectorwise to arrive at various physical targets, which are then related with financial allocations to result in physical achievements. These will require a team of organized personnel that can carry out these programs, making the best use of financial resources to achieve maximum results.

Since the beginning of the planning process, plans have been formulated for the welfare of the Scheduled Tribes as the improvement of the quality of life has been one of the objectives of the five year plans. Accordingly, financial allocations were also made in the Five-Year Plans though investment was not very significant in relation to goals.

During the first four five year plan periods, the goal was to develop socio-economic conditions of the tribal people, but the policies, programs and the machinery for its implementation could not do much. As a result, some tribal communities received some benefits while the others remained untouched. In some places these forces of development have sometimes adversely affected the tribals. The experiences of different development programs being run in rural areas and more particularly for the tribal people provided a good base for a new phase of tribal development which began in the Fifth five year plan and continued thereafter.

At this stage, let us review the policies and programs taken up in the earlier plans for the development of the tribal people of the country.

Soon after independence, the First five year plan was started in 1951. Under the comprehensive program for rural development, Natural Extension Scheme Blocks were started in 1951. This was followed by 56 Community Development Programs which were established on 2nd October, 1952. Each Community Development Project covered 300 villages and a population of 2 lakh with an area of about 400 to 500 sq. miles. Each project was divided into three Development blocks covering 100 villages with 60 to 70 thousand population. The period of the project was 3 years initially with an allocation of Rs. 12 lakhs per project. It was expected to create a self-sustained growth through these Community Development blocks. All aspects of the Community life were envisaged as the tasks in the program. But this experiment met with little success. The reasons were that the emancipation of tribal communities was a complex process with serious socio-political and economic implications. The powerful feudal and vested economic interests therefore had to be fought against and new modes of role relations had to be established to ensure tribal claims. These sporadic and isolated attempts could have only nominal impact on the welfare of the tribals.[10] Modifing the Community Development concept for the tribal region after this early experience, 43 special Multipurpose Tribal Development blocks were started in India in 1954. It was realized that it would not be possible to start and sanction such an intensive program throughout the tribal region within a short period. Thus the Ministry of Community Development and the Ministry of Home Affairs constituted funds of Rs. 12 lakhs and Rs. 15 lakhs respectively in addition to normal allocations to Community Development projects and a less intensive model of Tribal Development Block was evolved. Altogether 489 such Tribal Development Blocks with more than two-thirds tribal population were established by the end of Third Five Year Plan. Those, tribal areas which had more than 50% tribal population but less than two-thirds continued to be served by the general program under the

Community Development Blocks. After a short period and with the opening of new departments for other types of developmental programs apart from Education, Agriculture and Public Health, the quantum of development effort by the Community Development and Tribal Development blocks remained constant, rather became less with time and gradually withdrawn, leaving the Blocks with only a small content.

In the beginning of the Fourth Five Year Plan considering the land-based rural economy, a series of pilot programmes were conceived for specific target groups; they included the Small Farmers Development Agencies (SFDA) and Marginal Farmers and Agricultural Laborers agencies. Then Drought Prone Area Program was also initiated. In all these cases, attention shifted from area development to development oriented individuals who needed special attention accordingly to certain criteria. Greater attention was on the weaker sections of the society. Some Tribal Development Agencies (TDA) were also established on the pattern of SFDA. During the Fourth Five Year Plan altogether six such agencies were started and two more added afterwards. Each TDA covered a group of T.D.Blocks. But with time, the agencies which were expected to comprise elements of economic development and social services became agricultural development programs with substantial investment on roads. Thus these programs could not outgrow their pilot phase.

An Important feature of the Fourth plan was the strengthening of protective regulations by amending the Debt Relief Regulation in the years 1970-71 to protect the tribals from exploitation. The idea of area planning emerged during the Fourth plan period but no serious effort was made to develop area development program or for implementing the same. Thus, the same institutional frame, personnel, composition, program content and plan strategies were continued during the succeeding annual plans after the Fourth Plan period was over.

Upto Fourth Plan period, it was noted that due to weakness in the policies, programs as well as the administrative machinery, achievement was not very significant in relation to the needs of tribal population. Considering the pattern of the tribal life and culture, the Government of India took the decision that from the Fifth plan onwards the major thrust for development of the tribal areas and tribal communities ought to be provided by each of the concerned sectors. As it was also noticed that sometimes area development was provided for at the cost of the tribal communities, therefore it was clearly laid down that the strategy would be area development with focus on development of the tribal communities. This strategy for integrated development led to the launching of the Tribal-Sub Plan in the Fifth plan period.

Therefore, after independence, four phases in the process of planning can be identified. In the first phase, the emphasis was on providing immediate relief to the general population who were denied such amenities during the colonial rule and also to build up the infrastructure for future growth. In the second phase, the emphasis was on resource mobilization and provision of social service infrastructure in the countryside. In the third phase, the emphasis shifted to reduction of disparity and growth with justice. In the fourth phase, programs for meeting the basic needs of the people were taken up and poverty alleviation programmes were stepped up.

In each of these phases, plans and programs have been drawn up for the tribals broadly keeping the national objective in mind. But the advantages of the community development projects of the first phase were mainly taken up by the non-tribals living in tribal areas. Tribal development projects towards the end of the first phase were not much of an improvement.

Tribal development blocks in the second phase gave some attention to these constraints. During the fifth plan, integrated tribal area development approach was adopted after identifying areas of tribal concentration at the level of blocks and districts in the states and UTs having substantial tribal population. In addition Modified Area Development Approach was adopted for pockets of tribals which included also the primitive tribes. To handle the ITDPs, MADA s and PTGs, the tribal sub-plans were drawn up for the respective states/UTs. But the states/UTs having a majority of ST population were left out of the scope of TSP.

The Indian experiment to uplift the tribal people has been unique in that there are very few countries in the world with such elaborate systems of preferential treatment and Constitutional provisions of special protections and privileges for the tribals. Yet the most crucial questions, namely right to land and land-based resources for survival of the tribals have remained unresolved. Denials of these rights have led to distrust and disquiet in tribal minds, often leading to unrest and agitation.

The tribal development programs taken up after independence were aimed at increasing the income of the tribal people and raising their standard of living. This included measures for stopping land transfer from tribals to non- tribals, debt redemption, liberation of bonded labour, agricultural development, provision of irrigation facilities and special efforts to protect the interest of the tribals in land and forest. But most of these programs in the tribal sector had little impact on poverty and educational backwardness of the tribals due to inadequate financial backing and organizational support. A decline in the outlay for tribal development from the First to the Fourth Plan in terms of the percentage of the total plan outlay can be seen on the earlier pages. Only in the Fifth Five-Year Plan, the percentage was raised to 3.1, but this included expenditure in creation of the infrastructure for development. During the Fifth Plan, the Sub-Plan concept was adopted but the Meso Area projects drawn up with great effort could not be implemented. Even the Integrated Tribal Development Projects could not produce the desired results.

The origin of the Integrated Tribal Development Projects (ITDPs) lay in the failure of NES and CDP. This scheme came into operation in 1972 by the Tribal Development Department of the Ministry of Home Affairs in consultation wit various state level tribal development departments. But, it followed the same line of experience as over the preceding years, which had proved that areas developed without developing the tribals therein, could not succeed.

In 1975, the scheme of the tribal sub-plan within the main plans of the State and Union Governments was started almost in all states but without the project officials to control and manage the development activities of the various State and Union Government departments.

Though development is popularly regarded as an economic process, equal emphasis should be placed on the qualitative aspects of human development. Sociologically speaking, development should be looked upon as an organized activity with the aim of satisfying certain basic needs and to psychologically orient the tribals to adopt new skills, attitudes and lifestyles, so that they build up the inner strength, and appropriate social and cultural infrastructure to stand the pressures of the new situation and get benefits from the new programs and maintain higher levels. From this point of view, development is a multidimensional process to progressively improve the social, cultural, economic and human conditions of the people.

Since India opted for planned development, special attention has been paid to the upliftment of tribals and tribal areas, by providing enhanced allotment of funds and evolving special development programs to integrate the tribals with the larger society.

During the Sixth Plan, a new strategy was adopted for tribals living in dispersed areas and an area approach for tribal development in those areas where tribals lived in large concentration and individual approach for small and primitive tribal groups.

There have also been some negative aspects of the development process. They are:

1. Major irrigation projects leading to large scale displacement of tribal people;
2. Depletion of forest resources affecting tribals at various levels of development;
3. Decline of cottage industries and pauperization of tribal

artisans;

4. Land alienation

**Land Alienation**

The tribals in India (67.8 million) constitute one third of the total tribal population of the world (207 million). They are distributed in some 582 tribes; of which 75 are primitive tribes. About 94% of them live in rural areas. Alienation of land and indebtedness are the major causes of poverty among the Scheduled Tribes. These two are so much inter-related that one cannot speak of one without the other. Infact, it is indebtedness, which ultimately leads to alienation of land.

The nature of land alienation in the Scheduled Areas is broadly of two types:-

(i) The first is the alienation of land to non-tribals and plains-men which has been the major form of transfer of land from tribals. This was because the protective laws meant for the tribals were not enforced properly.

(ii) The second type of land alienation is state induced tribal land alienation. The case of Samatha Vs the State of Andhra Pradesh is a classic example of how the state has been violating its own constitutional duty in the Fifth Scheudle areas. In the name of economic development through industrialisation, the State has been alienating tribal lands for its development projects and the private industries. It also leads to large scale displacement. Research shows that the number of displaced tribals till 1990 is about 85.39 lakhs (55.16% of total displaced) of whom 64.23% are yet to be rehabilitated. *(Source: Walter Fernandes, 1994)*

Land is a state subject. Though the British began the process of conferring legal titles of land ownership to individuals in the tribal areas towards the end of the 19th century, it became all pervasive only in the post-colonial India. In respect of unrecorded lands, the traditional peasants are treated as encroachers and liable to be evicted.

As regards common village lands like pastures, village forests, sacred groves, streams etc, many State Governments have usurped these for development projects. The tribals who used to gather several minor forest produce from the forest areas have been deprived of the same. In 1987, the Committee on Forests and Tribals of the Ministry of Home Affairs suggested that as between 30-50% of the total income of the tribal families came from the land based resources, the State should recognize their rights of access to and control of these resources.[10]

Tribal families living in over 5000 forest villages possess no right on the land they cultivate. In 1984, the Ministry of Agriculture had advised the State Governments to confer long-term heritable but inalienable rights for 15-20 years in respect of land occupied by tribals in these villages. But nothing substantial has been done in this direction.

The development projects have also encroached upon the tribal land resources as most of the massive irrigation and power projects, steel plants, forest and wildlife projects etc have mostly come up in the tribal inhabited areas. The National SC and ST Commission has noted that out of the 1.7 million people displaced by 119 Central and State government projects, a staggering 0.8 million i.e. nearly half belonged to Scheduled Tribes.[11] According to a World Bank estimate, about two million tribal people currently face resettlement to make way for hydropower projects alone. This number continues to increase year after year. As yet, there is no national policy on resettlement of displaced persons.

There may be an argument that the massive expenditure on the welfare and development of tribals may be more than compensating the deprivation caused with regard to land. But an appraisal of the outlay and expenditure during the Five year plans belies this. Contrary to common belief, actual expenditure on the welfare of tribals has remained less than one percent of the plan outlay during the first four plans, although they constitute about 8% of the total population of India. During the First Five year plan, the allocation was 1.0% of the budget but the actual expenditure was only 0.8%. Between 1951-74, per capita annual expenditure on tribal welfare was as little as one and a half rupees at 1951 prices. After the introduction of the tribal sub-plan, it increased to around five rupees at that price level.

Another point to ponder is that whatever is spent on tribal welfare is heavily biased in favor of education which is 48% as against economic development which is 28%. Although many major irrigation projects are located in tribal areas, no more than 5% of the tribal land is irrigated. Even after massive investment in education, the literacy level among tribals is only 29.6% as against 52.2% for the country as a whole and for females it is only 18.2% as compared to overall female literacy for the country (39.2%). More than half of the rural tribal population has been found to be below poverty line as per the survey done by the Ministry of Rural Development in 1993-94. The per capita income of the tribals continues to be one of the lowest in the country and their alienation from the land continues. As on January 1999, the tribals were alienated from 9,17,590 acres of tribal land and only 5,37,610 acres of such land was restored as per the latest statistics of the Ministry of Rural Development. As per the annual report (2000-2001) of the Ministry of Rural Development, 3.75 lakh cases of tribal land alienation have been registered so far, covering an area of 8.55 lakh acres of land, of which 1.62 lakh cases have been disposed of in favor of tribals covering an area of 4.47 lakh acres.

The complexity of the land problem of the tribals stems from: (a) nature of association of the tribal people with their land; (b) frequent loss of control of the communities over these resources on the introduction of the new land use pattern; (c) self image of the tribal elites and their perception about their actual or potential role in the decision making process at various levels of the national life (d) conflict between traditional and modern elite in the perception of goal of economic and social development, and (e) absence of political preparation for changing production relations, stalemate in productive resources, production technology but rapid change in consumption norms.[12]

The policy implications of the types of relations with the land are diverse. They are based on: (a) on understanding of the structure and organization of customary rights; (b) changes under the impact of contact, technological change, government policy, growth of ideology and other measures, and (c) review of the legislative and executive measures with reference to recognition of the customary rights in land and forests.[13]

The objectives of the land reforms policy are:

i. Abolition of intermediary tenures ;

ii. Tenancy reforms aimed at security of tenure, regulation of rent and conferment of ownership rights on tenants ;

iii. Ceiling on land holdings and distribution of surplus lands;

iv. Consolidation of holdings;

v. Compilation and updating of land records.[14]

Land Alienation is one of the most complex problems in the tribal areas. The dispossession of the tribals from their land has become quite common. Due to economic backwardness, the tribals often have to mortgage their land or sell it as a result of which they became landless.

The Working Group on Development and Welfare of Scheduled Tribes during the Eighth Five Year Plan (1990-95) observed, "It has been found that the Scheduled Tribes are generally unaware of the protective laws in respect of alienation of lands. Further, the unscrupulous money-lending and the unproductive quality of land in the tribal areas were prime causes of alienation of tribal lands."[15]

The Working Group therefore suggested for elimination of exploitative practices and improvement in the productivity of lands. Further, a campaign should be undertaken to make the tribals themselves aware of their rights and modes of legal redressal.[16]

***Agriculture*:** Some of the problems faced by the tribal cultivators in the field of agriculture were:

1. Lack of irrigation facilities
2. Insufficient land (small size of operational holdings)
3. Irregular monsoon

4. Lack of agricultural inputs like HYV seeds, fertilizers etc.
5. Non-possession of ploughing cattle by many cultivators
6. Late and untimely disbursement of crop loans by the government and financial institutions
7. Marketing and processing facilities.
8. Shifting cultivation.

Shifting cultivation is still practiced by the tribal population on the higher slopes of the hilly areas of the country. As estimated, more than 6 lakh tribal families in the States of North-East, Orissa, Andhra, Uttaranchal and Jharkhand practice shifting cultivation, which is ecologically unsound. The problem of shifting cultivation is a very complex one involving economic, social and psychological aspects of the tribal communities and needs to be tackled with care and caution.

Lack of irrigation has been another major problem for the agricultural development of the tribal area. Experience shows that irrigation is a key factor of agricultural modernization and is a pre-condition for the successful introduction of the new and high-yielding varieties but the hilly areas are devoid of irrigation facilities.

**Education:** Education is the most important element in the development of any community. It has special significance for the weaker sections of the society like STs. For them, education is not only an input for their economic development, but also for promoting in them self-confidence to face new challenges. The Scheduled Tribes have fallen victims to the exploitation of the middlemen, merchants and money-lenders on account of their illiteracy and ignorance. The need for their educational development therefore, assumes prime importance to save them from economic exploitation and to help in their all round development.

Educational advancement can be taken to be the best indicator of the development of any community. The most important single indicator in this regard is the literacy rate.

The National Policy on Education (1986) states in regard to the education of the Scheduled Tribes:

The following measures will be taken urgently to bring the Scheduled Tribes at par with others:

1. Priority will be accorded to the opening of primary schools in the tribal areas.
2. There is a need to develop the curriculum and devise instructional materials in tribal languages at the initial stages, with arrangements for switching over to the regional language.
3. Educated and promising tribal youths will be encouraged and trained to take up teaching in tribal areas.
4. Residential schools including Ashram schools, will be established on a large scale.
5. Incentive schemes will be formulated for the STs keeping in view their special needs and lifestyles. Scholarships shall be provided for higher education with special emphasis on technical and professional courses. Special remedial classes will be provided to improve performance.
6. Anganwadis, formal and non- formal education centers will be opened on a priority basis.[17]

Considering that in spite of the availability of schools in most of the tribal villages, the tribals did not send their children to schools, essentially for economic reasons, it is necessary that some supplementary income earning avenues and other incentives are provided and local tribal youths with requisite qualification are appointed as teachers of these schools.

The Tata Institute of Social Sciences, Mumbai, conducted a study on this subject in Maharashtra during 1984-85. They found the following reasons for the drop-outs among the STs:-

1. The child being required to work at home,
2. Poverty and inability to afford education and
3. Their lack of interest in education.

The National Policy in education, 1986 had laid down

that the investment in education should regularly increase to reach a level of 6% of the National Income but the following table will show that after the Fourth Plan, the percentage of allocation started declining.

## Health and Nutrition

The tribal communities in general and primitive tribal groups in particular have been disease-prone in certain aspects and have little access to basic health facilities. Their misery is compounded by poverty, illiteracy, ignorance of causes of diseases, hostile environment, poor sanitation, lack

**Percentage of National Allocation on Education during the Five Year Plans**

| *Plans* | *Years* | *Percentage of total plan outlay* |
|---|---|---|
| First | (1951-56) | 6.96 |
| Second | (1956-61) | 6.40 |
| Third | (1961-66) | 7.78 |
| Annual Plans | (1966-69) | 4.77 |
| Fourth | (1969-74) | 5.21 |
| Fifth | (1974-79) | 3.27 |
| Sixth | (1980-85) | 2.58 |
| Seventh | (1985-90) | 3.54 |
| Eighth | (1992-97) | 4.88 |
| Ninth | (1997-2002) | 2.37 |

of safe drinking water etc. Some specific diseases of tribal areas are sickle-cell, anaemia, tuberculosis, leprosy, Diarrhoea, Cholera and reproductive tract infection.

Infant mortality is also high in tribes as compared to non-tribes and only 26% of the children in tribal areas received all vaccine. Thus tribal people need special attention for improving their health, reproductive and child health status.

The National Health Policy (1993) while recognizing the

heterogeneous tribal population and their varied health problems, accorded a high priority for extending the health services to those residing in the backwared rural areas, with a concentration of STs. The strategy adopted for meeting the health care needs include provision of preventive as well as curative services through the primary health care institutions and at the village level through health guides and trained dais. However due to local geographical conditions and less accessible areas of tribal habitations, the mobile dispensaries and health centres shall serve more useful purpose than the static ones.

**Addiction to Liquor and Drugs**

A very important problem which concerns the tribals is addiction to spirits, drugs and highly intoxicating liquors and drinks. While the indigenous during prepared by fermentation of rice, millets, mahua and other grains are nutritious, the distilled liquor which is sold by the government license holders is highly intoxicant and has little food value. The only practical solution is the banishment of liquor contractors from the tribal areas so that the tribals may be left free to brew their own liquor and fulfil their cultural needs.

Drug addiction is a serious health problem with several tribes. Singpho tribe of Arunachal Pradesh who have been addicted to opium are now left with only 1,000 persons though they numbered about 40,000 about 150 years ago. It is said that opium has diminished the tribe's fertility, increased the death rate and led them to the vicious circle of poverty as they had become too indolent.

The speedy spread of health education among the tribals is urgently required to wean them away from the wrong practices which they have acquired and to inculcate in them the basic principles of health and sanitation.

**Economic Progress**

For improving the economic condition of the tribals, it is of utmost importance that special efforts need to be organized and mounted to provide gainful employment for sufficient duration of the years. Considering the socio-economic background, the level of education and skill endowment etc of the tribal communities, such efforts also need to be innovated and tailored according to their needs and the prevailing conditions of the area. For all those daily wage earners like non-agricultural laborers and construction workers some type of regular and settled wage or income earning activities need to be organized. Similarly, a large number of idle or non-earning members in tribal households also require suitable training and skill formation so as to enable them to increasingly take up different type of secondary and tertiary occupations of their own on a permanent basis in the nature of small scale, home industries, animal husbandry, business etc to strengthen the economic base and supplement their family income.

**Indebtedness**

Indebtedness is a symptom of the economic malaise among the tribal communities. At the household level, it is indicative of poverty, unemployment or living beyond the means available. The tribal households are prone to indebtedness. It is generally believed that indebtedness is endemic among them due to the precarious nature of their very means of livelihood.

Under the Fifth Schedule to the Constitution, the Governors of States with Scheduled Areas have been given powers for making regulations for placing restrictions on money-lending activities in such Scheduled Areas. Relevant laws/regulations exist in 16 TSP States/UTs to regulate the business of money lending and to give debt relief. However, the legal measures to curb the activities of money-lenders and traders have failed to have much effect on the severity of the problem due to the ineffective enforcement machinery and lack of alternative sources of credits for meeting consumption and productive needs. Lack of sound national policy to extend consumption credit to poor tribals has tended to make them dependent on the landlords and money-lenders, which also results in their debt-bondage.

**Bonded Labour**

Bonded labour system was abolished by law throughout

the country with effect from 25th October 1975 by an ordinance which was later replaced by an Act of Parliament namely the Bonded Labour System (Abolition) Act 1976. The responsibility of identification, release and rehabilitation of bonded labour rests with the State governments. No information on the number of tribal bonded labourers identified, released and rehabilitated is available though as on 31st March 1993, the total all India figure stays at 2,51,439 which includes STs also. This is an important area and efforts should be made on a regular basis to identify and rehabilitate bonded labourers in general and STs in particular.

**Forests and Tribals**

Among Nehru's Panchsheel for tribal development, one of the points was that 'tribal's rights in land and forests should be respected'. This was only right as the forest to a tribal is a community resource, a means of sustenance that needs to be judiciously used, maintained, nurtured and renewed.

About 53% of the total land in India (328.7 hectares) is covered by forests, out of which about 63.34 million hectares (19.27%) is notified forest and only about 11% of the total area comprises of dense forest.

Forests have been in existence since much before human beings appeared on the earth, and whereas forests can exist and thrive without human beings, human beings cannot exist and thrive without forests. For centuries, the tribals have depended for their livelihood on the forests that meet nearly all their needs. For a tribal, his whole life is closely linked to the forest in all its forms.

In the Indian Constitution, duty has been imposed under Article 48(A) and Article 51(A)(g) on the state and the citizens to protect and safeguard forests. India has had a forest policy from the British days when in 1894, the National Forest Policy was drafted. This policy helped the British acquire and own all the forest lands in the country, which were until then, the community holding of the tribals. Thus the tribals, who had depended on the forests for their livelihood, were deprived of their right over the forests.

Later in order to safeguard and preserve the forest wealth and to consolidate all the existing laws relating to the forests, the Indian Forest Act, 1927 was passed. Through this Act, the reserved forests were almost closed to the tribals while in the protected forests, they had their existing rights except those prohibited by the State government. Later more and more protected forests were converted into reserve forests and exploited for their raw materials. The State government was also given vast powers to regulate almost anything with regard to the protected forests.

The tribals being ousted from their forests, lost their means of livelihood, they in turn were forced to destroy more forests for their survival. The ancient tribal culture and practice of balance between human and ecological needs, changed into what can be termed as destructive dependence on forests.

The next forest policy was prepared in 1952. This was in a way an extension of the erstwhile British forest policy because the forests were treated as raw material for commerce and industry, and no notice was taken of the needs of the forest dwellers who depend on the forest for their survival. In 1956, the forests were nationalized.

The Forest conservation Act, 1980 continued to be biased in favor of Commerce and industry and ignored the demands and needs of the tribals. This Act stipulated that the state government could not direct dereservation of forests or convert the use of forest land for non-forest purpose without the prior approval of the Central Government. But any policy on Conservation of forests is incomplete without the participation of the forest dwellers. The B.K.Roy, Burman Committee (1982) on 'Forests and Tribals' has brought out the symbiotic relationship between the tribals and forests very well. It stated that the forest policy should meet the ecological needs and raw material needs of the tribals.

The tribals have their own indigenous methods of identifying the imbalances in the forest eco-system and to tackle the same.

The third National Forest Policy (1988) emphasized protection, conservation and development of forests. It says that the domestic requirement of the tribals and other poor in or near forests should be the first charge on the forest produce and the tribal people be closely associated with the regeneration, plantation, development and harvesting of forests so as to provide them gainful employment.

The main thrust of the Government's Forest Policy should be to ensure the conservation of forests and the development of the tribal community therein. This can be achieved by winning the confidence of the tribals and earmarking certain areas as their community property. An attempt should be made to involve them in forest projects like forest development and conservation. Each and every policy should aim at conservation of forests and its growth together with the subsistence of the tribals and their betterment.

**Development or Change**

Development is usually conceived as an aspect of change that is desirable, broadly predicted or planned and administered or at least influenced by the governmental action. Thus the concept of development consists of :

(a) An aspect of change,

(b) A plan or prediction; and

(c) Involvement of the government for the achievement of that planned or predicted goal.

The term 'development' is also used for the process of allowing or encouraging people to meet their own aspirations. It therefore must relate to transforming the entire society enmeshing together its economic, social, political and administrative aspects for an all round balanced upward change.[18]

The main aim of development is to increase national as well as per capita income and to raise the living standard of the people and to secure justice, freedom, equality and security for them in the society. The focus of development is now increasingly on :

(a) Equitable distribution of wealth and income;

(b) Full utilization of manpower;

(c) Better utilization of natural resources; and

(d) Protection of human environment etc.

Thus the major dimensions of development are;

(a) Economic

(b) Social and

(c) Political

Backwardness of an area is often attributed to the paucity of resources. Tribal development aims at increasing the incomes and strengthening the material aspects of tribal culture through better utilization of the environmental resources i.e. forests, minerals, flora and fauna, agriculture and animal husbandry etc.

Economic development in terms of an increase in per capita income is no longer regarded as the only development objective. It may pave the way for a substantial improvement in the quality of the people. It also means bringing about improvement in the social being of the people and as such lays stress on provision of health services, education, housing, improved status of women and workers and reduction of poverty, disease and ignorance.

Though all the tribal areas are not at the same stage of socio-economic development, nevertheless, it can be said that there are some basic similarities in all these areas on the basis of which certain common policy can be formulated. The tribal areas are characterized by their aloofness, a lower level of economic activity and a closed social structure.

Administratively, the programs for the welfare of the tribals fall under three categories;

(a) Centrally operated programs;

(b) Centrally sponsored programs, and

(c) State sector programs.

The scene of tribal development can be viewed against

the backdrop of the five year plans in the country. During the First Five Year Plan period, more emphasis was given to categories and areas to bring overall changes through community development programs. People's participation and proper motivation were the two most important factors. During the Second Five Year plan, a massive program of integrated development was initiated by organizing 43 special Multipurpose tribal blocks in areas having tribal concentration. Top priority was given to education followed by communication, agriculture, animal husbandry and health. In the Third Five Year plan, 489 tribal development blocks were provided financial assistance from the center and state sectors and emphasis was given on food production. During this period, economic upliftment was given top priority followed by education, health and housing.

These priorities remained unchanged during Fourth plan. However, much emphasis was given to "Area and Regional approach". The most innovative program during the Fourth five year plan was the introduction of six pilot projects in the backward tribal areas covering 40,000 tribal families. These projects laid stress on providing improved seeds and agricultural implements as well as fertilizer and irrigation facilities.

The tribal sub-plan strategy formulated in 1974-75 made concerted effort to quicken the pace of development in the tribal areas. Prior to that, the situation was not satisfactory as the Ministry of Home Affairs, Government of India noted in its report, "that in the name of tribal development, we have spent a lot of money during the last several plans but when accounting was made, it was found that actual benefits trickling down to the tribals have not been consistent with the promise we have made. Expenditure has not resulted in the benefits that should have accrued to this population. Unfortunately, the development programs for the tribal areas did not yield the desired result...".[19]

Therefore, it can be said that the tribal development programs of the government during the plan periods are appreciable but the achievements have been unsatisfactory. There may also be a view that the development programs taken up for STs are not appropriate for them and hence badly implemented.

**Empowering the Scheduled Tribes: An approach to the Tenth Plan (2002-2007)**

Guided by the conclusions that were recorded in the Mid-term appraisal of the Ninth Five Year Plan (1997-2002) stating that "A small bunch of bureaucratic programmes had done little to avert the precipitious pauperization, exploitation and disintegration of tribal communities and therefore, most of the persistent problems like poverty, indebtedness, land alienation, displacement, deterioration of forest villages and the tribals living therein, shifting cultivation etc, continue to persist even till today as the 'Unresolved issues of Tribal Development, the Tenth Five year plan lays down its first priority in finding solutions to these very unresolved issues. Solutions to this effect can best be found only when the deprivation and exploitation of tribals is eradicated. The Tenth Plan will, therefore, adopt eradication of deprivation/exploitation of tribals as the centre-point in its approach, while pursuing simultaneously the Ninth Plan commitment of empowering the tribals.[20]

**Summing UP**

An assessment of the present stage of tribal development programs in many tribal areas presents a not very happy picture. Despite the creation of tribal development blocks, ITDPs and the adoption of the Tribal Sub-plan strategy, the fact remains that:

1. The majority of the tribal areas have been isolated and backward,
2. The tribal areas are characterized by socio-economic exploitation by non-tribals,
3. The tribal lands are still alienated and indebtedness is on the increase,
4. The tribal literacy rate remains at the low level, and
5. The tribal agricultural technology remains unchanged.

## Reference

1. Verrier Elwin – Nehru's forward to 'A Philosophy for NEFA', Shillong, 1964, p. XI
2. Alexander Verghese. Seminar (282) February, 1983, p. 34.
3. First five year plan document, Planning Commission, New Delhi.
4. *Ibid.*
5. Second Five Year Plan document, Planning Commission, New Delhi.
6. Third Five Year Plan document, Planning Commission, New Delhi.
7. Report of the working group on the empowerment of the scheduled tribes, Planning Commission, New Delhi, 2001.
8. J.P.Singh and N.N.Vyas (ed)- Tribal Development, Himanshu Publications, Udaipur, 1989, p. 17.
9. Report of the working group on the empowerment of the Scheduled Tribes, Planning Commission, New Delhi, 2001.
10. B.K. Roy Burman- Perspective for administration and development of Scheduled Tribes, NICD, Hyderabad, 1975, p. 46.
11. Report of the National Commission for SC & ST (28th report) New Delhi, 1988, pp.254-255
12. Ashok R. Basu- Tribal Development programs and administration in India, National Book Organization, New Delhi, 1985, p. 92.
13. Shilu AO Committee Report, 1969, p. 25.
14. Government of India, Occasional Papers on Tribal Development No. 7, Ministry of Home Affairs, 1977.
15. Report of the Working Group for the Eighth Five-Year plan, Planning Commission, New Delhi, pp. 35-37.
16. *Ibid.*
17. National Policy on Education (1986), Ministry of H.R.D., GoI, New Delhi.
18. Ashok R. Basu-Tribal Development programs and administration in India, National Book Organization, New Delhi, 1985, p. 92.
19. Government of India, Occassional Papers on Tribal Development No.7, Ministry of Home Affairs, 1997.
20. Report of the Working Group for the empowerment of the Scheduled Tribes, Planning Commission, New Delhi, 2001.

# 4

# Tribal Sub-plan Strategy

The Constitutional obligation in free India to make the tribals catch up with the non- tribals in the race for social, political and economic prosperity, which is the kernel of planned action in the different Five year plan periods, cannot be fully appreciated if the special situation in tribal areas (ecologically, socially, politically and administratively) is not fully discussed.

Article 46 of the Constitution contains all the safeguards for members of the Scheduled Castes and Scheduled Tribes. Thus, the goal set by the Constitution assures a progressive life to the members of these weaker sections of the community. Our goal is to 'emancipate them from all forms of exploitation'.

Keeping up with these objectives, the Five year plans were launched with special priority for the Scheduled Tribes and other weaker sections of the society. They aimed at increasing their income, employment and facilities for health, education and housing. Upto the Fourth Five year plan, a sum of Rs. 358 crores was spent on the welfare of backward classes through special schemes alone. The introduction of Tribal Sub-Plan strategy in the Fifth Five year plan gave a fillip to the outlay and expenditure on STs in the planning process. Earlier, except for the education sector, under which stipends and scholarships were given to the ST students, the welfare content in other sectors was general and diversified.

In the First plan, the main emphasis was on health, housing and communication, but in the Second plan, the emphasis shifted to economic development (agriculture, cottage industries, forests, cooperative societies and the setting up of multi-purpose tribal blocks). The Third plan renamed these blocks as Tribal Development Blocks with priorities for economic upliftment, education and health, housing and communications. The Study team on 'Tribal Development Programs' set up by the Planning Commission in 1969 (Shilu AO Committee), did not feel enthusiastic about giving a clear verdict whether the progress was "appreciable or marginal" but felt that the delay in the implementation of the considered recommendations of the Dhebar Commission (1961) has worsened the position which these recommendations were intended to correct and failure to pay attention to and profit by their advice on matters pertaining to the formulation and implementation of tribal development programs has resulted in the failure of ambitious schemes and consequent waste of valuable resources.[1]

Experience shows that most of the programs in the backward classes sector in the absence of adequate financial backing and organizational support, had little impact on the poverty, educational backwardness and social disability of the backward classes.

This was sought to be corrected in the Fifth Five-year plan through the Sub-plan strategy where utmost priority was accorded to drawing up an integrated area plan after identifying specific tribal areas and their problems.

The Fifth Five-year plan (1974-79) should be regarded as a watershed in the history of tribal development. Much thinking and preparation went into the concept of tribal development before the commencement of that plan period. In 1972, a Task Force on 'Development of Tribal Areas' was set up with Prof. L.P.Vidyarthi as Chairman to

(a) Review the nature and the level of development that has taken place so far;

(b) Suggest a perspective of development for a fifteen year period and

c) Formulate proposals for the Fifth plan indicating priorities, policies, programs and outlays in the light of the perspective.

The task force pointed out the problem of development of Tribal Areas and linked it to the backwardness of these areas, the poverty of the people and the integration of tribals with the rest of the population. They suggested that areas with a high concentration of tribal population should be identified and grouped, the combination of ecological, occupational and social parameters properly assessed for policy formulation and implementation and a steady flow of benefits assured to the Scheduled Tribes. In their view, the obvious emphasis would have to be on the primary sector of the tribal economy, i.e. agriculture and forestry; at the same time, there should be a frontal attack on the alienation of land, indebtedness, lack of credit and marketing and excise policy.

Later in the same year, an expert committee on tribal development headed by Prof. S.C. Dube submitted its report (1972) defining the new strategy for tribal development in the Fifth plan which is as follows :-

(a) The problem of tribal development should be defined at the national level and national efforts required for tackling it should be worked out.

(b) The precise part assigned to each state and to each department in this task should be fully defined and the central sector should play an important supplementary role.

(c) A review of important policies especially those covering forest, industry, mineral development and excise administration should be taken up.

(d) An integrated area development approach in consonance with the development of the people be adopted. The development programs should give high priority to programs minimizing the incidence of exploitation and helping local communities to build up their inner strength.

(e) Special schemes for extremely backward areas,

neglected and isolated tribes and tribals affected by major projects should be formulated.

(f) Strengthening and streamlining of administrative and economic institutions should be taken up urgently and evaluation should become an integral part of the administrative structure.

These ideas led to the birth of the concept of a sub-plan for the tribal regions of a state within the overall framework of the state plan. The objective of the tribal sub-plan has been the development of the area with focus on the Scheduled Tribe population within the sub-plan area. The concept includes identification of Development Blocks within a state having more than 50 per cent Scheduled Tribe population and launching of a massive effort for tribal development within the "sub-plan area". The unit of planning, an integrated Tribal Development Project (ITDP) in a state comprised an aggregate of Development Blocks. The ITDP being smaller than the district and bigger than a Development Block appears more feasible for planning. Guidelines laid down that planning should be based on the needs of the area and the people and hence, the process has to be commenced at the grass-root level, i.e., the Development Block and funneled upwards to ITDP, State and national levels.

The sub-plan concept is based on the use of the financial resources as investment in the tribal areas and effort has to be mounted to translate this investment into concrete benefits leading to increase in the income of tribal families. For this purpose, funds are given by the Central Government as Special Central Assistance to the State Tribal Sub-plans in pursuance of the Constitutional provisions making tribal development the special responsibility of the Central Government.

During the Fifth plan, the introduction of Sub-plan concept provided a proper focus on tribal development. For the first time, 16 states and 2 Union Territories prepared the Tribal Sub-plan highlighting the objectives and the priorities as well as earmarking funds for tribal development in the various sectors like agriculture, animal husbandry, minor irrigation, cooperation, forestry, small and village industries, education, health etc; the twin objectives were preventation of tribal exploitation and positive economic development.

Tribal Development Agencies- four in Orissa, two in Madhya Pradesh, one in Andhra Pradesh and one in Bihar, totaling eight came into being in the beginning of the Fifth plan. Their aim was to make massive investment exclusively for tribals from central funds, while making use of the state outlays for development of both tribals and non-tribals.

For the preparation of the Tribal Sub-plans, the Planning Commission issued a set of guidelines to the states. The guidelines spell out the long-term objective of the Tribal Sub-plan as :

(a) Narrowing the gap between the levels of development of tribals and other areas, and

(b) Improving their quality of life.

Among the immediate objectives were:

(a) Elimination of exploitation in all forms

(b) Speeding up the processes for social and economic development

(c) Building up the inner strength of the people, and

(d) Improving their organizational capabilities.

The guidelines laid down the criteria for identification of sub-plan areas, the approach and strategy for their development and also the pattern of funding and formulation of programs in these areas. It also stated that the sub-plan areas in each state should comprise a number of viable projects. For each such Integrated Tribal Development Project (ITDP), an integrated area development plan focussing attention on the specific problems of the area and the tribal people, was to be formulated. The sub-plan areas in each state thus comprised a number of viable projects.

In addition to the Scheduled Areas, each state identified the Tehsils/Talukas/Blocks having a concentration of 50 per cent or more of the tribal population. From these, suitable planning areas were carved out at macro, meso and micro-levels, keeping in view the natural resources, physical features, level of development of the tribes inhabiting the region and other socio-economic considerations to suit the planning functions at these levels. It was laid down that these areas should, to the extent possible, confirm to the existing administrative boundaries. By the end of the Fifth plan, 179 projects (ITDPs) had been identified in the entire tribal sub-plan area in the country. Some of the main points of strategy in the Fifth Five year plan were :-

***(a)*** ***Preventation of exploitation:*** For this purpose, integrated credit-cum-marketing services were developed in the sub-plan area. These services covered marketing of agricultural and minor forest produce, supply of inputs and essential consumer commodities. Credit and marketing structures in these areas was reorganized into Large Agricultural Multi-purpose Societies (LAMPs) in accordance with the recommendations of the Bawa Committee set up by the Ministry of Agriculture, Government of India, to study the problem.

***(b)*** ***Development of tribal agriculture:*** The most important aspect of tribal agriculture development were ownership rights, completion of land records, land development and introduction of improved methods of agriculture.

***(c)*** ***Generation of employment opportunities:*** This was done through programs relating to horticulture, animal husbandry, poultry, piggery etc and encouragement of cottage industries based o local raw materials.

***(d)*** ***Provision of basic infrastructure:*** This included growth centers, communication, schools, health centers, rural electrification, marketing and credit organizations besides training facilities and manpower planning.

***(e)*** ***Special groups and their problems:*** Even within the tribal areas, there were primitive tribal groups who needed special attention and help. States/UTs were advised to formulate suitable schemes for their welfare and development.

Implementation of the special strategies for tribal development namely the Tribal Sub-Plan (TSP) and the Special Central Assistance (SCA) to TSP began during 1974-78 period. These were considered to be two effective instruments to ensure flow of population-proportionate funds to STs from general development sectors.

Detailed guidelines were issued by the Ministry of Home Affairs, which earlier looked after Tribal welfare regarding the Tribal Sub-Plans. It said that "A Sub-Plan should be drawn up for these areas which may present an integrated view of their problems, the broad objectives and outlines of the various programs like physical inputs, financial outlays, legislative and administrative frame. All activities of a government and semi- government organizations, financing and credit institutions and special sector programs may be fully integrated in the Sub-Plan which should present a total picture of the development of the region."[2]

The long-term and short-term objectives of the Sub-Plan were also enunciated. The long-term objectives were

(a) To narrow the gap between the levels of tribal and other areas; and

(b) To improve the quality of life of the tribal communities.

Among the immediate objectives were the checking of exploitation in all its forms, speeding up the process for social and economic development, building up the inner strength of the people and improving their organizational capabilities.

Thus the idea was that the Sub-Plan would envisage a total picture of development. The guidelines of the Planning Commission also stated that all activities of the government and semi- government organizations, financing and credit institutions and special sector programs may be fully integrated. As per the guidelines issued by the Ministry of Home Affairs and the Planning Commission, the Tribal Sub-Plan area was initially delineated into 42 Integrated Tribal Development Projects (ITDPs) - 31 major and 11 medium projects.[3]

Under the Tribal Sub-Plan, four broad categories of

development programs were thought of; economic, infrastructural, human resources and others.

Under economic development programs, all kinds of programs which assist the tribal people in raising their level of income, were included.

The tribal areas lack basic infrastructure. Therefore, infrastructural development programs including building of roads, bridges and culverts extension of electricity lines and provision of irrigation were taken up.

The human resources development programs include all forms of education – elementary, secondary, vocational and technical. It also includes training for self-employment and preparing for various representative organizations which lead to a job. Safe drinking water was also included under the broad category of human resources development.

Under the other category, programs such as updating and improvement of land records were taken up.

Economic problem of the tribals, would have first attracted the attention of the government after obtaining freedom but due to age old conventional policy decisions taken about the tribal development, of keeping the tribals isolated and undisturbed in remote geographical setting, did more harm than good. This continued for sometime in the earlier Five-year plans and ended with the inception of Tribal Sub-plan.

In tribal sub-plan areas, the transfer of tribal land to non-tribals has been banned in most of the States. However this has done little to control the changing of land through concealed tenancy systems. The Working Group on the development and welfare of SC and ST during Eighth Five year plan (1990-95) had mentioned a study report of the Department of Rural Development, Government of India which said that the awareness level of the tribals was so dismal that very few STs were found aware of protection laws in respect of tribal lands.

In the Tribal Sub-plan approach, the problem of tribal development was divided broadly into two parts viz. Areas of tribal concentration and of dispersed tribals. In the former case, the area development approach, with focus on tribal development was accepted, whereas in the case of dispersed tribals, the approach was family-based. In pursuance of this policy, all the areas with 50 per cent tribal population were identified for which separate Tribal Sub-plans were prepared. During the Fifth five-year plan, the strategy of TSP was adopted in 19 states and two Union Territories where 191 ITDPs were in operation. Even then, 40 per cent of the ST population lived outside the TSP area. Therefore, other norms have been evolved to cover the tribal villages under MADA pockets and village clusters identified on the basis of a village's population being 50 per cent or more of tribals. Full districts covered under TSP area are having ITDPs.

The Fifth Plan marks a new phase in tribal development in India. The new strategy has come to be known as the 'sub-plan strategy' for tribal development. The preparation of tribal sub-plans by the state governments has resulted in the pooling of considerable data about areas of tribal concentration at the micro-level. All compact areas of 10,000 tribal people or more in all states and tribal pockets of tribal concentration in those states, which have largely dispersed tribal population, have been brought within this frame. For the former, Integrated Tribal Development Projects have been set up.

An Integrated Tribal Development Project is a medium-term plan for the concerned area corresponding to the Five year plan of the state. Preparation of annual plans and their translation in the form of Annual State Budget are two crucial stages in the implementation of these projects. First, the preparation of annual plans has to be initiated at the project level well ahead of the annual plan at the state level and, an approach of gradual change has to be adopted so that the plan can come in full consonance with the ideal frame for the area within a period of five to seven years.

In the tribal areas, the area development programs have to be so designed that they keep the man in focus. The tribal development efforts have been given high priority and started with the areas having tribal concentration. In this scheme of things, the dispersed tribals remained outside the ambit of an intensive program of development. It was therefore, necessary that an effective program for this most vulnerable group is taken up in right earnest.

The first effort in this direction was made in the Fifth Five year plan, when the issue of tribal development was broadly divided into two parts: (a) development of tribals living in the area of their concentration, and (b) development of dispersed tribal population.

The approach and strategy of tribal development in these two cases were quite distinct. In the case of predominant tribal areas, the emphasis was on finding out satisfactory solution to the common problem which confronted all developmental efforts namely that the area development program do not necessarily mean development of the people living in that area. This has a special significance for tribal areas in view of the socio-economic situation of the tribal communities. Development of infrastructure should not become an end in itself but become a means of achieving the final goal of the development of the community. Any investment on infrastructural development must subserve the basic objective of the development of tribal communities living in that area.

Another important distinguishing characteristic of the tribal situation in predominantly tribal areas as compared to those areas having dispersed tribal population is with reference to the ownership of resources. In the predominantly tribal areas, the community has full command over the local resources, at least in practice, if not in law. On the other hand, the command over resources in the case of dispersed tribals is extremely limited. The case of dispersed tribals is therefore to be treated on a different footing. Infrastructural development in areas with dispersed tribal population cannot be treated as a part of tribal development programs. In any program for tribal development in these areas, attention has to be focussed on the individual and the group; taking the group or the family as a unit. The approach, here, cannot be that of area development. Here, we have to start with a man, build up the program from below and incorporate it in the general development scheme of the area.

In the Fifth Five year plan, as a part of the new strategy for tribal development, four objective criterias were adopted to analyze the problem and satisfactorily solve it in the given time frame. They were:

(i) The size of the community,

(ii) The stage of their economy,

(iii) The extent of isolation, and

(iv) The level of literacy.

Thus small pre-literate tribal communities, living in remote inaccessible areas and subsisting at a pre-agricultural stage of economic development were categorized as primitive tribal groups who now number 75. The focus on development of these communities has to be on their well being.

After accepting the need for a special program for development in areas of tribal concentration, the next step was to identify those areas and delineate them. The case of those areas was clear which were included in the Fifth and the Sixth Schedule of the Constitution. As the Scheduled areas enjoy a special Constitutional status, it was decided that all the Fifth Schedule areas should qualify for inclusion in the new tribal development program, irrespective of the size of tribal population until such time as a decision was taken to de-schedule them.

However, there were substantial areas of tribal concentration in many states which were not covered under the Fifth Schedule. In the first instance, it was decided that all the areas with more than 50 per cent tribal population should be included under the new tribal development program. Thus, all predominantly tribal areas, as recommended by the Scheduled Areas and Scheduled Tribes Commission (Dhebar Commission) in 1961, were covered under this program.

The next immediate question after this basic decision was to define the smallest unit in terms of administrative jurisdiction, geographical area and/or population which could be considered for inclusion in the Tribal Sub-plan. It may be recalled that Community Development Blocks had been carved out in the fifties on objective criterias of population and area, and gradually a block has been accepted as the smallest unit for developmental administration in the country. Therefore, the block was taken as the basic unit for the purposes of delineating areas of tribal concentration as a starting point.

The Shilu AO Committee (1969) appointed for reviewing the tribal development programs observed that the Tribal Development Block was not a suitable unit for planning and implementation for the tribal areas because of its small size. This was accepted in the new approach as well and a new unit at the MESO level was envisaged to be established. It was also decided that a group of Blocks might constitute an Integrated Tribal Development Project that will be the meso level unit for planning and implementation of the tribal development programs.[4]

In the actual exercise taken up by the States, the Integrated Tribal Development Projects (ITDPs) were formed so as to cover a tehsil or a taluk in most of the cases, and in some cases a district as a whole. Thus, in the Fifth Plan, the areas under the Fifth Schedule of the Constitution and Development Blocks with more than 50 per cent tribal population, disregarding the non-tribal population in the industrial and urban centers, if any, were covered under the new extensive program for tribal development in the tribal sub-plans. The special problems of the development of hill areas had been engaging the attention of the Planning Commission since the early sixties, particularly with reference to the hill districts of Uttar Pradesh (Uttaranchal). But no concrete program was formulated until the Fifth Five year Plan; when it was decided that a special program should be taken up for the development of hill areas. The hill areas for this purpose were defined as regions more than 4,000 meters high above the sea-level. Thus, the hill area development program was taken up in the hill districts of Uttar Pradesh. It was also decided to exclude the areas covered by tribal sub-plans from hill area program. An exception was, however made in the case of Jaunsar-Bawar in Dehradun district. It is the only area with a predominantly tribal population in the Uttaranchal. It was, therefore, decided that the Jaunsar-Bawar area should form a part of a larger project comprising the compact areas taken from the districts of Dehradun, Uttarkashi and Tehri Garhwal, ignoring the formal distinction between Scheduled Tribes and others and that it should be covered by the hill area development plan of Uttar Pradesh.

It is thus clear that in the Fifth Five year Plan, a large proportion of the tribal population was covered under special developmental programs taken up under the tribal sub-plan and the hill area program. With this it was possible to cover almost 63 per cent of the total tribal population under the tribal sub-plans of the 18 states and Union territories during the Fifth Five year Plan.

In the Sixth Five year Plan, all pockets having a population of 10,000 or more and having more than 50 per cent tribal concentration, were covered under the Tribal Sub-plan. Thus about 80 per cent of the total tribal population was covered under the Intensive area programs. Even then 20 per cent of the tribal population remained outside the perview.

The guidelines for the preparation of the tribal sub-plans were formulated by the Planning Commission and it was envisaged that " the sub-plans should attempt in broad terms, answers to the main issues facing the tribal communities in these areas". The sub-plan, as a conceptual frame, included all aspects of tribal situation. The administrative needs for the new developmental programs were specially underlined. According to the guidelines, "the pattern of administrative organization should be worked out in detail for achieving the functional coordination and efficiency. At this stage of development, protective and developmental functions cannot be distinguished in the tribal areas, particularly in view of the fact that in the new strategy, elimination of exploitation has been accorded the highest priority".[5]

The tribal development administration represents the instrument for translation of policy decisions in operational terms. In the new strategy, it was explicitly accepted that while the sub-plans would provide the economic and social inputs, the protective and administrative aspects would be taken care of under the appropriate constitutional provisions. Consequently, it was decided that, as far as possible, the sub-plan area should become co-terminus with the Scheduled Areas. In pursuance of this decision, the Scheduled Areas were extended to cover the Sub-plan areas in the State of Madhya Pradesh, Bihar, Orissa, Gujarat, Rajasthan, Maharashtra, Andhra and Himachal Pradesh.

Here, it may be useful to state some of the important features of the new policy frame as reflected in the guidelines for the preparation of the Sub-plan. These elements can be summarized as follows:

(1) Development in the tribal areas should be conceived in comprehensive terms. All developmental activities in the tribal area should come under the discipline of tribal sub-plans.

(2) Resources for development from all sources should be pooled and the priority for different programs should be worked out keeping in view the overall resource availability and the needs of the tribal areas.

(3) Problem-solving approach with clear objectives should be adopted, treating the system as a flexible element which could be suitably adopted. There should be no occasion for compromise on basic objectives.

(4) Development of tribal areas has to be an integral part of the total development of the State and the nation. The major thrust for development of these areas has to be provided by the various sectoral authorities themselves. The basic investment for development of tribal areas, therefore, should flow from the normal State plans.

(5) The Union Government has a special responsibility in terms of the Constitutional provisions. Each Central Ministry is responsible for development of the tribal areas in relation to its functional jurisdiction. However, all sectoral efforts taken together may still leave critical

gaps and may not provide the full answer to the problem. The Ministry of Tribal Affairs has now the overall responsibility for all aspects of administration and development of tribal areas as envisaged in the Constitution.

(6) The socio-economic situation in different tribal regions and sub-regions within the same area varies considerably. Therefore, each situation would require a specific solution. The basic unit of planning and implementation of tribal development programs should be homogenous as far as possible and viable enough to perform these functions. The ITDP comprising a group of Blocks as Constituent micro units should be accepted as the operational unit.

(7) Development programs in the tribal sub-plan should be built from below. These plans should represent an organic form fully integrated, both horizontally and vertically at different levels.

(8) Specific problems with reference to physical feature, sociological system or economic condition for each identifiable sub-unit within the ITDP should be answered by preparation of micro-plans within the framework of ITDP.

(9) The primitive tribal groups should be identified and a special program with adequate flexibility should be built up for them. This program should cover communities living within the sub-plan areas or outside.

(10) The administrative system for the tribal areas should be simple so that the system is within the comprehension of the community that it is supposed to serve. Adequate administrative and financial powers should be delegated and responsibility at each level should be specific.[6]

## Composition of Sub-plan Allocations

It is necessary at this stage to examine critically as to what should really go in the tribal Sub-plans. The investment actually made within the tribal areas except on major projects, should be accounted for in the tribal Sub-plan.

In 1985, the Government of India felt a need to introduce an element of control/ guidance to dissuade investment of this assistance in sectors where benefit are not directly and substantially co-relatable to tribal population. With this end in view, it was suggested by the Government of India that the Special Central Assistance may be divided into two components:

A major portion of SCA representing 75 per cent of the total may be sanctioned as an additive and gap filler to the state plan efforts as hitherto continuing the emphasis on schemes benefiting families.

Secondly, about 25 per cent of the total provision of the SCA should be utilized as incentives to be given to the States excelling in performances in the tribal development field.

The SCA was meant primarily for family oriented income generating schemes, while giving adequate weightage to infrastructure incidental to such schemes. Further SCA was intended as an additive to State plan effort and is not intended to be a substitute for existing plan schemes.

Besides SCA, funds are also made available to the state /UT governments under first proviso to Article 275(1) of the Constitution for the following:

(a) Resettlement of tribals practicing shifting cultivation

(b) Schemes for development of forest villages

(c) Development of tribals suffering from special disease

(d) Reclamation of ravine areas intended to be especially allotted to the Scheduled Tribes.

Detailed guidelines were issued regarding the formulation of projects under Article 275(1). Under such project proposals, the program of family oriented schemes and infrastructure development were to be clearly demarcated. Similar guidelines have been issued for the schemes to be funded out of the SCA. The schemes to be taken up include family oriented income generating programs and development of infrastructure like road, buildings, irrigation works etc.

Government of India lays great emphasis on furnishing of accounts and the utilization certificates of the funds given under SCA. In this regard, a quarterly return has also been provided but the State governments have been found to be lacking in sending their utilization certificates.

Now after a lapse of more than 25 years, it may be pertinent to ask how far has the tribal sub-plan succeeded as an instrument of affirmative action? The consensus is that the results have not been commensurate with the investments made. There is also an agreement that while the objectives of the tribal sub-plan are laudable and its strategy well conceived, implementation has been far from satisfactory. Indeed, the general feeling is that corruption and inefficiency have been rampant and the quality of output is low.

In the report of the working group for the Tenth Five Year Plan, it has been mentioned that the central ministries and the State governments have not taken the tribal sub-plan seriously and most of them have not earmarked funds for TSP on one pretext or another. Moreover there has been no systematic monitoring of the fund flow and the TSP flow has been defined in various ways without indicating how it has actually benefited the ST population. For example, even a road passing through some tribal areas has been shown as TSP road though it is part of the State highway with most of its length running through non- tribal areas.[7]

When we come to the issue of sectoral priorities in the tribal sub-plan, the position is equally dismal. Even a casual scrutiny of the plan and budget document pertaining to any year from the Fifth to Ninth plan period will make it clear that the sub-plan lacks a sense of direction. Virtually, all the State government departments have received a slice of the cake. This thin dispersal of resources has led to dissipation of efforts and loss of impact.

A better way to quantify funds would be on the basis of certain selected indicators of development covering both infrastructures and human resources development. This could then be developed into a composite indicator of backwardness, which can then be used as a multiplier to determine district wise allocations. It would be a good idea to limit future allocations to Education, Health, Agriculture, local government work and beneficiary oriented income generating schemes only.[8]

One of the advantages of the STs is that their population is located in compact areas, which are called the Scheduled areas. As such, it is much easier to concentrate on all round development of STs through an area approach. For development of STs to be meaningful, we have to not only implement the convergence approach but also ensure that there is a proper mechanism to enforce it, not only for the state governments but also for the Central ministries.

One important point, about the tribal sub-plan is that the funds earmarked for these areas should not be diverted to other areas. But since shortfalls do arise in certain sectors, suitable adjustments are made by the concerned departments.

The Government of India had suggested to the State governments that they may consider pooling all outlay under different sectors together under one Area Demand for the Tribal Sub-plan as a whole. This was introduced in Maharashtra and Gujarat in 1976 and has now been adopted in Rajasthan, Himachal Pradesh and Madhya Pradesh. In this arrangement, various schemes under the tribal sub-plan area of all departments continue to be shown under the tribal sub-plan major functional heads. All items relating to the sub-plan under different functional heads are pooled together under a single Demand. The Demand is presented to the State Legislature by the Minister for Tribal Affairs. The responsibility for operating the budget under each functional head continues to rest with the concerned heads of Departments with the Tribal Development Department authorizing any diversions.

**Planning from below**

The planning in tribal areas has to begin at a level that is near enough to the people. The unit for these plans has to be much smaller than a district. Even within a block, plans may have to be prepared for appropriate sub-regions. The focus of such planning has to be on the development of the tribal community.

Tribal communities, in terms of skills of their individual members, are perhaps the highest skilled groups. Planning from below, to be realistic, must start with identification of these skills. It should proceed with careful selection of skill-points on whose foundation new skills can be built up. This would also bring the unfamiliar and new elements of specialization in those skills within the easy reach of the groups concerned.

Any essential pre-requisite in planning for the tribal areas is a clear understanding of the relationship of the tribal with his/her environment. The tribal community draws its sustenance from its own immediate environment. The relationship between the forest and the tribal is an important example. The fact that forests have been playing a crucial role in the local economy and may continue to do so for quite some time, has to be recognized, if a micro-plan has to have any meaning for the tribal group.

Thus, planning from below in the case of simple societies is a delicate exercise of simulating a process of change gradually building on their traditional system, which in due course should be able to replace the earlier dependence-relationship in a limited area by a set of more formal and modernistic relationships with their neighborhood and the regions beyond. Development should represent a process of natural growth from the traditional to the modern within the assimilative potential of the people in the area while utilizing the traditional tribal institutional structure for initiating a change.

Another basic issue in planning for development is the optimum utilization of the limited resources. Any investment has two aspects : the activity and the area. Experience has shown that if the location for investment in different sectors is properly coordinated, the same resources can go a much longer way. Land and forests are the two key resources in the tribal areas. A vast majority among the tribals are agriculturists. With the opening up of the tribal areas, however, the situation has changed. In many areas, the tribals are losing command over the resources and a class of landless laborers has emerged. In some areas, the tribals still practice shifting cultivation.

One of the crucial elements in the new strategy for tribal development, which stands out in the above discussion, is that the programs and the priorities have to be decided consciously for each area and for each community, taking into account the specific situation in each case. Also certain known facts about the tribal situation cannot be ignored and the planning at the local level must confirm to the broad policy framework keeping in view the parameters. There are certain characteristics common to all tribal areas. Elimination of exploitation should be provided the highest priority. For this purpose, a review of the forest policy is required so as to give the community a share in the forest produce. Alienation of land and indebtedness are other major problems that need to be tackled through suitable legal and administrative measures. A greater use of the provisions in the Fifth Schedule of the Constitution is needed to simplify the administrative system and to cut the procedural lags. These provisions may also be used for establishing a clear chain of command with specific responsibility and built-in accountability.[9]

**Summing up**

The problem with the TSP strategy has been that it has been interpreted as merely an area approach. It has become an instrument of infrastructure development in many States like Maharashtra, Orissa, Bihar and M.P. Such a high investment on infrastructure leaves inadequate funds for family-oriented and poverty alleviation programs. The result was that beneficiary-oriented schemes did not receive more than 20 per cent outlay under TSP during the Seventh Plan period. There is need to provide more attention to such programs.

The second drawback is that there is minimal participation of the tribal beneficiaries in the entire planning process. The planning process should start at village or gram panchayat level and the panchayat plans should be aggregated to form a block development plan. This should be integrated in an ITDP plan and the Tribal Sub-plan. As originally conceived the TSP strategy envisaged administrative, organizational and financial integration to promote speedier development of STs. Even now administrative and financial integration has not been effected in many States.

As per the TSP stipulation, funds are decreed to be non-divertible and, within a plan period, non-lapseable. Yet there are instances where TSP funds have been diverted to other channels and in some others, allowed to lapse.[10]

We have crossed 55 years of our independence and now it is our prime duty to examine a few questions. Have our tribals benefited by the government's activities and programs? What is their present status and condition? How have the Five year plans and the tribal sub-plans affected their lives? Does the program benefit the officials more than the people? Have we been able to associate our Adivasi brethren in the governance of the country or even in running their own developmental programs?

The need for tribal development has been well understood and well emphasized at different levels. We are completing fifty two years of planning in India but unfortunately the tribal development programs are lacking both at planning and implementation level. Many good programs have failed at the implementation level because the person concerned with implementation are generally unsympathetic to them.

We should also not presume that a good plan necessarily produces good results. There are several intervening variables between planning and implementation as we have seen earlier. Without the requisite political will, excellently drawn plans can be left to adorn office shelves.

## Reference

1. Shilu Ao Committee Report, 1969, p. 25.

2. Government of India, Occasional papers on Tribal Development No.7, Ministry of Home Affairs, 1977.

3. *Ibid.*
4. Shilu Ao Committee Report, 1969, pp. 25-26.
5. Sixth Five year plan document, Planning Commission, New Delhi.
6. Dr. B.D. Sharma-Planning for Tribal Development, New Delhi, 1984, pp.77-79.
7. Report of the working group for Tenth Five year plan, Planning Commission, New Delhi, 2001.
8. Dr. B.D. Sharma—Planning for Tribal development, New Delhi, 1984, pp. 99-121.
9. *Ibid.*
10. Ibid.

# 5

# Working of ITDPs, SCA to TSP and Grant under Article 275(1) of the Constitution

## Introduction

The tribal situation in the country presents a varied picture. Some areas have a large tribal population, while in other areas, the tribal people formed a small proportion of the total population. There are some tribal groups which are still at the food-gathering stage; some others practice shifting cultivation; yet others pursue primitive forms of agriculture. Some areas are still inaccessible. Keeping these things in view, the Planning Commission issued guidelines for the adoption of sub-plan strategy during the Fifth Five year plan. It envisaged drawing up of sub-plans to present an integrated view of the problems of Scheduled Tribes, the broad objectives and strategies, an outline of the various programs, physical inputs and financial outlays etc. It should in short, present a total picture of the development of the region.

Even now, over 45% of the ST families continue to exist below the poverty line. For meeting this challenge, it is necessary that our planning system should be so flexible that we could plan taking community or family as a unit. And no policy could be successful unless it is sincerely and honestly implemented. The Maheshwar Prasad Committee on Administration in the Tribal Areas recommended several measures to be taken in the sphere of selection of officers and creation of a special cadre for tribal areas besides special allowance for personnel posted to the tribal areas.

For a realistic formulation of the development plan, a clear understanding of the socio-cultural factors which might impede or accelerate the processes of change will be essential. The sub-plan should also present a clear picture of the resource configuration of these areas based on the available data, techno-economic surveys and other research studies.

The Constitution envisages the fostering of a faster pace of development for the tribals so that they can be brought to the same level as the non-tribal groups. In the predominantly tribal areas, there is the area-approach with focus on development of the tribal communities, while community-oriented programs have been evolved for the primitive groups.

The two special strategies of Tribal Sub-plan (TSP) for STs and the Special Central Assistance (SCA) to TSP have been receiving special attention right from their initiation in the early seventies, as these are the most effective mechanisms to ensure additional flow of funds for STs from the other general development sectors in proportion to their population.

The first sub-plans, prepared during the Fifth plan, covered around 65% of the tribals in the country. Preparation of programs with reference to the specific needs of each area is Central to the sub-plan strategy. In the Fifth plan, the quantum of outlay from the State plan was arrived at keeping in view (a) the total population (b) the geographical area, (c) the comparative level of development and (d) the state of Social Services.

While quantification of the outlays from the State plan was made in the Fifth plan, the level of investment from the Central programs did not pick up as envisaged. The Central Ministries were required to quantify the flow of benefits from their programs to the tribal areas but the exercise did not yield much result except in the case of specific programs that were taken up in the tribal areas.

In the tribal sub-plan, the role of the Central Ministries is equally crucial since they have to assume the overall responsibility for the development of the tribal areas in their respective sectors. It is necessary for them to prepare specific schemes where they feel that the Government of India must supplement the efforts of the State governments in their respective sectors. They should also make their own arrangements for monitoring of these programs in the tribal areas. For this purpose, a special cell should be created which could be the part of the monitoring system of the Ministry.

As per the information available, earmarking of funds under TSP is being followed by 25 Ministries/Department at the Centre and at State level, only 23 States/Uts are adhering to this.

The ITDPs were conceived under the TSP strategy as the operational unit for achieving administrative integration for speedier tribal development. The underlying assumptions in the establishment of ITDPs were :

(i) The Social fabric of the tribal area is relatively simple. The administrative structure for implementation of a developmental plan has to be within the comprehension of individuals whom it is intended to serve. The tribals should be required to deal with as limited number of officials as possible.

(ii) The administrative structure has to be integrated at an appropriate level so that both regulatory and development administration can work in unison for speedy development.

(iii) The administrative powers, working norms and financial requirements should confirm to the prevailing special conditions in these areas.

(iv) There is a need for total administrative effort within a limited period of time. This is possible only if the administration is structured on the model of a single line agency.

(v) There should be a high power development authority which should have the entire administration of these areas under its full control. This authority should have sufficient decision making powers so that important matters are not required to be referred to the State government.

vi. The traditional panchayat system must be strengthened and assigned a participative role for development.

**Formal Structure of ITDP in the District**

At the district level, a project authority has been constituted for each ITDP. The authority is expected to bring in an element of collective leadership.

Village Level Worker

Extension officers — B.D.O — Extension officers

District level Officers (DAO, DAHO,DFOetc.) — Project Administrator ITDP — District level officers (Executive Engineers, CMO etc.)

Collector or Deputy Commissioner

Divisional level Officers — Divisional Commissioner — Divisional level technical Officers

Development Departments — Tribal Commissioners — Regulatory Departments

The ITDP is the operational level for the purposes of planning and execution of TSP. The Project officer has a very important role in association with other departmental and technical personnel of the project and other non-official members and representatives of Panchayats to evolve a meaningful project as required under the TSP. There should be programs of action which are well integrated and need-based. These should be formulated keeping in view the special conditions of the project area, socio-economic and cultural aspects of tribal people, clearly spelling out the inter-sectoral and intra-sectoral priorities; phasing them over the years and also bringing in necessary adjustments or modifications whenever needed.

However, it has been found that the ITDPs lack dedicated and committed officers and workers. The quality of personnel is therefore, crucial to the implementation of the development programs.

The ITDP is a unit of planning and a Development Block is the unit of execution. Generally, a Project Administrator is in charge of an ITDP and a B.D.O (Block Development Office) remains in charge of a Development Block. Administrative linkages in the ITDPs would roughly be as follows

In this manner, a unified line of command has been set up, though it cannot be said that it has fully served its purpose.

At the project level, a committee consisting of officials and non-official members has been constituted for planning and overseeing functions.

It is fully realized that the, implementation of the policies and programs at the ITDP level depends on the quality of personnel engaged in their execution. The men and women entrusted with the responsibility of tribal development have to be chosen not only for their competence but also for their sensitivity and dedication. They should also be provided suitable training.

An Evaluation report on ITDP (1987) in Gujarat conducted by the PEO of the Planning Commission mentioned that in Gujarat, increased indebtedness was traceable to such factors as:

- Economic imbalances,
- Rise in the prices of agricultural inputs and consumer goods,
- Heavy expenditure on social functions, and
- Limitations of institutional infrastructure to take care of

the various credit needs of the tribal population. Another report identified the reasons for increased indebtedness in Orissa as:

i. Abject poverty,

ii. Misery and ignorance among tribals,

iii. Callous and indifferent attitude of government and bank officials,

iv. Steep increase in the prices of essential commodities etc.

This study also showed that only 8% of the beneficiaries from the sample taken by them, having income below Rs.1500 per annum, had crossed the poverty line. The remaining 92% and 80% of the beneficiaries from the income range of Rs.1500 and Rs. 2500 were still struggling to reach the income level of Rs. 3500 per annum. The shortcomings were generally attributed to administrative failures like wrong identification of beneficiaries and the wrong selection of schemes. There have also been other factors like :

(i) Lack of proper infrastructure in the rural areas for timely supply of inputs for the schemes and adequate marketing outlays etc.

(ii) Failure to carry out proper survey of the target households.

(iii) Too much emphasis on the achievement of physical targets without proper concern for the factors necessary for the successful implementation of the programs.

(iv) Lack of adequate attention to TRYSEM as an integral part of the IRDP.

(v) Lack of pragmatic approach.[1]

Another evaluation study conducted by the Planning Commission in 1997 in Gujarat and 6 other states namely Andhra Pradesh, Bihar, M.P, Maharashtra, Orissa and Rajasthan revealed the following points:

1. Except in Maharashtra and Andhra Pradesh, the Project officers of ITDPs have very little direct role in the planning and implementation of the tribal development programs.

He/ She does not have any direct control in allocation of resources and fixation of priorities within the Project area.

2. Monitoring has been found to be the weakest link in the implementation of ITDP program. The study has therefore suggested that the existence of monitoring and evaluation cells should be made a precondition for release of funds under the ITDP.

3. There is no uniformity in the staffing pattern in various ITDPs. The staff strength in the concerned ITDP varied from 3 in Bihar, to 217 in Orissa. Since all ITDPs are required to carry out surveys, coordination and monitoring of tribal development programs, some norms may be evolved regarding the minimum staff strength.

4. There is also a need of posting of committed, competent and dedicated officers in the ITDPs. This is lacking in most of the states. Even training programs for ITDP officers are not being regularly organized.

5. As per the central guidelines, the states are required to allocate state plan funds to TSP atleast in proportion to the percentage of tribal population in a state but except for Bihar and Orissa, other states are allocating much less to the TSP.

6. A large proportion of the TSP funds is being allocated to agriculture, minor irrigation and power in all these states. But inspite of that it has been found that the delivery system of the ITDP schemes in agriculture is weak.

7. The performance in the health and education sector was not found satisfactory in that the availability of teachers and health staffs in the villages was found to be insufficient.

8. Poverty, illiteracy, isolation and the lack of knowledge of their rights render the tribals vulnerable to exploitation. Land alienation is still a serious problem. There is an urgent need to generate awareness among the tribals so that they are involved in the planning process.[2]

In the Fifth Five-year plan, the need for an integrated approach in planning and implementation through ITDPs was accepted unequivocally. The policy frame under the Tribal Sub-plan was made quite explicit on this issue with a view to guard against any formal hurdles which could possibly appear while translating these policies into appropriate operational programs. Integration as an element in the strategy of development has an important distinguishing feature. It basically requires re-arranging the ongoing activities.

The new tribal development framework was envisaged as all inclusive and no aspect of tribal life and no issue relating to the tribal areas could be outside it. The tribal sub-plans have a much wider ambit compared to the State plans or even the National plan. They can cover the non-plan items and the non-developmental facets of a local situation, should an element be considered essential for achieving the basic objective.

The basic objective of the tribal sub-plan is to evolve a program of total development for the micro-region with focus on development of tribal communities living there. Integration, in the context, has a wide canvas. Beside the organizational coordination, the central point of attention in any integration exercise should be the program content.

There are four major facets of integration which may have to be kept in view while preparing an integrated plan of action for the development of a region. They are :-

1. Synchronization of the areas of operation of different programs.
2. Integration of programs with a clear total perspective.
3. Organizational integration;
4. Financial integration

Under the TSP approach, planning in the tribal areas was envisaged at three levels. The State's Tribal Sub-plan was to provide a broad policy frame at the macro-level and the existing Block was taken as the micro unit for planning. These micro units served as the building block for a meso level structure which was to serve as the primary unit for planning and implementation. Thus a number of Blocks or parts thereof together formed an Integrated Tribal Development Project (ITDP) under the Tribal Sub-plan.

While delineating the new units of ITDPs, it was considered desirable, though not necessary, that they should cover as far as possible full administrative units so that the problems about redefining the areas of jurisdiction, etc. of various functionaries are minimized. The formation of ITDPs was taken up currently with the delineation of the Tribal Sub-plans. It envisaged that an ITDP should comprise a group of Blocks taking due note of the natural resources, physical features, level of development of the tribal communities living in the area and other socio-economic conditions having relevance for planning functions at the meso level. The ITDPs that have finally emerged are generally co-terminus with a tehsil or taluk or a district depending upon the size of the area and the degree of tribal concentration in each state and its different regions.

In the Fifth Five year plan, a total number of 180 tribal development projects were established in different states. It was envisaged that an average ITDP should cover a population of about two to three lakhs. However, in practice the size of the ITDP varies considerably both in terms of their area and population because of the varying situation in different states.

The coverage under the tribal sub-plans had been increased during the Sixth Five year plan by including smaller units than a Block. The boundaries of the ITDPs carved out during the Fifth Five year plan were readjusted, wherever necessary, and new projects were established following the same principles. Suitable administrative changes were made to harmonize the jurisdiction of ITDPs and other area-specific schemes. This process was facilitated by extending the Scheduled Areas to cover the entire Sub-plan area giving the tribal project a distinct juridical status.

The geographical synchronization of administrative units and the areas of operation of various developmental programs provide a rational frame for organic fusion of all programs in each micro area which is the central theme of the sub-plan strategy. The various schemes sponsored and financially supported by the Union and the State governments carry their mark of origin to the point of execution in a variety of forms. This distinction is artificial and does not hold any significance for the beneficiary. What is significant and of interest to the beneficiary is the package of schemes for the common tribal and his family. There are two distinguishing features of any program viz. the source of its financing and the organization for its implementation.

The ITDP was supposed to be a point for full integration of administrative and development effort in the tribal areas. It was also envisaged that all programs emanating from different level and different sources in the State or the Center should coalesce at the level of ITDP and flow from there as a set of balanced and well-defined schemes without markings of their origin. For example, if there are more than one program sponsored by different organizations covering the same item, they should not have different conditions.

The ITDP, thus, has characteristic of both an area program as also a target-group program. It is an area program for the development of the tribal region and it is a family-based program addressed to the development of the tribal communities living in that area. Briefly the areas which have been identified for special treatment in the ITDPs under the tribal sub-plan program are as follows :-

1. Agriculture sub-regions in the hilly areas
2. Forest-rich areas
3. Zones of influence of industrial and mining complexes
4. Extremely backward tribal pockets;
5. Areas with high proportion of landless labour; and
6. Other areas with distinctive resource potential for development of pastures, horticulture, animal husbandry etc.

The beginning which was made with the tribal sub-plans and the ITDPs in the Fifth plan was the first massive effort of its kind in micro-level planning with a clearly defined objective. It was, therefore, necessary that all investments in the area should get reflected in the ITDP plan. The investments in some of the area-specific central programs are taken credit of in the sub-plan outlays. The same applies to the Integrated Tribal Development Program. But the working of these continuing programs have shown that in many cases, tribal areas in a district were not getting their due share in the scheme.

In the preparation of ITDPs, two sets of exercises were taken concurrently. Firstly, the project plans for a five year period with reference to the financial parameters and broad policy decisions about the development strategy were prepared according to the phased program. Secondly, a detailed listing of the schemes being implemented in each area by different agencies was completed. About 20% of the total investment in any year may pertain to new programs.

It was expected that each ITDP would become a viable area-development program with focus on the development of tribal communities. Since the ITDP is now the unit of planning and implementation, there should be adequate administrative and financial power with the project authority so that once the projects are approved and provision is made in the budget, sanctions can be issued at the project level and program implementation becomes effective. The problem of participation of people in development is closely linked to the nature of development.

On the basis of the past working of ITDPs the following suggestions are made:

1. A major portion of the pool funds under the TSP should be distributed among the ITDPs in the states on an equitable basis.
2. There should be complete financial, programmatic and administrative integration at the ITDPs/ ITDAs levels.
3. Multiplicity of organisations in TSP areas should be eliminated.
4. In an ITDP, there should be a single line administration on the pattern of Andhra Pradesh.
5. ITDP area should cover rural and urban areas of the

ITDPs in the district. All officers at the Project/ District level working in an ITDP should be placed under the direct control of the Project officer regardless of whichever department they may belong to.

6. Adequate administrative and financial powers should be vested in the Project officers so that the Project officer can be made accountable for the progress of development programs in the ITDPs.
7. The Office of the Project officer, ITDP should be strengthened with adequate supporting staff and other necessary facilities for planning, monitoring and implementation.

**Special Central Assistance**

The first important step for creating a meaningful package of programs under the tribal sub-plan is the acceptance of the integration of the total financial investment for the tribal areas. There are four sources of financing for tribal development; namely State plans, Central plans, institutional finance and Special Central assistance. In formal terms, the Special Central assistance was not created as a separate stream of funds necessarily distinguishable upto the last point. It was passed on in the form of a general authorization to the appropriate authorities to use additional funds upto a given limit for a variety of purposes. The additional funds could be used for speeding up any of the ongoing programs of special relevance to the tribal areas, adapting them wherever necessary, or to fill in a gap if considered desirable by the local administration.

The Special Central Assistance is provided by the Ministry of Tribal Affairs to the State Government as an additive to the State TSP. SCA is primarily meant for family-oriented income-generation schemes in sectors of agriculture, horticulture, sericulture, animal husbandry and cooperation. A part of SCA (not more thatn 30 per cent) is permitted to the used for development of infrastructure incident to such income generating schemes.

SCA is intended to be additive to State plan efforts for tribal development and forms part of TSP strategy. It is released for the economic development of the following:

(a) Integrated Tribal Development Project (ITDP) area in which ST population is 50 per cent or more out of the total population.

(b) Modified Area Development Approach (MADA) pockets containing 50 per cent or more ST population.

(c) Clusters containing 50 per cent or more ST population.

(d) Primitive Tribal Group (PTG).

(e) Dispersed Tribal population outside (a), (b), (c) and (d) above.

(f) Assistance for margin Money Loan Programme for the Tribal Finance and Development Corporations in the States.

(g) Special projects for the development of tribals.

The decision to allow the use of Special Central Assistance assumed special significance in the context of limited adaptability of the normal plan programs. In most states, the Special Central Assistance comprises about 20% of the total sub-plan outlay.

**Article 275(1) of the Constitution**

The issue concerning the level of administration in the tribal areas could not be expected to claim due attention in a general plan exercise. But with the steady rise in the level of investment under tribal sub-plans, the quality of administration became a critical element not only for the success of the programs but for the welfare and protection of the tribal people. It, therefore, required separate and urgent attention.

The First proviso to Article 275(1) envisaged a very special dispensation for the Scheduled Areas. It envisaged a continuous appraisal of the needs of the administration of the tribal areas. The required finance became a charge on the Consolidated Fund of India.

To promote the welfare of Scheduled Tribes, Article 275(1) provides for grant-in-aid to States/UTs for implementation of development programs in addition to general development outlays accruing to the tribal people and areas.

The Central Government releases funds every year under Article 275(1) to the states in proportion to their shares in tribal population. Thereafter, the State governments release these funds to their line departments through the Department of Welfare. However, according to the information received from the various states the flow of funds from the state to the project authority is not done as per the guidelines. Therefore, the Ministry of Tribal Affairs in consultation with the Planning Commission has decided that from the financial year 2001-2002 funds will be released to the states on the receipt of actual projects so that there is no danger of the diversions of funds and also that the projects are completed in time.

The formulation of such specific schemes as implied in the guidelines requires rigour in planning and an appropriate implementation method. The pre-requisite to the identification and formulation of such schemes is an assessment of the felt-needs of the tribals.

The reporting mechanism and maintenance of records and utilisation of funds under these grants are weak in most of the states. If a success is to be made of this program, the monitoring mechanism needs to be made more effective. As per the earlier guidelines the funds provided in Article 275(1) were to be utilised for the following schemes:

(1) Resettlement of tribals practising shifting cultivation;

(2) Development of forest villages;

(3) Development of tribals suffering from special diseases;

(4) Reclamation of ravine areas intended to be specifically allotted to Scheduled Tribes;

(5) Specific Health schemes (a) Not already funded by existing plan schemes (b) On going plan scheme, where some of the specific aspects and problems are not taken care of and which need additional funds;

(6) Enrolment subsidy for tribal memberships in LAMPS and Primary cooperatives to ensure cent percent enrolment of STs during Seventh Plan;

(7) Intermediate processing of MFP/SAP by LAMPS and other cooperatives;

(8) Income generating schemes of tribal women's organization;

(9) Special machinery for detection of land alienation, money lending, bonded labor cases and filing of court cases under appropriate legislation;

(10) Compact Area Programs for vulnerable and sensitive tribal areas;

(11) Specific Tribal crafts training cum production centers;

(12) 'Nasha' Nivarana Samskara Kendras for propagating prohibition amongst tribals through voluntary organizations;

(13) Residential schools for primitive tribes;

(14) Development of alienated lands restored to the Scheduled Tribes; and

(15) Any other specific schemes relevant to the tribal population not covered under existing plan schemes.[3]

The Union of India provides this financial assistance for the purpose of promoting the Welfare of Scheduled Tribes or raising the level of administration of the Scheduled Areas to that of the administration of the rest of the areas of that State.

In the changed scenario of globalisation and liberalization of the national economy, the government has issued the following guidelines on 2nd July 2002 to strengthen the mechanism for the release of money under Article 275 (1) and its proper utilisation. It says that:

(i) Grants under Article 275 (1) will be an additionality to Normal Central Assistance (NCA) to State Plans to meet the cost of such schemes/projects as may be undertaken by the States and approved by the Ministry of Tribal Affairs for the purpose of the welfare and development of the Scheduled Tribes or raising the level of administration of the Scheduled Areas.

(ii) The grants will essentially be used for creation and up gradation of critical infrastructure required to bring the tribal areas at par with the rest of the country. The infrastructure will be upgraded so as to enhance capacity of the economy in tribal areas to meaningfully and more effectively absorb funds, including institutional finance and thereby create opportunities conducive to income and employment generation. Due emphasis will be given to infrastructure in the sectors critical to enhancement of human development indices such as in health, education, income generation, etc.

(iii) The specific projects/schemes along with physical and financial plans showing sector-wise and year-wise phasing of activities for funding under Article 275 (1) should form an integral part of the overall TSP and, therefore, be prepared along with the Annual Plan of the State. The entire TSP of each of the State would be discussed and approved by the Ministry, preferably at the time of finalisation of the Annual Plan of the State. The flow of funds under Article 275 (1) to the relevant sectors in each of the State would be determined and approved accordingly.

(iv) Peoples' participation is the central thread around which the entire fabric of tribal development is to be woven. The approach towards tribal development should, therefore, ensure harnessing this extra-ordinary strength of community living/participation inherited and inculcated by the tribal population. While planning and implementing the schemes out of the grants under Article 275 (1), due regard should be given to the provisions of The Panchayats Act, 1992 and of The Panchayats (Extension to the Scheduled Areas) Act, 1996.

(v) Adoption of an integrated and holistic approach for preparing micro plans for ITDP/MADA/Clusters through multi-disciplinary teams is sine qua-non-for effective targeting of the projects/schemes. The long-term micro-plans, showing year-wise and sector-wise physical and financial components, should earmark the funds flowing from the State Plan, SCA, Article 275 (1) and under various Central Sectors/Centrally sponsored Schemes of different Ministries of the Central Government.

(vi) Each State, Region, ITDA, MADA and Cluster requires

a specific plan, based on the felt local needs such as low literacy, poor health services, critical gaps in sectors like irrigation, roads, bridges, electricity, technical/ vocational institutes, forests, sports promotion, etc. Efforts should, therefore, be made to identify thrust areas for each ITDA, MADA and Cluster and on that basis for the region or the State, as a whole.

(vii) The thrust areas so identified should form central theme of the planning and specific projects accordingly prepared. Attempts should be made to dovetail resources available so as to ensure perceptible changes in the tribal areas as against the practice of spreading resources too thin under sectoral programmes in a disintegrated fashion.

(viii) Expenditure on items recurring in nature is strictly prohibited. However, an amount maximum up to 2% of the Grant may be used for project management, training, MIS, administrative expenses and monitoring and evaluation.

(ix) The concerns/issues effecting women should occupy central position in preparation of the projects/schemes, including the involvement of women right from planning to the implementation stage. The projects should be so planned that substantial benefits, at least 30% in proportion, are targeted for women.

(x) It has been observed that the Finance or the Planning Departments of various States often take a long time in release of funds to the implementing agencies, thereby defeating the very purpose of adopting a project approach. The release of funds by the Ministry would, therefore, be strictly linked to the actual performance in the implementation of the schemes, including timely submission of utilisation certificates.

(xi) On the basis of ITDA-wise integrated plans prepared through micro-planning, projects can be taken up to bridge the gap in infrastructure in critical areas such as education, health, SSIs, forest, forest villages, drinking water, electrification, communication, rural marketing, agriculture, animal husbandry, sports promtion, food processing, processing of MFPs, human resource development in technical and vocational spheres, water harvesting, resettlement of displaced persons, tribal land management, etc. Needless to add, only those projects will be approved which fulfill the broad parameters as enumerated in these guidelines and are normally not specifically taken up under the State Plan or other schemes of different Ministries of the Government of India. The maintenance of infrastructure maximum up to 10% of the entitlement of the State would also be permissible, subject to prior approval of the Ministry on the proposal.

(xii) The initiative for imparting quality education to the tribal students through 82 Model Residential schools started in the IXth Five Year Plan period would be continued as far as establishment of these schools are concerned and proportionate recurring and non-recurring grants will continue to be provided as per the existing norms. The other academic institutions with similar objectives such as Navodaya Vidyalayas would also be supported, if such Vidyalayas are set up for tribal students.

(xiii) The TSP component of various departments/sectors under the State Plan should be put in a different Demand Head in the budget of the Tribal Development Department of the State. An amount equivalent to 10% of the total allocation under Art 275 (1) will be earmarked and retained at the Ministry's level. This amount will further be allocated for innovative projects amongst only those States, who adopt the TSP approach in letter and in spirit by ensuring that the entire TSP funds, at least in equal proportion to the population of tribals in the State, are placed in one budget head under the administrative control of the Tribal Development Department of the State Government for more integrated and focussed planning and implementation of projects/schemes. This 10% earmarked fund will be used as an instrument to bring about changes in the institutional framework for adoption of TSP and be allocated only amongst the States actually releasing, in the previous financial year, at least more than 75% of the approved Tribal Sub-plan funds to the implementing agencies through the budget head of the Tribal Development Department of the State. In case of the tribal majority States, utilization of 75% of the grants released under the Central Sector Schemes of this Ministry would qualify for consideration of innovative projects.

(xiv) The remaining 90% of the funds will be allocated amongst the States on the basis of the ST population in each State as a percentage to the total tribal population of the country.[4]

The above guidelines had become necessary as the requirements of the Scheduled Tribes population needed to be addressed in a more focused and integrated manner, keeping in view their stage of development after fifty years of the planning process. They lag behind the rest of the population in terms of the human development indices. It is also to be noted that the infrastructure development in the tribal areas has not been at par with others and it is necessary to direct resources in a synergetic manner to bridge the gap in infrastructure in critical areas so that the capacity of the economy in the tribal areas to meaningfully and effectively absorb funds is substantially enhanced.

## References

1. Evaluation Study conducted by the Planning Commission, New Delhi, 1987.
2. Evaluation study conducted by the Planning Commission regarding the functioning of the ITDPs (1997), pp. 5-16.
3. Guidelines issued by the Ministry of Welfare, Government of India, New Delhi (1986).
4. Guidelines for release and utilisation of grants under proviso 1 of Article 275 (1) of the Constitution of India issued by the Ministry of Tribal Affairs, GoI, New Delhi, 2002.

# 6

# Forest and Tribals

The population of Scheduled Tribes in the country is 6.78 crores as per 1991 census. Thus they constitute 8.08 per cent of the total population. Traditionally, the lifestyle and customs of tribes have direct relationship with the forests. Most of the identified Scheduled Tribes are forest dwellers. They derive their livelihood from the forest produce. The Committee on Forests and Tribals in India (1982) reported that 2 per cent of the total tribals reside in forest villages and 5 per cent of them have occupied forest land while nearly 12 per cent of the total tribals are shifting cultivators.

The forest cover of the country as per the 1997 assessment of the Forest Survey of India is 6,33,397 sq. kms. Majority of the tribal population are heavily dependent on forests for their livelihood. While the tribal population has grown by more than 30 per cent during the decade 1981-91, about 33 million ha. Forest cover in the country has become degraded. This is a danger signal as the degradation of the forests directly affects the life of the tribals.

The National Forest Policy 1988, considering the symbiotic relationship between the tribal people and the forests envisages that the customary rights and concessions enjoyed by the tribals should be fully protected. The policy has the objective of meeting the requirements of fuel wood, fodder, minor forest produce and small timber of the rural and tribal population. The policy says that "the life of tribals and other poor living within and near forests revolve around forests. The rights and concessions enjoyed by them should be fully protected. Their domestic requirements of fuel wood, fodder, minor forest produce and construction timber should be the first charge on forest produce. These and substitute materials should be made available through conveniently located depots at reasonable prices."

The policy further envisages that "having regard to the symbiotic relationship between the tribal people and forests, a primary task of all agencies responsible for forest management, including the forest development corporations should be to associate the tribal closely in the protection, regeneration and development of forests as well as to provide gainful employment to people living in and around the forests".

The National Forest Policy 1988 realized the importance of participatory action between the Government and the local communities including tribals for the rehabilitation and protection of degraded forests and provided the following: "the holders of customary rights and concessions in forest areas should be motivated to identify themselves with the protection and development of forests from which they derive benefits. The rights and concessions from forests should primarily be for the bonafide use of the communities living within and around forest areas, specially the tribals."

Forestry operations, both planting and harvesting, are important sources of employment to the tribals. The National Commission on Agriculture had estimated that forestry sector generated 2.3 million man years of employment which was projected to reach 5.5 million man years by the year 2000. There are other estimates also which show that non-timber minor forest produce will alone generate about 1.1 million man years of employment which can be increased to 3.2 million man years. It is also estimated that for every person directly employed in forestry, four get employed outside because of forward linkages.

The Minor Forest Produce (MFP) have special importance for tribals as they are the main source of income for them. It has been estimated that collection of minor forest produce provides cash earnings to the tribals between 10-40 per cent of their total household earnings depending on the extent of forests in the area. In some districts like Bastar, they go up to 85 per cent of the total earnings.

The Central Government having recognized that MFP have vital role in sustenance of tribals, enacted the Panchayat (Extension to the Scheduled Areas) Act, 1996 which has the provision of conferring ownership right of MFPs to Panchayats/Gram Sabhas in Scheduled V areas. Further the Ministry of Environment and Forest had constituted an Expert Committee to suggest the detailed mechanism for the implementation of this Act. The Committee submitted its report in February 1998 and it has been forwarded to all States/UTs.

The Forest Survey of India assesses the country biennially using satellite data. The State of Forest report, 1997 has for the first time studied the forest cover of the tribal districts of the country. There are 149 tribal districts identified but the forest cover information of only 137 districts have been analysed. From this assessment, it can be inferred that the total forest cover in the tribal districts in 417,174 sq. kms. which constitutes 65.86 per cent of total forest cover of the country. It further shows that the loss of cover in the tribal areas is 4,899 sq. kms. and 5,937 sq. kms. compared to 1995 and 1993 reports respectively. This report also showed that 35.2 per cent of the total geographic districts are under forest cover.

According to World Development Report, 2000-2001, over 1 million hectares of forests are cut every year and only 10 per cent of forest land has adequate tree cover. The consequences of this extensive deforestation are increasing floods, silting of dams and changes in the micro climate. The land area prone to floods has doubled in the past 10 years and stands at about 40 million hectares. The forest in India cover an area of 7,43,584 sq. kms. or 22 per cent of the total geographical area of India. Among the states, only Tripura has 60.8 per cent and Orissa has 43.74 per cent of the total area under forests. In all other states, it is less than 40 per cent. Again, many of these forests are in poor condition and according to some very recent official estimates, the forests do not cover more than 13 per cent of total area of India.

This leads us to look into the programs for development and protection of forests in association with tribals and other village communities.

The tribal socio-economic life is intimately connected with forest ecology. Forest is an inseparable part of tribal life. Most of the tribal communities live in and around forests. The forests provides them with edible fruits and leaves, roots and tubers, honey and water etc. and their life is closely linked with the forest. The symbiotic relationship which exists between the tribal people and the forests is not confined to the economic activities alone, but also covers medicines, recreational activities, their whole social and cultural life. This symbiotic relationship depends upon the balance of their needs and the ecological needs of the forests. This mutual dependence ensures sustainable protection by the tribals towards all vegetation. The forest serves as the life support system for the tribals and they take all preventions against destruction of forest and forest wealth. Their traditions and folklores remind them of the consequences of any harm done to the forests and reinforce their close relationship and peaceful harmony with nature.

1855 was a landmark year in the history of the government control over forests. In this year, Lord Dalhousie, the Governor-General issued a memorandum on forest conservation. The Forest Act of 1865 came soon after and it regulated exploitation, management and preservation of forest.

The Forest Act of 1878 divided the forest into:

1. Reserved forests.
2. Protected forests and
3. Village forests.

The practice of trespass and cattle grazing were restricted in the Reserved and Protected forests. Certain acts were declared as forest offences and made punishable.

The Forest Policy Resolution of 1894 declared that the

sole object of the administration of State forests was for public benefit. It emphasized the advantages of limiting the rights and privileges of individuals enjoyed by them as per customs and traditions for the sake of public good. It also specified that whenever any demand for cultivable land was made on forest areas, it should be given.

Through the Indian Forest Act, the Government of India gradually increased its control over the forest areas. It also declared certain items as forest produce.

The National Forest Policy 1952 clarified the government's views regarding the relationship of tribals with the forests. It said, "Village communities in the neighborhood of a forest will naturally make greater use of its products for the satisfaction of their domestic agricultural needs. Such use, however, should in no event be permitted at the cost of national interest." This placed restrictions on the freedom which the tribals formerly enjoyed in respect of their use of forest products.

The National Forest Policy of 1988 was oriented towards maintenance of environmental stability, conservation of natural heritage of the country, checking of soil erosion, checking sand-dunes in desert areas, increasing the forest cover in the country, meeting the requirements of fuel, fodder, minor forest produce and small timber of the rural and tribal population, increasing the productivity of the forests and encouraging efficient utilization of forest produce.

In regard to the rights and concessions, the policy was very much oriented towards the development of the tribal people. It stated that the life of the tribals and other people living within and near forests revolve around forests. The rights and concessions enjoyed by them should be fully protected, their domestic requirements of fuel wood, fodder, minor forest produce and construction timber should be the first charge on forest produce.

Forest resources consist of two types of products:

1. Major forest products and
2. Minor non-wood forest products

The Major forest products consist of timber, small wood and fuel wood including charcoal. The Minor non-wood forest products include all products obtainable from the forests other than wood.

**Forest Rejuvenation and Tribal Area Development**

If tribal economic development is to be a reality, then the forests have to be rejuvenated. The decision to plant various species of trees should be left to the local tribal people as they alone can sustain the forests and guard them. The future of the tribal people is linked to restoring the degraded forest lands with appropriate technology and with the participation of the tribals themselves. The restoration of the degraded forest land will ensure sustained employment round the year and improve the environment.

There is an urgent need to change the Indian Forest Act 1927 and the changes should accord recognition of tribals as partners in the management of forests. In short, this Act should become user-friendly.

The National Commission on Agriculture (1976) had found the potential of revolutionizing the economy of tribals in minor forest produce and called for nationalization of forest produce with a view to check the exploitation of tribals and to ensure a fair price for primary tribal collectors of forest produce. This facilitated formation of Tribal Development Cooperative Corporations in States having sizable tribal population for the procurement and marketing of minor forest produce at protective and remunerative prices, through the primary cooperative societies consisting of tribals. Government of India has also set up in 1987 the Tribal Marketing Development Federation of India Ltd. (TRIFED) as an apex body of State tribal development corporations at the national level. This body now helps in procurement and marketing of minor forest produce.

After the Bhuria Committee Report, the Panchayats (Extension to the Scheduled Areas) Act was passed in 1996 and the ownership of minor forest produce has been vested in the Gram Sabha in the Scheduled Areas of eight states coming within the Fifth Schedule of the Constitution.

Despite these developments, there are still several areas in which the National Forest Policy and the various enactments relating to conservation of forests and wildlife continue to come in conflict with the bonafide needs of the tribal communities. These need to be looked into so as to protect the interests of the tribal communities fully.

The National Conservation Act 1970 came to the conclusion that deterioration of the forest cover primarily was due to forest dwellers. Hence, further restrictions were placed on the tribal rights. Notable among these is the regulation of the rights of the forest dwellers over some of the minor forest produce. Unemployment and under-employment was considered to be the major cause of encroachment of the forests. The Forest Conservation Act, 1980 puts a blanket ban on use of any forest land or any portion thereof for non-forest purposes. This Act was felt to be a hindrance for undertaking development works for large number of tribals living in forests which deprived them of basic infrastructure facilities like roads, dispensaries, schools etc.

The National Forest Policy 1988 tried to restore the balance as may be seen from the broad objectives of the policy given below:

(i) Association of tribal people, in protection, regeneration and development of forests and to provide gainful employment to people living in and around forests.

(ii) Replacing private contractors with Government agencies like tribal cooperatives, labour cooperatives, Government corporations etc.

(iii) Marketing arrangements

(iv) Development of forest villages on par with revenue villages

(v) Implementation of family-oriented beneficiary programs.

The Panchayat (Extension to the Scheduled Areas) Act has clearly assigned the ownership of minor forest produce to the Panchayats at the appropriate level. The State Acts have simply defined the MFP products as per Indian Forest Act, 1927. Only the states of Gujarat and Maharashtra have made necessary amendments in their Panchayat Acts to this effect. In Gujarat, it has been vested the Village Panchayat and the sale proceeds of MFP shall be paid into and will form part of Village Panchayat Fund. In Maharashtra, the ownership of MFP has been granted to the Gram Sabha and State Panchayat. The other Scheduled Area States should also make suitable amendment in the State Act to give effect to the provisions under the Central Act.

**Forest Villages and Joint Forest Management**

The concept of forest villages was developed by the British. The existing habitations in the forest were declared as forest villages or people were brought from outside for establishing forest villages. The lease of the land was to be renewed on yearly basis. The tribals did not have permanent rights. This system continued after independence also. After the decision of the Kerala High Court in 1974, the Government of India advised the state governments to treat it as a revenue village and to give full rights to the people over the land cultivated by them. It is estimated that 2 lakh tribal families in 16 states live in forest villages.

The Forest departments in various states/UTs have now come up with a new concept of Joint Forest Management.

The Forest Department pays wages to the tribals and others for undertaking afforestation and its protection and the tribal communities are given a share in the produce. This concept has once again given certain rights on the forest land to the tribals and their families. As on 1.9.2000, 10.25 million hectares of forest land in the country was being managed and protected by 36,165 Village Forest Protection Committees. It is necessary that all forest villages are recognised as revenue villages so that tribal community can be empowered in the real sense. Suitable action is recommended on the following issues:

(a) As a policy, tribal communities living close to the forest should e involved in regeneration, afforestation, protection and management of forest areas under Joint Forest Management by ensuring following conditions:

- ❖ Adequate forest areas are entrusted to well defined user groups;
- ❖ Stake-holders have voice and choice in decision making ;
- ❖ Security of tenure as well as long-term access to benefits from the resources are assured.

(b) Forest villages should be intensively developed and heritable but inalienable rights on the lands should be given on priority basis. Agro forestry and social forestry should be promoted for meeting the food, fodder, fuelwood, timber and bamboo requirement of the people.

(c) Rehabilitation of shifting cultivation should be planned by promoting eco-restoration under the Rural Works programs.

(d) Organized commercial cultivation and collection of medicinal plants should be encouraged to ensure "Herbs for all and Health for all".

(e) Wildlife conservation should harmonize its activities to ensure development of tribal communities also. No one should be displaced from the protected areas without appropriate settlement and rehabilitation.

Environmental degradation in tribal areas is a cause and effect phenomenon. Poverty, low income, lack of livelihood sources, non-awareness about the environment etc are causes of environmental degradation. Therefore, a two-way approach is required- one to solve the rural problems through developmental process and the other to protect environment through community participation by creating awareness among them.

Deforestation has been responsible for soil-erosion, dwindling of forest cover, floods and droughts, desertification, non-availability of forest produce, pollution and impoverishment of tribals. This can be averted by increasing forest cover through JFM program by ensuring that suitable forest patches are entrusted to tribal communities for greening.

The Forest Policy should also ensure that tribals should not be displaced from the "Protected Forest Areas" and resettlement and rehabilitation of tribals should be ensured by adopting eco-development around protected areas.

In pursuance to the National Forest Policy, 1988, the Ministry of Environment and Forests started the following programs for the protection and development of forest-based biomass required for the sustenance of tribals and local poor living in and around forests:

**Association of Scheduled Tribes and Rural Poor in Regeneration of Degraded Forests on Usufruct Sharing Basis**

The above program was started as a 100 per cent centrally sponsored scheme in the VIII plan with an outlay of Rs. 735 lakhs. The scheme was continued in the IXth plan with an outlay of Rs. 1500 lakhs. The scheme is implemented through the State Forest Departments on the basis of the projects formulated by them. During the VIIIth plan, nine states namely A.P, Bihar, Gujarat, Karnataka, M.P, Maharashtra, Orissa, Rajasthan and West Bengal implemented this scheme in tribal dominated areas. Apart from the wages for the work done, the tribals benefitted with intermediate products and sharing in final harvest. They were also entitled to collect Minor Forest Produce (MFP), dead and fallen wood and fodder. The impact of the scheme in the areas of implementation was found good by the Ministry and more states came forward to undertake it during the IXth Five Year Plan. The target for forest regeneration during the VIIIth plan was put at 10550 hectare with the financial allocation of 735 lakhs. By the end of the plan period, the achievement has been 8330 ha.

**Joint Forest Management**

The National Forest Policy, 1988 envisages people's involvement in the development and protection of forests. The requirements of fuel wood, fodder and small timber for house-building purposes are to be treated as first charge on forest produce. Further effort is to made so that tribal people are motivated to identify themselves with the development and protection of forests from which they derive benefits. In order to achieve it, the Ministry issued guidelines on 1-6-1990 for involving village communities in the development and protection of degraded forests on the basis of their taking a share of the usufruct from such area. The concept of Joint Forest Management (JFM)thus took shape. 20 states have already issued their resolutions for operationalising the JFM. As per the implementation reports, about 1.30 million ha. of degraded forests in the country area being managed and protected through 20134 Village Forest Committees (VFC). The area under JFM is managed by the VFCs and Forest Department. Sometimes, local NGOs are also involved in implementation of activities under JFM. All states permit 100 per cent intermediate forest produce from thinning, lopping and minor forest produce to VFCs. However, the share to the beneficiaries from final harvest of timber varies from State to State.

A number of other schemes under implementation in the National Afforestation and Ecodevelopment Board are also in operation for development and conservation of forests. Most of these schemes are implemented in tribal areas.

**Tribal-Forest Interface**

There are some other important issues in the Tribal-Forest Interface. The Ministry of Environment and Forests has issued guidelines on 18th September 1990 which deals with regularization of those encroachments on forest lands before 25th October 1980 which fulfill the criteria given in the guidelines. The relevant paragraph 1.1 of the guidelines, which clarifies the cases of encroachments is reproduced below:

"Such cases are those where the State Governments had evolved certain eligibility criteria in accordance with local needs and conditions and had taken a decision to regularise such encroachments but could not implement their decisions either wholly or partially before the enactment of Forest Conservation Act on 25-10-80". But some of the States are still trying to regularise the encroachment even after the above cut-off date, e.g., the Madhya Pradesh Government has brought out a legislation which provides for regularisation of encroachment on forest lands upto the year 1983. So the tussle continues.

Apart from this, there are disputed claims over forest land arising out of forest settlement. Local inhabitants living in and around forest areas have laid claim to certain notified forest lands contending that they were in occupation of such areas prior to the initiation of forest settlements and their rights were not enquired or commuted before notifying these lands as forests under respective laws. The claimants are requesting that title of such lands should be conferred on them. It has been felt by the Central Government that there may be bonafide claims which may have been overlooked causing widespread discontentment among the aggrieved persons. Such instances ultimately erode the credibility of the Forest Administration and sanctity of the forest laws, especially in the tracts inhabited by tribals.

Seized of these complexities, an inter-ministerial committee examined the issue and after consultation with the state governments stressed the need to resolve such dispute with utmost urgency and suggested the feasible course of action to redress genuine grievances without jeopardizing protection of forests and forest land. Guidelines were issued to deal with such cases in 1990 and States/ UTs have been advised to identify the claims according to this guideline under the following catagories:

(a) Claims in respect of forest areas notified as deemed reserved forests without observing the due process of settlement as provided in Forest Acts provided that these pretain to

❖ Tribal areas; or affect a wide cross section of rural poor in non-tribal areas; and
❖ The claimants are in possession of the disputed land.

(b) Claims in tribal areas wherever there is prima-facie evidence that the process of forest settlement has been vitiated by incomplete or incorrect records/maps etc. and the claimants are in possession of the land and such forest settlements pertain to a period after 1947.

(c) Claims in tribal areas wherever the process of settlement is over, but notification under Section 20 of the Indian Forest Act 1927 is yet to be issued; provided the claimants are still in possession of disputed land.

After these claims have been verified by a Committee at the local level, the State/UT Government will consider restoration of titles to the claimants. These proposals will be finally approved by the Ministry of Environment and Forests along with proposals of compensatory afforestation.

The guidelines issued by the Ministry of Environment and Forests on 18th September 1990 also provide for settlement of disputes regarding pattas/grant involving forestland. The cases will also be examined by a local committee at the district level comprising of local DFO, SDO (Civil) and a representative of the Tribal Welfare Department. The disputes are to be resolved at the district level to the extent possible and in case of difficulty, orders of the State/UT Government or the Government of India may be obtained.

**Forest Villages**

Historically, Forest villages were set up in remote and inaccessible forest areas to provide uninterrupted man-power for forestry operations. With the passage of time, many such areas have become accessible and human habitation has increased. Therefore some of the State governments converted forest villages into revenue villages well before 1980. Nevertheless, there still exist between 2500 to 3000 forest villages in the country and there is a demand to notify them as revenue villages.

The guidelines issued by the Ministry in 1990, which have been referred above, also provide for the forest villages into revenue villages after denotifying requisite land as forest. Proposals in this regard are to be submitted to the Central Government under Forest Conservation Act, 1980. But the process of conversion of forest villages into revenue villages is so cumbersome that in Madhya Pradesh alone, over 1,00,000 tribal families live in about 500 forest villages but possess no rights to the land they cultivate. The Madhya Pradesh Government passed a law to give them security of tenure, but the Forest Conservation Act, 1980 has struck down this law. The result is that the tribals, although not being displaced from lands that they have cultivated for decades, cannot get loans from banks or the National SC/ST Finance and Development Corporation as they are not legal owners of this land. Similar problems have been observed in the eastern Terai districts of UP where the Forest Department had settled a large number of poor villagers on forest lands to do Taungia plantation.

### New Forest Policy and Tribals

It is generally believed that the new Forest Policy issued in 1988 heralded a new era in forest management. According to this policy, forests are not to be commercially exploited for industries but these are to conserve soil and environment, and meet the subsistence requirements of the tribals and other rural poor. Derivation of direct economic benefit from the forests has been subordinated to the objective of ensuring environmental stability and maintenance of ecological balance. It discourages monocultures and prefers mixed forests. The focus has shifted from 'commerce' and 'investment' to ecology and satisfying the minimum needs of the people, providing fuelwood and fodder, and strengthening the tribal-forest linkages.

But many of these provisions have not been put to effect as the new forest policy is non-statuary and advisory statement, not backed by law. It is distinct from the Forest Conservation Act, 1980 which is binding on all State Governments. Further there are a number of contradictions between the new Forest Policy and the amended Forest Conservation Act, both of which were enacted in December, 1988.

The Forest Conservation Act prohibits plantation of horticulture crops, palms, oil-bearing and medicinal plants on forest lands unless prior permission of the Government of India has been taken. It also curtails the rights and concessions to forest dwellers by relating them to the 'carrying capacity' of forests.

It has also been observed that after 1993, the commitment of the Government of India to the new Forest Policy and Joint Forest Management has considerably weakened. The tribals right of entry and usage in reserve forests will now be subject to carrying capacity and can be curtailed or 'rationalized' by the Government. Further, sacred groves can also be acquired by the government. The Government is also trying to debar the nomadic groups from exercising any rights on forest lands.

In the above discussion, we have so far seen that forest and tribals are inter-dependent on each other- one for its protection and care and who can do it better than tribals whose life revolves around it and the other for their source of livelihood as they are dependent on the forest produce.

To sum up, the following measures need to be taken in this sphere:

(i) Conferring heritable but inalienable rights on tribals cultivating lands in forest villages as per government decision in 1984;

(ii) Enforcement of guidelines/circulars on purchase of MFP from Panchayats/Gram Sabhas and market reforms;

(iii) Removal of restriction on tribals rights of access, collection of forest produce and clearly define their rights in JFM and community forestry schemes.

(iv) Involving tribal panchayats in processing of MFP to give them benefit of added value;

(v) Collection of forest produce should be enhanced through:

- Change in silvicultural practices of managing forests;
- Change in the nature of species being planted onpublic lands from timber to usufruct based trees;
- Publicity about the tribals in forest and communityland and greater control over market;
- Tribals should not be displaced from sanctuaries and national parks;
- Protection of tribal's rights to collect forest produce

from these areas (sanctuaries and national parks);

- ❖ Developing a strategy of wildlife protection in harmony with tribals and with their active cooperation;
- ❖ Basic minimum services need to be extended to tribals located in forest areas.

(vi) Alternative technologies of energy and housing that reduce dependence of local communities on wood must be promoted by the State, with the active participation of NGOs.

(vii) State-supported cooperatives of landless tribals should be set up for processing and marketing of various non-timber forest produce.

(viii) The most important pre-requisite for the success of the above initiative is the progressive empowerment of the tribal people, so that a new leadership can be provided to the Panchayati Raj institutions in the tribal areas.

(ix) Agro forestry and social forestry should be promoted for meeting the food, fodder, fuelwood, timber and bamboo requirements of the people. Commercial forestry should be promoted for economic development of the tribals. Marketing assistance should be made available to them. Cultivation of bamboo and herbs should be encouraged.

# 7

# Panchayati Raj System in Scheduled Areas

Introduction of planning, having the twin objectives of growth with social justice provided an opportunity for realizing the objectives of the Constitution. Panchayati Raj institutions were created to bring the process to the grassroot level. For the development of the tribals, the development administration was assigned an important role.

After independence, the government was faced with three tasks:

(a) Removing the communication gap between the tribals and the regional community in the framework of national integration.

(b) Protecting the resource base and the cultural apparatus, which can provide the basis of collective effort for meeting national challenges.

(c) Initiating measures for meeting the immediate needs of the tribal population and for facilitating the process of participatory development.

To meet the objectives, three strategies were adopted in the Constitution:

1. The Fifth Schedule enumerated measures for the administration of the tribal areas in the states that have large pockets of tribals. In such areas, the Union Government could give directions to the State and the Governor was given a special power for overseeing the

administration of the Scheduled Areas.

2. The Sixth Schedule was meant for tribal majority states in which provision was made for the establishment of autonomous District Councils which could make laws for the management of land and forest, shifting cultivation, appointment of chiefs and headmen, inheritance of property, marriage and divorce, social customs and anything related to village administration.
3. Article 275(1) of the Constitution provides for grant-in-aid to the States for promoting the welfare of Scheduled Tribes and raising the level of administration of the Scheduled Areas.

It has to be appreciated that the bulk of tribal population lives in Scheduled Areas notified as per Fifth Schedule and tribal areas notified as per the Sixth Schedule of the Constitution.

The Fifth Schedule constitutes an integral scheme of the Constitution with direction, philosophy and effort to protect the tribes from exploitation. Its objective is to preserve tribal autonomy, to ensure social, economic and political justice for preservation of Peace and good governance in the Scheduled Areas. All actions of the State must be in furtherance of the above Constitutional objective.[1]

## 73rd Amendment Act and Powers and Functions of Panchayati Raj Institutions

Before the 73rd amendment to the Constitution, the Panchayats were assigned some traditional functions such as maintenance rather than developmental responsibilities. The 73rd Amendment made PRIs responsible for maintenance as well as developmental activities. Article 243 G enlists the power, authority and responsibilities of Panchayats. In conformity to the 73rd Amendment Act, all the States have amended their respective Panchayat Acts and enlisted the functions assigned to the different levels of PRIs in the respective states. The functions enlisted in the State Panchayat Acts are classified into three categories:

1. General Administrative functions;

2. Developmental and Social and
3. Maintenance, as per the nature of these functions.

The Constitution Seventy third Amendment dealing with Panchayats recognised the need for special provisions for scheduled areas and tribal areas. It empowers Parliament to enact legislation providing for exceptions and modification in respect of these areas. The existence of different traditional systems of self-government in different tribal areas makes the exercise a complex one.

The 73rd Amendment Act should be implemented in its true spirit in all the States having Scheduled Areas. The Gram Sabhas should be given the right of decision-making on all resources within their villages.

The institutions proposed for the Scheduled and tribal areas should be vested with adequate powers to deal with problems of tribal people like land alienation, indebtness, deforestation, ecological degradation, displacement, excise policy, alcohol and drug addiction, out flow of minerals, hydel and water resources etc. access to natural resources in tribal areas should remain with the tribal people for utilisation on a sustainable basis.

The 73rd amendment gave a significant role to the Gram Sabhas. Without sufficient awareness and enlightenment on the part of tribals about the local self government institutions, the objectives of the amendment cannot be realized.

There have been attempts in the Fifth and Sixth Schedule States in the North-east to link the traditional grass root structures to the Constitutional Autonomous District Councils. In many areas, the traditional village structures are still not redundant but the elected Panchayat system has either been superimposed or both the systems are running parallel at the village level. One finds this situation in the Manki-Munda system in the Jharkhand, the Manjhi-Gomang system in Orissa and the Patel-Manjhi system in M.P. [2]

A significant development in regard to the self-government in the Scheduled Areas is the extension of the provisions of Part IX of the Constitution to the Scheduled Areas through the Panchayats (Extension to the Scheduled Areas) Act 1996. This legislation is unique in requiring the states to confer larger powers and authority on the Gram Sabhas and Panchayats in Scheduled Areas and also reserving the posts of chairpersons exclusively for the Scheduled Tribes in these areas.

**Panchayati Raj system in Tribal Areas**

The major task of Panchayati Raj in the tribal development is to develop standards and sensitivity in the society that helps to identify leadership potential in these terms. Tribal development efforts and programs face various impediments that spring from organizational and financial constraints. By proper involvement of the local people, at least three objectives of tribal development can be achieved: viz. (a) laying down maximum standards of productivity or efficiency for those who own or use precious natural resources; (b) minimum standards of performance by public agencies by asking them to be responsible to the local people and (c) creating a scientific temper which implies a changing of the mind and old habits of thought and action. In most of the tribal development programs, not enough care is taken to involve the local tribal councils.

Poverty, underdevelopment and unemployment are consequences of a social and economic process. It has been found that because of various pulls and pressures, the facilities and inputs intended for the tribals are largely siphoned off along the way. Due to the absence of viable organization at the village level, there is hardly any check.

It has now been recognized that tribal development cannot be administered from above, it has to be organized from below. Development as contrasted with mere growth, is a long drawn out process and has to be viewed on a long-term perspective from various points- legal, social, cultural and economic. While the realization of these issues has grown considerably, institutional arrangements have, however, not been developed adequately.

The Panchayati Raj structure, conceived of as an instrument of consultation, participation and self-management, has not proved universally suitable for tribal areas. The chief reason seems to be its inability to confirm to village and regional tribal traditions and ethos. It ignores the part played by traditional tribal institutions composed of persons chosen through consensus by village and regional assemblies. An ingrained allegiance to the traditional tribal leaders like the village headmen and to the traditional socio-political network does not facilitate wholehearted acceptance by the tribal of the new panchayat bodies. In Jharkhand, the Manki-Munda system is still alive and the Santhals, the Saora and several other tribes have preserved their traditional set-ups. In Jaunsar-Bawar area of Uttaranchal, the Village Sayanas still play an important role in revenue collection. So there is an urgent need to blend the statuary Panchayati Raj institutions and the traditional tribal bodies in such a way as to create a viable, harmonious and efficient system.

It has been found that in some tribal regions existing Panchayati Raj system comprising three tiers of Gram Panchayat, Panchayat Samitis and Zila Parishads have been accepted by the tribal people. But in other regions, the traditional organizational structure and leadership are still influential. The Panchayati Raj system has not been a success uniformally. There is need, therefore to ensure that the traditional systems are allowed to play their due role.[3]

## Panchayati Raj system and the Scheduled Areas

With the promulgation of the Indian Constitution, the tribal affairs were accepted as a national task above party considerations. This was reinforced by specific provisions in the Constitution like Articles 164(1), 224, 275, 338, 339 and the exceptions made even in the Fundamental rights contained in Articles 15, 16 and 19.

The President at the Center and the Governors in the States were assigned the task of operationalizing these provisions. The Governor under the Fifth Schedule has been assigned the task of sending annual reports to the President regarding the administration of the Scheduled Areas in that state. The executive power of the Union extends to the giving of directions to the State as to the administration of the said areas. The Governor also has the authority to direct that any law of the State shall not apply to the Scheduled Areas or shall apply with such exceptions and modifications as he may deem necessary. The President can give directions to the states as to the drawing up and execution of schemes for the welfare of the Scheduled Tribes in the states. The financial needs for the execution of various welfare and developmental programs as also for raising the level of administration of the Scheduled Areas to that of the rest of the state, have been fully provided for under the First Proviso to Article 275(1) of the Constitution and made a charge on the Consolidated Fund of India. A National Commission of Scheduled Castes and Scheduled Tribes has been provided for under Article 338 to investigate and monitor the safeguards provided for the SCs and STs under the Constitution or any law in force.

After the submission of the Bhuria committee report, it was decided in 1996 not to extend the provisions of Part IX concerning Panchayats and Part IX A concerning municipalities as such to the Scheduled Areas and consider making necessary exceptions and modifications before extending them.

The Provisions of Panchayats (Extensions to the Scheduled Areas) Act (in brief the Extension Act) envisages the community at the village level in the form of Gram Sabha as the basic building block of the new system. It also puts on record the fact that the Gram Sabha is competent to manage the affairs of the community in accordance with its customs and tradition. This provision is unique and stands out in contrast to the general scheme of delegation and devolution of powers, including that for the panchayats under Article 40 and 243 G.

Here then is a framework which has the potential for building up of the inner strength of the tribal community. In the area of protection of their rights, it is now the Gram Sabha which has to assume the pivotal role in the spheres of land alienation and providing effective protection to the tribal people. The Gram Sabha has to ensure that tribal land is not alienated and wrongfully alienated lands are restored to the real claimants. Even the State government cannot acquire land without their consent.

The Extension Act, thus, for the first time has started a process of unfolding the potential of the Fifth Schedule. A beginning has been made at the village level and parameters for transformation at higher levels in the Panchayat system have been set. The pattern of the Sixth Schedule with some modifications has to be adapted at the district level. Thus the Gram Panchayats and the Zila Parishad have a chance to emerge as an institution of self-governance in the Scheduled areas. The State, in due discharge of its Constitutional responsibility of providing effective protection to the tribal people, has to assume a supportive role with the people themselves occupying the center of the stage.

The pre-independence tribal scene had the following elements :-

1. A system of self-governance guided by the traditions and customs of the people
2. Considered intervention at the highest level in matters concerning the system and the legal frame; and
3. Realization of the need for protection of tribals exemplified by the 'excluded area' approach and 'inner line' permits.

The community at the village level in the tribal areas is a functioning unit. It has managed its affairs in accordance with its customs and traditions and in a spirit of democracy. The Dhebar Commission (1961) succinctly brought out this in its report in the following words:

"The decision of their councils is law to the tribals. The sanction behind it is both necessity and faith; necessity because there in far flung areas social equilibrium and stability have to be maintained by some responsible agency and the council is that agency; faith because with tribals their social customs and religious rites are the essence of their existence."[4]

The above ideals had been enshrined in our Constitution as Article 40. It said: -

"The State shall take steps to organize village panchayats and endow them with such powers and authority as may be necessary to enable them to function as units of self-government."

Yet no explicit provision was made in the Fifth Schedule to ensure that necessary space was created within the formal system for this living entity at the village level, the village Council or the Gram Sabha and that the new edifice was built there as in real terms.

The only frame at the local level which could be of help was that of the Gram Panchayat. The 73rd amendment succeeded in bringing the collectivity of the people in the form of Gram Sabha in the formal Constitutional frame vide Article 243(b). But the amendment was silent on the powers of the Gram Sabha. Article 243 A envisaged that the legislature of a State may provide the Gram Sabha with such powers and perform such functions, as deemed necessary.

The vital decision in the case of the tribal people was to exclude the Scheduled Areas from the purview of the new provisions concerning panchayats and later about municipalities which were enshrined in the Constitution through the 73rd and 74th amendment respectively. Accordingly, a provision was made under Article 243 M(4)(6) as :-

"Parliament may by law, extend the provisions of this part to the Scheduled Areas... subject to such exceptions and modifications as may be specified in such law, and no such law shall be deemed to be an amendment of this Constitution for the purposes of Article 368".

The new law for the Scheduled Areas envisages village community as the basic unit of the self-governing system. Sec 4(d) deals with the competence of the Gram Sabha. It says :

"Every Gram Sabha shall be competent to safeguard and preserve the traditions and customs of the people, their cultural identity, community resources and the customary mode of dispute resolution."

This provision, in effect, transforms the entire legal edifice of the Scheduled Areas. The Community in the village, that is the Gram Sabha, managing its affairs in keeping with its traditions and customs, is now at the center of the stage. The management of the Community resources is now the responsibility of the Gram Sabha. All powers concerning any program whatsoever now vest in the Gram Sabha. The Gram Sabha will also certify the authenticity of all expenditure. The Gram Sabha and the Panchayats at appropriate level will have the power to exercise control over institutions and its functionaries in all social sectors. Even the non-governmental institutions and their functionaries are covered under this provision.

Thus the pivotal role of the Gram Sabha has now been acknowledged. It has been especially protected against any intrusion by any other authority whatsoever including the State itself. The scope of the role of Gram Sabha will get enlarged once the people gain experience in the new setting and acquire confidence in dealing with various matters concerning their life in the new formal frame.

The Panchayati Raj system has therefore infused a new spirit in the tribal areas. The scheme of the Fifth Schedule has also become explicit after the enactment of the provisions of Panchayats (Extensions to Scheduled Areas) Act 1996. Section 4(d) of this Act provides that :-

"Notwithstanding any thing contained in Part IX of the Constitution, ... every Gram Sabha shall be competent to safeguard and preserve the traditions and the customs, their cultural identity, community resources..."

Under clause 4(m)(iii), the power to prevent alienation of land in the Scheduled Areas and to take appropriate action to restore any unlawfully alienated land of the Scheduled Tribes has been entrusted to the Gram Sabha and Panchayats at the appropriate level. Appreciating the spirit of the Extension Law, the Supreme Court in 'Samatha Case' has observed :

"It would indicate that the tribal autonomy of management of their resources including the preventation of alienation of land in the Scheduled Areas and taking of appropriate action in that behalf for restoration of the same to tribals, is entrusted to the Gram Panchayats."

Gram Panchayat in the Scheduled Areas is now the chief executive body of the Gram Sabha, answerable to it and functioning under the general control, superintendence and direction of the Gram Sabha.

The Extension Law has taken due note of the possibility of the laws being incongruous with the spirit of the Fifth Schedule, not being adapted by the state or Central government. For example, the only state which has amended all laws involving acquisition of land for public purposes is Maharashtra. The implication of this is that all laws which are inconsistent with the provisions of the Fifth Schedule as reinformed by the Extension Law, are deemed to have become inoperative with effect from 24.12.1997.

The Constitution specially envisages the establishment of panchayats for the rural areas at three levels – village, intermediate and district. These panchayats according to Article 243 G may be endowed with ' such powers and authority as may be necessary to enable them to function as institutions of self government.

As stated earlier, the Scheduled Areas were kept outside the purview of both part IX and part IX A with a provision for extension of these provisions to the said areas by law, with suitable exceptions and modifications by the Parliament, under Article 243 M and Article 243 Z respectively. The provisions of Panchayats at all the three levels have been extended to these areas with effect from 24.12.1996 with exceptions and modifications as given in the Extension Act. The provisions concerning municipalities have not been extended so far.

The difference between the institutions beyond the Gram Sabha in the Scheduled Areas and elsewhere in the country, thus are related to two basic elements :-

(i) The competence of Gram Sabha as made explicit in the

Extension Act; and

(ii) The pattern of district-level administration as envisaged in the Sixth Schedule.

The Gram Sabha as envisaged in the Extension Act for the Scheduled Areas, is the best possible to the ideal of village-republic. The present institutional framework of Panchayats is hierarchical. It has also been made clear that the relationship between the Gram Sabha and the Gram Panchayat shall be the same as between the Parliament and the Government. The specific powers given to the Gram Sabha include land acquisition, prevention of land-alienation and restoration of illegally transferred lands, management of water-bodies, working of minor minerals, ownership over minor forest produce, control over money-lending, regulation of village markets, control over use, storage etc of intoxicants and enforcement of prohibition.

The list of items given above in relation to the Scheduled Areas shows that the concerns of Panchayats at all levels henceforth will cover the substantive issues of governance.[5]

**Democratic Decentralization**

The concept of decentralization is invariably used to mean the transfer of planning, decision making and administrative authority by the Central Government to its field level organizations, local governments and local administrative units. Decentralization, thus refers to the creation of local bodies in which the people and their representatives are given formal powers to decide upon a range of public matters. Democratic decentralization and decentralized planning are expected to achieve the broader objective of empowerment of the poor.

The experience of Panchayati Raj has however been far from happy. The reasons are not difficult to find. They are :-

1. Lack of political will
2. Lack of expertise at the local level,
3. Lack of development orientation and problems of re-orienting the bureaucracy.

Some scholars have expressed the view that the modern statutory Panchayati Raj System has not been found entirely suitable for tribal areas of the country. The traditional tribal societies were accustomed to regulation of their domestic, social, religious, economic, socio-political and even judicial affairs through the combined wisdom of the village elders. Introduction of Panchayati Raj System has also witnessed conflicts between tribal and non-tribal leaders and in some areas power has been captured by non tribal people in the tribal majority areas.

Now all states having Scheduled Areas have brought into force the necessary legislations to give effect to the provisions in the Extension Act, 1996. But all is not well with the implementation of the Extension Act. There is need to redefine planning and implementation strategies as the rationale behind the Extension Act was to empower Gram Sabhas to approve and sanction all matters pertaining to tribal society and economy. The role of Panchayats at different levels should be merely to execute decisions taken by the Gram Sabha.

As none of the State Acts contain any specific provision for making the Panchayat an institution of self-government by providing adequate safeguards so that the Panchayat at higher levels do not assume powers and authority of the Panchayats at lower level and the Gram Sabhas; this needs to be considered by the State governments urgently.

Coordination needs to be ensured in the activities of TDCC/ITDA/ITDP/Block/financial institutions and the Panchayats to ensure harmonious and balanced utilization of resource (men, money and material) for achieving plans/ programs/ project targets.

Some studies have indicated that the major problems faced by the Gram Panchayats are related to the shortage of drinking water, electrification of hamlets, lack of link roads in villages, inadequate health and educational facilities, drainage system, soil conservation and land development. These basic needs require priority in planning and execution.

An integral part of the success of Panchayati Raj system would be that Gram Sabhas function as a guiding organization in Scheduled Areas and their recommendations and decisions are mandatory for the Gram Panchayats.

Thus, the Extension Act has been one of the important legislative measures of recent times which recognized the tribal people's mode of living, their culture and traditions. There are still some reservations and hurdles in implementing the Act in its entirety. But it is hoped that the provisions of the central and conformity legislations would enable the tribal people to have access to basic livelihood resources and enable them to lead a life without exploitation and with honor and dignity.

**Working of the Panchayati Raj in Jharkhand**

A comparative study of the Working of traditional and Statuary Panchayats in the tribal areas of Ranchi district by Ram Naresh Trivedi (1970) clearly and distinctly reveals that the need of the hour is neither to reform and streamline the traditional panchayats nor to substitute the Statuary Panchayats by traditional panchayats but to make the Statuary Panchayats more acceptable and really beneficial to the tribal people.[6]

By the time the country became independent, traditional Panchayats of the tribal people were not so virile and powerful as before, but, at the same time, not so decadent and powerless as was the case with the non-tribal traditional Panchayats. Consequently, alongwith the Statuary Panchayats, the traditional Panchayats continued to function in the tribal areas. Being different in origin and functions from each other, the traditional and Statuary Panchayats came to be looked upon as rival and competitive machineries of the village government.

Traditional Panchayats, for maintaining the solidarity of the society and based on the customary rules of the tribal community, have been in existence in each tribal village since long. These traditional Village Panchayats, however, had more or less no administrative responsibilities. Their source of income was very meagre. They were not concerned with the law and order, development programs and other administrative powers and responsibilities.

Prior to independence, the Parha (Divisional) and Hatu (village) Panchayats, whose main functions were to decide social and religious matters, were much powerful in the tribal areas of Ranchi. The main objective of the Parha (Divisional) and Hatu (village) Panchayats was to maintain the solidarity of the society. The tribal people had great faith in their Traditional Panchayats.

A tribal village even at present is a unit of much cultural importance. It is one of the important units of social structure and at the same time the exclusive agency of supervising the life of the tribal community, of maintaining law and order among them and also of giving some sort of direction to the purposes of the villagers either individually or collectively.

Munda and Oraon are the two main tribe of Ranchi district. Parha Panchayats of the Mundas are of two kinds:

1. Parha of the Khuntkatti area; and
2. Parha of the Bhuinhari area.

The Mundas were the first to settle in the tribal areas of Ranchi district. It is they who cleared the dense forests and made them virgin cultivable lands. These settled lands came to be known as "Khunt-Katti Hatus" i.e. is a village of original settlers. With the passage of time, these lands were acquired by the Raja and they came to be known as "Bhuinhari areas". Those Mundas who migrated to areas outside the Raja's control and founded villages came to be known as "Khunt-Katti Patti".

Writing about the Parha Panchayats among the Mundas, S.C.Roy says "Each Parha in the Bhuinhari area has a standing Panchayat. Parha Panchayat is a fixed and standing body having permanent officials. The principals who conduct its business are the Parha Raja and his Dewan."[7]

A Parha Panchayat in the Khunt-Katti area is composed of one or two headmen (the Munda or the Pahan or both) from each of the different villages constituting the Parha. The Manki (Head of the Parha) is the only permanent official of the Parha in such areas. His post is hereditary. Whenever the Parha Panchayat is summoned to settle disputes, the Manki invites the village heads to attend the Panchayat.

The organization of Parha Panchayats among the Oraons is very elaborate. S.C.Roy[8] traces the origin of the Parha system among the Oraons to a desire of the villages in one neighbourhood for a common system of protection against natural and supernatural forces. The Parha is a loose confederacy of a number of villages with a central organization known as Parha Panchayat.

Parha Panchayats have been playing a vital role in the political and socio-religious organizations of the Mundas and Oraons since their settlement in the tribal areas of Ranchi District. The main functions of the Parha Panchayats are the following:

1. To maintain law and order in the villages under its jurisdiction.
2. To settle socio-religious and boundary disputes between the villages.
3. To hear appeals against the judgements of the Hatu (village) Panchayats.
4. Breaches of sex taboos viz. incest, adultery etc. between the numbers of the same clan.
5. Any dispute between the village head and the village priest.

In course of field work, it was observed that the above stated powers and functions of the Parha Panchayats applied more in the case of Oraon-Parhas rather than in the case of Munda-Parhas. In short, it can be said that the scope of activities and breadth of power of the Oraon-Parhas are wider and greater than those of the Munda-Parhas. This is so because whereas the former has jurisdiction over all kinds of cases, the latter very rarely take up the cases arising out of breaches of sex taboo. However, so far as the power of settling the disputes is concerned, the Munda Panchayats seem to be more powerful than the Oraon Panchayats. This is so because Oraon Panchayats are not the final authority in settling almost all cases coming under their jurisdiction. Appeals against the judgement of the Oraon Hatu Panchayat may be made to the Parha Panchayat. But the Hatu Panchayats among the Mundas are the final authorities in settling almost all cases coming under their jurisdiction.

Though the Hatu Panchayats were to look after the enforcement of the customary laws, yet the ultimate and chief burden of such maintenance rested with the Parha Panchayats. It was the duty of the Parha officials to see that breaches of customary laws did not go unpunished and unchecked. They were able to maintain the observance of the customary laws, in the absence of police, because of the belief among the tribal people that the violation of customary laws made the gods angry which may cause epidemics or other calamities or disasters to themselves, to the clan or the village. These beliefs and fears had a very deep and lasting effect on the mind of the tribal people and kept them law-abiding.

It was also said that the customary laws of the tribals were transmitted from one generation to another without their being written or codified or without any formal teaching of such laws or without any training to those who were to maintain them. The tribal children, as they grow, attend the Panchayat meetings regularly and this enabled them to know about the customary laws and the penalties for their violation. In this way, by the time a tribal attains adulthood, he knew all about the customary laws of its clan or tribe and also the ways and means to settle the cases arising out of the violation of such customary laws.

Thus, it can be said that though both the Parha and Hatu Panchayats are in existence and they are performing certain functions also, yet their functions and utilities cannot be said to be of any real importance, except so far as the preservation of the time old tribal customs and manners are concerned. The establishment of the Statuary Panchayats and the gradual increase in the association of the tribals with their functioning has further accelerated the pace of the decline of the Traditional Panchayats.

**Statuary Panchayats in Ranchi District**

In the tribal areas of Ranchi district, the Statuary Panchayats were not established in the pre-independence period. They came to be established in the year 1948 with the enactment of the Bihar Panchayat Raj Act, 1947 (Bihar Act No.7 of 1948).

Statuary Panchayats came to be established in the tribal areas of Ranchi district under very unfavourable circumstances. The Jharkhand party and the authorities of the Traditional Panchayats did not take kindly to it as they visualized them as their potential enemies, particularly due to the fact that the office bearers of these Panchayats were to be the elected representatives of the people, whereas they themselves were occupying the hereditary posts.

In the early years, the Traditional Panchayats continued to enjoy their hold over the tribals regarding their social and religious customs and sex offences. The Traditional Panchayats had much influence upon the people and nobody dared to go against the village head and the village elders. The village heads still retained some influence in the area.

The Traditional Panchayats presently look after only the social and religious matters. Such matters have not been brought to the Statuary Panchayats so far. The Statuary Panchayats mainly look after the developmental works and settling of disputes. Therefore, even if both the Panchayats co-exist in such a manner that the traditional Panchayats look after the social and religious disputes only (which they are doing presently) and the Statuary Panchayats look after the developmental works and settling of disputes (other than social and religious), there will be no clash in the discharge of their respective functions.

Urbanization and industrialization has led to the weakening of the traditional Panchayats in the urban areas of Chotanagpur. Traditional Panchayats in its present form do not appeal to the educated tribals. However effective and powerful the traditional Panchayats might have been in the past, they are in a state of decay and decline today.

It is a well known fact that the success of the Village

Panchayats depends on the enthusiasm that is aroused and the feeling of oneness that is generated in the village community and the confidence it enjoys among all sections of village life.

## References

1. D.Mukherjee-Issues in Tribal Development Administration (Management in Government), July-September 2000, pp. 75-81.

2. Bhupinder Singh and Niti Mahajan (ed)- Role of Democratic Decentralization, Panchayati Raj in TSP areas, Inter India Publications, New Delhi, 1999, p. 27.

3. B.D.Sharma- Planning for Tribal Development, New Delhi, 1984.

4. U.N.Dhebar- Report of the Scheduled Areas and Scheduled Tribes Commission (1960-61), Publications Division, Government of India, New Delhi, p. 501.

5. B.D.Sharma- The Fifth Schedule (Vol I and II), Sahyog, Pustak Kutir Trust, New Delhi, 2000, pp. 29-30.

6. Ram Naresh Trivedi- Working of the Panchayats in Ranchi District (1970), pp 10-22.

7. S.C. Roy: The Mundas and their Country, Ranchi (1912), pp. 419-421.

8. S.C. Roy: The Oraons of Chotanagpur, Ranchi (1915), pp. 414.

# 8

# Uttaranchal-the Land and the People

The state of Uttaranchal has an area of 53,179 sq. kms. and a population of 70,50,634. It extends in length 225 kms. from North to South and in breadth 310 kms from West to East. It lies in the central zone of the Himalayas. It has 13 districts namely Dehradun, Uttarkashi, Tehri Garhwal, Rudraprayag, Chamoli, Hardwar, Pauri Garhwal, Bageshwar, Pithoragarh, Almora, Nainital, Champawat and Udham Singh Nagar. It was formed on 9th November, 2000 with Dehradun as capital. It has a great potential for tourism and development of forest products. Forests are rich with species like pine, spruce, oak, rhododendron and medicinal and aromatic herbs. Annual earning from forest products are Rs. 135 crores. The rivers Ganga, Yamuna and Ramganga are the major rivers flowing through this region which is enriched with mineral deposits like magnasite, lime stone, dolomite and talc. The rivers generate resources for hydroelectric power to the tune of 1,000 M.W.

The Scheduled Tribes population of UP was 2.88 lakhs in 1991 as against 1.99 lakhs in 1971. As per 1981 Census, the largest tribal community in Uttar Pradesh were the Tharus (47.53 per cent) followed by Jaunsaries (26.04 per cent), Buxas (16.85 per cent) and Bhotias (9.39 per cent). The Rajis were the tiniest being only 0.20 per cent of the total ST population of the State. The decadal growth in the population of Scheduled Tribes in the state has shown lower rates as compared to general population i.e. 2.10 per cent growth rate of population was reported in the case of Scheduled Tribes during 1981-91 against 2.29 per cent in the case of general population in the corresponding period. The provisional figures of 2001 census indicate that in the last decade, the population of this state has increased by 15.60 per cent as compared to the increase of 23.12 per cent during 1981-1991. The provisional figure of 2001 census shows a population of 84,79,562 of which 43,16,401 were male and 41,63,161 were female. Thus the number of females was 964 per 1000 males. According to the 1991 census, population of the Scheduled castes and Scheduled tribes constituted 17.48 per cent and 2.68 per cent of the total population of Uttar Pradesh. After the formation of the new State, the population of STs has gone up to 4 per cent of the total population of Uttaranchal.

As per 2001 census, the literacy rate of Uttaranchal is 72.3 per cent; it being 84.0 per cent among males and 60.3 per cent among females. This compares favorably with the literacy rate of 59.58 per cent as per the 1991 census. About 76.82 per cent of the total population live in the rural areas, the population density per sq. km. being 133, and agriculture continues to be the mainstay of the people. Out of the total 55,63,174 hectares of the state's area, about 62.31 per cent is under forest cover. For agricultural purposes, only 7,62,000 hectares are available which is 14.24 per cent of the total land area and of the total agricultural land, only 40.66 per cent area is irrigated. Here it may also be mentioned that in the hilly regions of the state, the irrigated area is less than 16 per cent of the net sown area.

The state of Uttaranchal is predominately hilly with 88 per cent of the total geographical area in the hilly region and the rest 12 per cent in the plains region. On account of its undulating topography, rugged terrain, varied climate and poor soil cover, the hilly region suffers from various constraints. The factors which severely inhibit the pace of development are: very limited arable land, overwhelming percentage of small and marginal holdings, fragmented land holdings, difficult agricultural conditions, sparse pattern of human settlement, severe soil erosion, deficiencies in infrastructure and amenities, inadequate institutional support, long gestation period of projects and low returns on investment. Furthermore, the rapid depletion of natural resources has aggravated the problems related to its environment and ecology. Inadequate development of technologies suitable for hilly areas, unscientific management of natural resources and unsuitable land use patterns have resulted in the low productivity on the one hand and depletion of natural resources and ecological degradation on the other.

Keeping in view, the level of backwardness of Uttaranchal, there is an urgent need to frame a policy for the proper development of the region. The foremost challenge is the problem of environment and ecological imbalance. This affects the tribal people of the region adversely. Forests are very important resource and play a very significant role in the process of economic development. As a result of indiscriminate felling of trees for commercial purposes and pressure on forests for domestic purposes ,the forest cover has greatly depleted. The problems of drinking water, fuel wood, fodder and soil erosion has emerged due to deforestation. A concrete policy is required therefore at the earliest for the protection and conservation of forest wealth.

Out migration of population, particularly among males from villages to the towns and cities is one of the most important features of the demographic structure in the hilly region of the state. Low income and inadequate employment opportunities due to weak agricultural and industrial base force people to migrate from the region. This can be mitigated to some extent by promoting self-employment schemes on the one hand, and the initiation of an industry-led development strategy on the other. Diversification of agriculture into high value horticulture crops hold considerable promise for the hilly region. The climate is also suitable for growing tea plants on a large scale. The establishment of small industries based on horticulture crops, forest wealth, tea-gardening, herbal and medicinal plants in Uttaranchal will open opportunities for employment of local people which in turn will increase the income level on the one hand and check out migration of people on the other.

Women constitute the backbone of Uttaranchal as hill agriculture is dependent on them. They are overburdened with work and fifty years of freedom have not led to any significant improvement in their life-style. Some value-added processes in agro-based industries and packaging etc. could easily be developed at the village level by imparting vocational and technical skills to the womenfolk. Vocational training can also be imparted in tailoring, kitchen-gardening, tea-gardening, vegetable growing, food preservation, mushroom growing, embroidery, knitting, weaving, painting etc. The development of handicraft based on locally available raw materials have good scope of providing employment and income generation.

Uttaranchal State has recently been given the position of 'Special Status' state by the central government. This will entitle it to receive 90 per cent of the central plan assistance in the form of grants and 10 per cent as loan. Best use of provisions under the category of special status could lead to economic development at a faster rate.

## Scheduled Tribes of Uttaranchal

In 1950,the number of Scheduled Tribes in India was 212. It increased in 1956 when the list was revised. Five Tribes of UP namely Jaunsari, Buxa, Raji, Bhotia and Tharu were included in the list of Scheduled Tribes in 1967. They are now the major tribes in Uttaranchal.

The tribal people of Uttaranchal are amongst the most primitive races in the country. Many of them live in strategically important border areas, which make their position sensitive. Their economy is closely linked with forests. Majority of them are below the poverty line, possessing meager assets and are exclusively dependent on wages, minor forest produce and agriculture. In Uttaranchal, tribes live in three well-defined regions. The Bhotia, Raji and Jaunsari live in the mountainous regions forming part of the Great Himalayas. The Raji, the tiniest among the hill tribes, are found only in nine villages in an area of almost 200 s.k. in Pithoragarh district. The Tharus are mainly concentrated in the Terai areas from Gorakhpur in UP to Nainital in Uttaranchal. The Buxas live both in the Terai and Bhabar areas in the districts of Nainital, Hardwar, Pauri-Garhwal and Dehradun. The Bhabar lies just below the Himalayan foothills as a narrow strip of five to twenty five kilometers in width, with an elevation of 1200 to 2200 feet above the sea level. The Buxas are supposed to be the original inhabitants of the Terai belt. Educationally they are more backward than the Tharus. Agriculture is their main occupation.

The Jaunsaris live in the Jaunsar area of Dehradun district. They include the Khasas, the artisan classes, Koltas and Bajgis. The Khasas comprising the Brahmins and Rajputs constitute the privileged class while the Koltas are made to serve them. They are also treated as untouchables. Khasas are traditional landowners while the Koltas and Bajgis (artisans) have no independent existence of their own. The Koltas are also suffering from bondage in some places. As per a study made by the Tribal Research Institute Lucknow, 90 per cent of Kolta families in Jaunsar-Bawar were indebted. As per Amir Hassan (1979) the incidence of indebtedness among Buxas was as high as 83 per cent.[1]

**Literacy Amongst Scheduled Tribes**

The analysis of 1991 census reveals that the literacy rate of Scheduled Tribes population in Uttar Pradesh is 35.70 per cent as compared to 41.60 per cent of the total population. The literacy rate of Scheduled Tribes males is 49.95 per cent whereas 19.86 per cent females are literate.

The low level of literacy among Scheduled Tribes in the state is because of nearly 20 per cent dropout at primary level and 80 per cent at Junior High School level of education. Due to low literacy level and high dropout rates, the tribal people are unable to take full advantage of reservation in government jobs.

**Employment Position**

Even after fifty-five years of independence the representation of the Scheduled Tribes in government services is abysmally low in UP. Against a reservation of 2 per cent, the highest representation of the Scheduled Tribes was reported in Class D posts (0.63 per cent) followed by

Class A (0.54 per cent) and Class B (0.50 per cent). The poverty rates of Scheduled Tribes in UP as compared to the total population at the national level and state level has been reported to be much higher. At the national level, poverty ratio of the Scheduled Tribes was reported to be 57.1 per cent as against 37.4 per cent among the total population. During 1993-94, the poverty rate of the Scheduled Tribes in UP was reported to be 66.6 per cent as against 45.3 per cent among the total population.

## Economic Classification of Workers

The total Scheduled Tribes main workers in UP were 0.86 lakhs in 1981 which increased to 1.03 lakhs in1991 registering a compound annual growth rate of 1.9 per cent. Again 84.36 per cent workers are engaged in primary sector and slightly more than 9 per cent workers were reported to be engaged in the tertiary sector. The percentage of workers engaged in primary sector was reported comparatively higher in cases of STs as compared to general castes. Similarly, percentage of workers engaged in tertiary sector was reported just half in case of STs than general castes. As compared to general and total workers, workers relating to STs are more dependent on agriculture. As per 1991 census, 70 per cent of the STs were cultivators and 13 per cent agricultural laborers, while only 17 per cent workers were engaged in non- agricultural economic activities.

## Land Holdings Amongst Tribals

No land settlement has been done for over 50 years in the area. The increase in population has resulted in the fragmentation of land holdings, making them uneconomical. During 1980-81, total land holdings of the Scheduled Tribes was reported to be 28.3 thousand comprising of 50 thousand hectare land area. Of these land holdings, 53 per cent land holdings were marginal. The land holdings of the Scheduled Tribes were reported just 0.51 per cent against the total land holdings of the State. During 1990-91, total land holdings of the Scheduled Tribes was reported to be 32.3 thousand comprising of 57 thousand hectare land area; out of these, 52.63 per cent land holdings were reported to be marginal.

These land holdings were recorded just 0.16 per cent against the total land holdings of the State.

**Land Alienation**

The problem of land alienation is quite widespread among Tharus and Buxas of Nainital and Udham Singh Nagar districts in Uttaranchal. It was detected in a survey conducted by the State Planning Institute during 1983 that more than 53,000 acres of land, including government and tribal land has been encroached upon mainly by outsiders who are Sikhs and Hindu Panjabis. Instead of making any serious efforts to evict the trespassers, the State government followed a policy of regularizing the encroachments on government land.

**Forests and Tribals**

The total forest area of Uttaranchal is 34,355 sq. kms. out of which about 23,682 sq. kms. is under the control of the forest department. Thus 67 per cent of the total area of Uttaranchal is covered under forests. Forests are categorised as 'reserve' (no local rights), and 'Protected' (with some local rights). For forest dwelling tribals in Uttaranchal, collection and sale of minor forest produce has been a good source of income. Among economic activities in the forest are collection of sal seeds, mahua flowers, herbs etc.

The marketing of agricultural produce varies from crop to crop. However, most of the tribals still carry the agricultural produce to the market place by animal-driven carts, bicycles or through manual load. The forest department continues its policy of harassing the tribals by implicating them in criminal cases or prosecuting them under the Indian Forest Act for unlawfully taking out fuel wood etc. This mindset needs to be changed and regeneration of forests, afforestation of wastelands and farm forestry is required. The task of regeneration may be given to the forest protection committees. The "Van Panchayat " is an ancient institution in Uttaranchal for forest management as it was created by the British as the dominant common property resource and its scope can be increased to include grazing and pasture lands. As per the available data the total number of Van Panchayats in Uttaranchal numbered 4665 in the year 1993 and Dehradun district had 159 Van Panchayats.

### Agriculture and Allied Sectors

63.8 per cent of people of Uttaranchal are farmers who cultivate about 12.4 per cent land. Agriculture is thus practised in a limited area and is mostly of traditional type having various constraints namely, difficult terrain, fragmented land holdings, vast climatic diversity and predominantly rainfed farming. The climatic conditions in Uttaranchal favour diversification from agriculture into horticulture, namely fruits, cut flowers, herbs, mushrooms and vegetables including potatoes. This needs infrastructural support in the form of soil and water conservation measures, irrigation facilities, credit and marketing support, etc. However, there is a lack of institutional support and local capital is scarce.

Agriculture in terms of net sown area occupied only 12.4 per cent of the reported area in 1993-94, but gave employment to nearly 80 per cent of the people in rural areas. On account of the small size of the land holdings and near total dependence on rainfall, yields are low.

Horticulture earns far more income than crop production. Micro-level village studies have shown that pear, plum, citrus fruits, walnut and almond are the main fruits which have a great potential. Constraints in developing fruit production include lack of availability of quality plants, lack of diesease and pest control measures, lack of marketing infrastructure and lack of labour in peak times.

### Other Sectors

In Uttaranchal, the income and employment generating activities of registered factories and household industries are almost negligible.

Tourism is one sector which can be developed to the greater advantage of the area. As per an estimate, tourists bring in Rs.12,000 crore annually and this can be increased to Rs.16,000 crore if it is declared a thrust activity.

### Government Assistance

As per government records, most of the tribal families

have received assistance under IRDP program. While the scheme of Indira Awas Yojana was significant as far as the number of beneficiaries was concerned, some tribal families have also received financial assistance through ITDP and Prime Minister's Rozgar Yojana. But on the whole, the tribal population continues to face difficulty in securing advances from government and financial institutions, a fact which was highlighted in our visit to village Sujau in Chakrata Block.

While implementing the programmes involving individual loans and subsidies, it is vital that adequate and timely availability of the assistance to the beneficiaries ensured, failing which the enthusiasm of the people is reduced and they face difficulty in repayment of the loan not being able to draw full benefit from the investments.

**Background of selected district (Dehradun)**

Dehradun district has an area of 3088 sq. kms. and a total population of 10,25,679. Out of that the ST population is 84,076 (8.20 per cent). As per 2001 census, the literacy rate of the district is 78.96 per cent with 85.87 per cent males and 71.22 per cent females being literate. Along with Nainital (71.22 per cent), it has the highest literacy rate in Uttaranchal. It has six development blocks. The total forest area constitutes 68.8 per cent of the total geographical area, which is quite high. The gross sown area was 39.68 per cent and net sown area was 16.97 per cent. The area under kharif was 57.43 per cent and under zaid crop was 2.89 per cent. Canals irrigate about 47.96 per cent of land. In Dehradun district, household business operations and animal husbandry are the main occupation. Of the entire population 32.56 per cent are main workers and 1.64 per cent are marginal workers. The district has two tehsils namely Chakrata and Dehradun. It has 763 villages of which 743 are inhabited. Chakrata tehsil has a high percentage of ST population (7.48 per cent) as against the total tribal population of Dehradun district (9.99 per cent) as per the 1981 census. The ST population is mainly concentraed in the rural areas of Chakrata tehsil (78.01 per cent).

In Dehradun district, land is uneven and most of the villages are situated at heights. In these village, assured irrigation through canal is not available. Thus the area under kharif is more than the area under zaid crops. Dehradun has a large area under potato, sugarcane and soybean besides paddy, barley and wheat.

Dehradun provides habitat to two different tribal groups, the Jaunsaris in the hills and Buxas in the plain portion of the district. In the hills most tribal villages are situated between heights of 3000 feet and 5000 feet above the sea level.

Tribal economy is beset with problems. Although the tribals are dependent on land, they are not able to grow good crops. Their methods of cultivation are mostly primitive. Their land is unirrigated and undulating. Problems of land alienation and insecurity exist in acute forms.

**Conditions During British Rule and After**

The British ruled the tribal areas of UP within the broad framework of policies laid down by the government. The district of Dehradun is divided into two parts, the hilly part and the Doon. The Jaunsar Bhabar pargana which was under the possession of the Rajas of Sirmur and later the Gorkhas, fell into British hands only in1815. Despite a number of settlements, the British found it expedient to revert to the indigenous system of rule through 'Sayanas' and 'Chauntras' who not only collected land revenues but were also responsible for its Khat-wise and village-wise allocation. To oversee their work, the area was put under the charge of a Tahsildar assisted by Kanungos and Patwaris. As the Patwaris were grossly underworked, they were entrusted with the police administration of the area with powers to investigate cases and arrest offenders.

Soon after Jaunsar-Bawar in Dehradun district came into British hands in 1815, first settlement operations took place, which was concluded in 1818. It was based on the tribute exacted by the Gorkhas, which constituted land revenue, allowance of 'chauntras' and 'Sayanas' and custom duty on all goods passing out of pargana through Kalsi.

It was during the Sixth settlement that there arose a dispute between the 'chauntras' and Government Surety as a result of which the institution of 'chauntra' itself was abolished. The result of this step was that during the Seventh settlement the functions of the 'chauntras' stood transferred to 'Sayanas' of a khat who were made jointly responsible for payment of the land revenue of the khat to the extent of their share.

In the eighth settlement made in 1859, for the first time, an attempt was made to measure cultivation. The total cultivated area was estimated to be 21,603 acres, out of which 164 acres were rent-free. As a result of this settlement the office of Government Surety was abolished.

On the enforcement of the Government of India Act of 1935, Jaunsar-Bawar was declared a partially excluded area. An important regulation made under this Act was the Khat Haripur Bias (Jaunsar Bhabar pargana) Tenants Protection Regulations, 1940 which aimed at ejectment of tenants especially the Koltas, Bajgis etc, who were prohibited to own land under the Dasturul Amal. During British time, the actual tillers did not have any legal right on the land and were debarred from owning land under the Dasturul Amal. It was for the first time in 1940 that they acquired occupancy rights. Similar rights were extended to the non-Khasa tribals living in the rest of Jaunsar under Jaunsar-Bawar parganas tenant protection regulation 1949. This regulation forbade ejectment of tillers of soil who had been in cultivating possession for a period of not less than three years.

The British way of administering tribal areas before independence is best summed up by Dr. B.D. Sharma in the following words: -

"They (the British) adopted the policy of lightly administering these areas. The normal administration of the provinces in which the tribal areas were located was not extended to them. In many regions, single line administration was established where all authority was entrusted in one individual who was the chief representative of the government in that area. The local custom was honored and there was judicial intervention only when it was considered inevitable."[2]

When India became independent, one of the first acts of the Constituent Assembly was to set up two sub-committees to investigate the tribal situation. The sub-committee known as the Excluded and Partially excluded areas (other than Assam) Committee was headed by Shri A.V.Thakkar (later known as Thakkar Bapa). On the basis of this sub-committee's recommendation, the Constituent Assembly laid down the principle that the new democratic government had a responsibility for the welfare of the tribal people and the development of the tribal areas. It also recommended that the Constitutional arrangements should include not only the tribal people living under the Excluded and Partially excluded areas but also those living outside such areas and wherever found. This meant a big change from the British policv in this area since it emphasized the need for viewing the tribal problem as a whole.

As a consequence of the repeal of British laws, the Excluded and Partially excluded areas were brought under normal administration. Article 342 of the Constitution provides for scheduling of tribes for a State as a whole or any part thereof. For administration of areas of tribal concentration, Article 244 of the Constitution empowers the President to declare any area where there is any substantial population of tribal people, as a Scheduled area. While tribal areas of North East were included in the Sixth Schedule, tribal concentrations in the rest of the country found place in the Fifth Schedule. Under the Fifth Schedule, the state under which a Scheduled area falls, exercises executive powers but the Governor of the state is vested with the authority - (a) to modify Central and State laws in their application to them and (b) to frame regulations for their peace and good governance and in particular, for the protection of the rights of tribals in land, the allotment of waste land and their protection from money-lenders.

It is thus clear that the constitution distinguishes between the tribals living in the Scheduled areas and other areas. Articles 15,16 and 19 enable the Parliament and the State Legislature to take into consideration the condition of the tribes in the matter of enforcing the provision relating to the equality of all citizens.[3]

However these Constitutional provisions were not made applicable to the tribals in UP as the state government took no steps to get its tribal population declared as STs till 1967 when five tribes numbering 2 lakhs were declared as Scheduled tribes. The remaining tribes still remain unscheduled. The government of UP fixed a reservation quota of 2 per cent in the Services for STs in 1970.

The Jaunsar-Bawar Security of Tenure and land Records Act 1952 provided protection to tillers, placing the law relating to the land tenures on a more stable footing and regularized the preparation of record of rights as a result of the records operation undertaken since1950.

The Zamindari was abolished in Jaunsar-Bawar with the enactment of Jaunsar-Bawar Zamindari Abolition and Land Reforms Act 1956, which was enforced only from 1st July 1961. This Act abolished the intermediaries with certain exceptions and replaced the tenures existing in the parganas with those bhumidars, sirdars and asamis as in other parts of the state of UP. The Act also established Gaon Samaj for land management and to admit new tenants to the land vested in it. The functions of Gaon Samaj are now being performed by the Gaon Sabhas.

The state government of UP identified five tribal concentrations in the hill districts and formulated ITDPs for them in the beginning of the Sixth Five-Year Plan. But the central government refused to provide Special Central Assistance to them. These were – two ITDPs in Nainital, one in Pithorgarh district, one in Chamoli and one in Dehradun district namely the Chakrata-Kalsi ITDP.

The Garhwal Anusuchit Janjati Nigam Limited was established in June 1975 as a subsidiary of the Garhwal Mandal Vikas Nigam for the overall development of the Scheduled Tribes residing in the Garhwal Division which comprises Uttar Kashi, Pauri-Garhwal, Tehri Garhwal and Dehradun districts. The affairs of the Corporation are managed by a five member Board of Directors with the Commissioner Garhwal Division as its Chairman.

**Problems of Hill Areas**

The environment problems of the hills are deforestation

and soil erosion, flash floods and decline in the yield of crops, fodder and other minor forest produce. Poverty in the hills is directly related to shortages of materials for basic subsistence. In many areas, intensive human and livestock pressures along with indiscriminate felling of trees for commercial purposes have already led to loss of soil and rapid depletion and destruction of forest cover. These activities have led to deterioration in the economic condition of the tribals. Development activities like construction of buildings, roads, dams, large and medium industries and mining etc. have aggravated environmental problems. Consequently perennial sources of water, springs and small streams have dried up in many areas.

**Planned Tribal Development in Uttaranchal**

It was only during the Second Five Year Plan that the tribals were able to attract the attention of the State Government which implemented a Rs.7 lakh plan for the development of a few selected tribes. During the Third five year plan, tribal development was, however, undertaken on a planned basis on a fairly large scale. In this plan, more than Rs. 1.5 crores were spent on their educational, economic and environmental improvement. Three Ashram schools were set up in Khatima (Nainital), Lakhimpur and Dudhi (Mirzapur).

In 1967-68, a new era emerged for the tribals of UP with the scheduling of five tribes namely Jaunsaris, Buxas, Rajis, Bhotias and Tharus and all the educational facilities available to the Scheduled Castes were extended to the Scheduled Tribes also.

In 1968-69, two pilot projects for the promotion of agriculture, industry and literacy were started for the Jaunsaris and Buxas. In 1969, the UP Zamindari Abolition Act was amended so as to bar transfer of land belonging to STs without the permission of the Collector of the district.

During the Fourth Five Year Plan, four special area projects were started at Chakrata and Kalsi (Dehradun), Khatima (Nainital) and Lakhimpur with a view to undertake all round development of the tribal economy, education and environment. About 111 credit Cooperative Societies were organized to provide credit and marketing facilities to the tribals and to supply them scarce consumer goods.

The aim of tribal development program during the Fifth Five Year Plan (1974-79) was to improve the quality of life of these primitive people and to narrow the gap between the level of development of these people and the general population. During this plan period ,most of the schemes initiated in the preceding plans were continued. Three institutions namely Kumaon Anusuchit Janjati Vikas Nigam, Garhwal Anusuchit Janjati Vikas Nigam and Terai Anusuchit Janjati Vikas Nigam were established in 1976 to help the tribal economy. The three corporations however failed to have an impact on the tribal economy due to lack of direction and program of work.

**Jaunsar-Bawar**

Jaunsar-Bawar lies is in the Himalayas, located at the north-western corner of the State of Uttaranchal. It forms the Northern half of Dehradun district. Its Southern side is adjacent to the Western Dun of the same district. The Western and northwestern boundaries are contiguous with Sirmur, Jubbal and Taroch, now in Himachal Pradesh. On the northeast, east and southeast, it is bounded by Tehri Garhwal. For administrative purposes, Jaunsar-Bawar forms part of Chakrata tehsil.

According to the District Gazetteer of Dehradun, the tract of Jaunsar-Bawar originally formed part of the territories of the Rajas of Sirmur or Nahan who were vassals of the Mogul Emperors. When the Gurkhas entered Kumaon and Garhwal in 1790, the Sirmur Raja made an alliance with them in 1803 and became their tributary. In 1814, the British declared war on the Gurkhas and expelled them from the Dun in 1815. Thereafter, Jaunsar-Bawar was administered by British officers who took orders from the Resident at Delhi.[3]

Jaunsar and Bawar were originally two separate Parganas. Later on, it was regarded as one pargana. It now forms the Chakrata Tehsil, with the cantonment town of

Chakrata as its headquarters. A Tehsildar heads the Tehsil and a Naib Tehsildar and 33 Patwaris assist him. There are 358 revenue villages in the tehsil. Now a Sub-divisional Magistrate I/C Chakrata and Kalsi is also posted at Chakrata. There is also a Block Development Officer at Chakrata assisted by Assistant Development Officers, one of whom is incharge of Social Welfare and the other of Tribal Welfare. There is another Block Development Officer at Kalsi who looks after the work there.

There are 39 Khats (the local unit containing a number of villages) – each having a Khat Sayana who is responsible for the whole Khat in all its relations with the government, especially in matters of revenue collections. Below him are the village Sayanas, each of whom combined in his person the functions discharged in the plains by the Lambardar and the village headman.

The whole of Jaunsar-Bawar is practically encircled by the Tons and Jamuna rivers except at the northwestern corner, where the Tons is joined by the Prabar river.

The forest in Jaunsar-Bawar is one of the most important sources of wealth. Now horticulture has also been seen as an important source of income with the production of ginger, potato, rice, wheat, mandua and tobacco etc.

As a matter of tradition, the village community in Jaunsar-Bawar is dominated, both socially and economically, by the Brahmins and the Rajputs. The lower castes, especially the Koltas and Bajgis, have been regarded as aboriginals.[4]

Chakrata and Kalsi are relatively underdeveloped tribal blocks in Dehradun district. As a whole, Dehradun district shows a very high level of development but Chakrata block continues to remain most underdeveloped. Dehradun district is the most urbanized district in the country as per 1991 census whereas in Chakrata block more than 90 per cent of the population lives in the villages. The block is completely mountainous with a total of 154 inhabited villages. Chakrata is predominantly a tribal block with 65 per cent Scheduled Tribe population and 28 per cent

Scheduled Caste population. The details of the population are given below: [5]

| Year | Total Pop | Total Pop. | | SC Pop. | | ST Pop. | | Literate | |
|---|---|---|---|---|---|---|---|---|---|
| | | Male | Female | Male | Female | Male | Female | Male | Female |
| 1971 | 32,834 | 18,242 | 14,592 | 1,732 | 1,516 | 15,025 | 12,566 | 3,324 | 336 |
| 1981 | 39,410 | 21,629 | 17,781 | 1,781 | 1,425 | 18,103 | 15,410 | 5,537 | 759 |
| 1991 | 49,097 | 26,341 | 22,756 | 7,291 | 6,353 | 16,705 | 15,224 | 8,446 | 2,175 |
| 1996 | 55,148 | 29,229 | 25,541 | | | | | | |

Employment is largely in the primary sector. Sex ratio comes to 873 per 1000 males which is in favor of males and literacy rate is lower among women. The average landholding is one and a half-hectare. Land can be transferred by a member belonging to ST to another ST.

Progress seems to have by-passed the Jaunsar-Bawar tehsil of Dehradun district. The local hill people are close-lipped for various reasons: some out of suspicion bred on their long experience of the plain's petty government officials bringing nothing but trouble and demands and some to protect their need-based commercial activities of poppy-farming and trade in prostitution. It is only the patient social worker who can penetrate this veil of secrecy through a confidence building exercise. We are indebted for much of these information to such workers which is based on their case studies in the hills.[6]

In the 1951 census, the population of Jaunsar-Bawar was given as 58,469. This is stratified into three social layers. The Brahmins and Rajputs occupy the top of the pyramid, the Bajgis and the other crafts' people make up the middle level, and the Koltas, who are one-fifth of the population and usually bonded, constitute the weakest bottom segment of the society. The Koltas are believed to be the original inhabitants of the area but were subjugated by the higher castes.

A characteristic feature of the Koltas in the traditional society of this region is their landlessness, though in the last two decades a few Koltas have come to own land.

However, their landholdings are highly uneconomic, meagre and insufficient to serve their needs.[7]

**Conclusion**

Having carried out the tribal development programme for a certain period, it is necessary to know whether the programme is having the desired impact on and conferring the planned benefits to the target group. There should, therefore, be a regular system of evaluation and monitoring of the various tribal development programmes.

This is all the more important as a separate state of Uttaranchal has been formed for the greater development of the hilly and remote areas which was earlier neglected.

The greatest challenge, before the new State, however, still remains that of channelising the political awareness generated out of its creation. If constant monitoring is done at the executive level, it can lead to better socio-economic performance as the problem is not one of lack of economic resources but of better management of resources, thus increasing the tempo of development.

## References


1. Amir Hassan, Tribes of UP, 1979, pp. 19.
2. Dr. B.D. Sharma- Administration for Tribal Development, Occasional Papers on Tribal Development, Ministry of Home Affairs, New Delhi, 1977, pp. 4-6.
3. District Gazetteer of Dehradun district (1911) p. 183.
4. Dr. B.D.Sharma- Tribal Development, the new strategy, Eleventh course on Tribal Development Administration, the I.I.P.A, New Delhi, 1982.
5. Integrated Area Development Plan for Chakrata Block (1996-2002) Centre for Micro-Planning and Regional Studies, LBSNA, Mussoorie p.20.
6. Avadesh Kaushal and I.A.S probationers of the L.B.S.N.A.A, Mussoorie, quoted in Chronicles of the Doon Valley by Prem. K. Thadhani, New Delhi, 1993, p.17.
7. S.C. Khairwal and I.A.S probationers of the LBSNAA, Mussoorie, Journal of the National Academy of Administration Mussoorie, Spring 1975, pp. 643-759.

# 9

# Impact of Tribal Development Programmes on the Condition of Tribals in Uttaranchal

The Commission for Scheduled Areas and Scheduled Tribes constituted under Article 339 (1) of the Constitution (popularly known as the Dhebar Commission) made a comprehensive survey of the tribal scene in the country in the year 1960-61 and their report presented in 1961 was quite wide-ranging in character.

For narrowing the economic gap between tribals and non-tribals, the commission felt that special arrangements should be made for undertaking rapid sample survey and collecting data which would enable the government to carry out development programmes within a fixed time limit. Secondly, in addition to the sample survey or survey of representative tribal areas and tribal groups, it suggested surveys and studies relating to specific problems faced by the tribal communities. Thirdly, they exphasised that evaluation of the government programmes should be done by an agency capable of taking an objective view and not by the agency in-charge of the implementation of the programmes.

The Dhebar Commission lamented the fact that hardly any survey or study has been conducted which would give an idea about the impact of the various development programmes upon tribal life. They found that there had been studies in certain sociological aspects of tribal life and sometimes about tribal culture and economy. But they emphasised that the problems that loomed large over the tribals were the problems of rights on land, rights in forests, exploitation by money-lenders, the impact of industrialisation on tribal life, health, education and communication. These problems remain the burning issues even today and merit serious study[1].

The Dhebar Commission was further moved by the validity of the first of the Panchsheel enunciated by Pt. Jawaharlal Nehru. In their view, welfare programmes for scheduled tribes should be in consonance and harmony with their way of life. This required first hand information on their economic status and way of life so that the development programmes could be attuned to tribal needs and aspirations. Hence, research into these aspects of tribal life is an essential prerequisite for effective planning. Further, an study of the effect of such schemes on the personality and the life style of the tribals should be done to gauge the extent to which such schemes and programmes have helped the process of integration of the tribals with the rest of the population. They stressed that research needed to be conducted into these aspects with a view to putting tribal development programmes on a secure basis[2]. These requirements do not appear to have decreased with the passage of time and are extremely relevant even today.

**Economic Development of the Region**

The Community Development Programmes were extended to Jaunsar-Bawar on 2nd October 1953, when a Community Development Block was inaugurated at Chakrata, but the initiation of the development work in the villages could be possible only after February 1954.

The jurisdiction of the Community Development Block Chakrata, at the beginning, covered the whole of Chakrata tehsil. Since March 1956, a separate NES Block was established at Kalsi to cover the lower half of the Tehsil, namely the Jaunsar area. The Chakrata Block was thus reduced in area to half its original size, but it continued to be a Community Development Block.

Among the two major parts of this region, Jaunsar and Bawar, it is the latter which has been remote and underdeveloped, and hence needs more of developmental facilites.[3]

The Panchayati Raj Act came into force in this region in December 1953. Under this legislation, the whole area of Jaunsar-bawar has been divided into 54 Gram Sabhas and 13 Nyay panchayats. There are 6 Nyay Panchayats and 23 Gram Sabhas in the Kalsi Block and 7 Nyay Panchayats and 31 Gram Sabhas are in the Chakrata Block. There is a post of A.D.O. Panchayat in both these Blocks.

The welfare measures taken up under the Community Development Programmes have been of diverese kinds and wide in range. The major activites can be grouped under the following heads:-

(a) Agriculture and horticulture

(b) Animal Husbandry

(c) Cottage industry

(d) Public health

(e) Education and Social education

(f) Women's Welfare

(g) SC/ST welfare

(h) Communications

(i) Cooperatives, and

(j) Panchayats.

From the point of view of permanent measures for rural development, Panchayats and cooperatives form the two basic issues. In Jaunsar-Bawar, the situation is complicated by the existence of a traditional village organisation in terms of Sayana and Khumri, which has functioned efficiently and exclusively in matters of local affairs, both administrative and judicial, since time immemorial.

Now with the coming of Panchayati Raj, it is difficult to differentiate between the Khumri and Panchayat of a village as both perform the same function though the Inter-village Khumri may be held between two villages among the parties concerned and the Gaon Sayanas. But the fact is that with the introduction of the Panchayati System, the powers and activities of the traditional Khumri have been curtailed.

A historical review of the development strategy in the hilly region reveals that the early planning period was characterised by a conspicuous absence of any well aimed development policy, while the planning era especially after 1962, shows a conscious effort towards changing the face of the hills by raising the levels of income and employment and by providing social awareness through mass education.

Still, all is not well with the planning process. While nature has given abundant resources to the region, these are not being developed fast enough. Because of differences in circumstances, the problems of the development of hilly regions and their exploitation is different from that of the plains. Consequently the strategy adopted in the plains cannot be applied with equal success in the hills. In the villages studied, the primary, secondary and tertiary sectors have failed to raise the levels of income and employment to an extent comparable with those achieved in the plains.

With the progressive implementation of the various five year plans, much has been achieved, yet much remains to be done. The problems of trafficking in women, bonded labour, out migration, alcoholism, low levels of employment and income etc, have not yet been completely solved.

The present study by and large reveals that there has been wrong planning, inadequate development strategy and wrong priorities. In fact any development plan of the region must take into consideration its peculiar problems related to the geographical, ecological, agro-climatic and socio-cultural features specific to the region. The plans modelled for the country as a whole have been implemented in this region without taking into account the specific requirements of the region. Even during the fifth and sixth five year plans, correct priorities were not set. Only during the seventh five year plan, formulation of a hill area sub-plan was undertaken for the hill areas of UsP. But this sub-plan has also failed to quicken the pace of development to the desired extent. Even in the Chakrata-Kalsi integrated tribal development project, programmes were not selected after due consideration of the local needs and constraints.

Tribals in this region have suffered from economic devastation due to ecological changes brought around by development measures in the tribal areas. It has resulted in the unemployment and dislocation of their socio-cultural life.[4]

Forests in the hills are not only an economic resource but constitute an essential life support system. The dependence of the tribals on forests for their day to day requirements, like fuel wood, fodder, etc., has resulted in a symbiotic relationship between the two. Sustainable scientific forest management holds the key to the prosperity of the region and betterment of the quality of life. Tribals generally collect the minor forest produce for their sustenance. One feature of minor forest product is that they can be used on a sustainable basis without adversely affecting the resource base. In this respect, they differ considerably from the major forest produce like timber. Education, health, nutrition and employment are some of the indicators of human resource development. Human resource development is a slow and time taking process which requires patience on the part of development agencies and has to be carried out in the context of local needs and priorities on a sustained basis. For example, education can focus on vocational training and skill development leading to income generating activities based on available resources in the area. The economic activities in the tribal blocks of Chakrata and Kalsi as well as in villages inhabited by the primitive tribes (Buxas) are not sufficient to match the demand for employment. As any economic activity, whether in the farm or non-farm sector, requires capital, there is a dearth of economic activity for want of capital in the area. Therefore, there is a need to look at the employment issue more closely in the light of local conditions.

Planning for sustainable employment opportunities in the region has to be on the basis of available and potential resources and skills in the area. However, based on a mountain specific approach to development, planning has to be the first precondition for ensuring desired economic growth with equity and justice on a sustainable basis. This is essential as the capacity of self-sustained and self-dependent development in the tribal area is very difficult to attain particularly in a tribal belt like Chakrata.

The success or failure of tribal development programs depend on the type of persons (government officials) and welfare bodies (NGOs) operating in the tribal areas. It is rather unfortunate that the people at large and those connected with their administration and welfare are neither fully conversant with the development in the tribal areas nor aware of the tribal problems. The apathy of the administration is also quite visible. For example the project officer's post in Chakrata-Kalsi ITDP is lying vacant for quite some time. Moreover no schemes are in operation for the development of Koltas and Bajgis who are amongst the poorest of the poor in Uttaranchal. Thus, there is an imperative need to increase the tempo of activity in the new state and to have more studies on the development of the tribals in Uttaranchal, as the information available is quite scarce.

**Brief Description of the Study Area**

***Chakrata:*** Chakrata Block forms the northern bigger half of the Chakrata Tehsil of Dehradun District. It is bounded by Himachal Pradesh in the north and north west, by Tehri Garhwal and Uttarkash districts in the east and north east and by Kalsi block and Doon valley in the south.

The term Jaunsar-Bawar denotes two once distinct Parganas and represents the typical rugged topography of the mountains and hills. It is in continuation of the other block of Kalsi, which together make the Tehsil of Chakrata.

The whole of the area is prominently agricultural, with animal husbandry as second occupation. Apart from these two main occupations, weaving, masonary, black smithy, carpentry, tailoring etc are practised by the lower castes.

The Rajputs are the land owning class in the area. They

occupy the best land in the village. Livestock is their subsidiary occupation. Like Rajputs, the Brahmins are also land owners and primarily agriculturists. They also pursue cattle rearing as their secondary occupation.

Koltas are landless labourers and tenants. They are mostly agricultural labourers; some work in road construction also. Before the settlements of 1956, they were bonded labourers to their Rajput landlords. Afterwards, they were given some land in Sirdari for their maintenance. The Koltas are also heavily indebted. They also do some weaving, masonary and leather work etc. The Bajgis are traditional drum beaters. Some of them have also become barbers and tailors.

**Economic Condition**

***Chakrata:*** Based on the survey conducted, it can be said that more than 96 per cent of the workers are engaged in cultivation and animal husbandry. Thus the primary sector is crucial for the development of people of this area in general who are also Scheduled Tribes. Diversification of agriculture into horticulture, floriculture, herbal farming etc is needed but it should be based on the requirement of the people in the villages. Accessibility is another problem and calls for urgent attention. The average landholding as per the Naib Tehsildar of Chakrata is one and a half-hectare of land and the land can be transferred by a tribal only to another tribal. The annual demand of land revenue was Rs. 93,000/- (the figure of last year) and the collection has been reported at 78 per cent of the demand. Loans of all types are also collected and the annual demand was Rs. 99 lakhs in the previous year, the recovery being Rs. 54 lakhs, which comes to 65 per cent of the total demand.

The Patwaris in Chakrata area are not only responsible for revenue collection, but are also entrusted with police functions. Similarly, Tehsildar and Naib-Tehsildar are also police inspectors for the area. Although the traditional system of Khat Sayana administration has undergone certain changes since the introduction of the Panchayati Raj, the Sayana system has remained the most important link between the villages and the outside world.

According to the Tehsildar of Chakrata, the minimum wage in the area was Rs. 70/- per day. The Koltas who work on the farms of the upper castes get Rs. 30/- per day in cash plus food given twice a day.

Although the bonded labour system was abolished in 1976 and all were liberated, yet the incidence of indebtedness specially loans taken for consumption purposes was quite high among the Koltas who are the poorest of all having no land and no permanent source of income. It is pity that no special scheme for the development of the Koltas and Bajgis have been framed as yet. A study of a typical village (Sujau) in Chakrata shows that on an average, the income of the villagers is at a subsistence level. In the hill areas, the per capita income is half that of the state average, as per the 1981 census. 80 per cent of the holdings are less than 2 hectares and 68 per cent are less than 1 hectare. The density of population per unit of cultivated land is four times that of the plains. About 23 per cent of the active age group of the hill area work as wage paid workers and as many as 80 per cent of them are migrant to outside the region. Families depend on remittances from their sons, who join the armed forces or migrate to the plains for jobs.

The average hill village is situated on a spur jutting out from the hill side in the middle of a slope, with its forests, grazing grounds and water sources above, and the cultivated field below. Their cattle are also kept in 'chanis' located mostly below the village. In this day to day struggle to subsist, the long-term view of resource conservation and management has been lost sight of by most of the inhabitants.

As per 1991 census, Chakrata Block has 153 village settlements and 84 per cent of these village settlement are in the population range of 100-500.

The rights of the tribals in the reserved forest have been stated in the report of the forest settlement done in 1921. There is however a flexibility in what is called concession conferred on the villagers by the forest department.

Traditionally, the people of Jaunsar-Bawar (which

includes Chakrata and Kalsi Blocks) are indifferent towards formal education. Though primary schools have been established in many villages and the number of Junior High Schools and Inter-colleges have increased, yet the attendance is quite low. The condition of the residential schools started by the government also leaves much to be desired.

Though, three Ashram type schools are run in Jaunsar-Bawar area, yet only a few Kolta families can afford to send their children to these schools. Instead they are forced to engage their children in grazing and household chores.

As the Koltas have little or no land, their income is barely enough to keep the body and soul together. They depend heavily on loans to meet their needs and when they are unable to repay the loan, they become the bonded labor of the creditors. Of the 21 cases examined, in 10 of them the indebtedness has been inherited. The indebtedness had increased in time in all but five cases. In 2 cases only, a serious attempt was made to repay the debt.[5]

Most Koltas are illiterate. Therefore, they are unaware of the entries made by the moneylender in the account books and are forced to put their thumb impression in the account books, thus making their case weak.

The roots of indebtedness go back to colonial rule. Before the U.P. Zamindari Abolition Act, this area was divided under the old revenue system into 37 "khatas" under the charge of "Sadar Sayanas" and the village under "Sayanas". These "Sayanas" who were responsible for the collection of land revenue, mostly belonged to the Brahmin and Rajput castes. They, therefore, distributed land among their own castes, keeping the lower castes deliberately landless.

*Kalsi:* Kalsi Block forms the Southern most part of Jaunsar-Bawar area. The whole area is mountainous with rough terrain.

It is bounded by two rivers the Jamuna in the east and south, by the Tons in the west and Chakrata block in the north. This area contains various rocks amongst which limestone, quartizite and shistose slates are most important.

Rainfall in this region is moderately high. The rainiest months are July and August.

The entire population (excepting those who have settled here from outside) has been declared tribal. The name of the tribe is Jaunsari and the name of the local dialect is also Jaunsari.

Majority of the population is engaged in agriculture directly or indirectly as owner, cultivatior, agricultural labour or bonded labour. In most of the villages, there is no household industry. Cattle and goat rearing is an important occupation.

All the high castes like Rajput and Brahmin are owner – cultivators, whereas most of the lower castes such as Koltas, Bajgis, Barhai etc have very small pieces of land given to them earlier by the upper caste landlords or by the government. It must be noted here that according to the 'Dastur-ul-Amal', only Rajputs and Brahmins can be owner-cultivators and no Kolta, Bajgi or other lower castes can get possession of the land. This has made the lower castes highly indebted - both inherited and self-borrowed and they often work as bonded labour in the filed of the creditors who are the upper caste landlords.[6]

The four major castes of Kalsi Block are Rajput, Brahmin, Bajgi and the Koltas. Rajputs constitute about 70 per cent of the total population and their main occupation is agriculture. Brahmins constitute about 10 per cent of the total population and are mainly agriculturists as well as doing priestly jobs.

The Koltas form about 15 per cent and are mainly agricultural labour. Bajgi is a common name for a number of castes like Nai, Barhai, Black smith and drummers. These people constitute about 3 per cent of the total population. Bajgis being a service class is looked down upon by the Rajputs and the Brahmins and their entry to their kitchen is prohibited. But, on the occasion of mass 'bhoj', Bajgis are served in the utensils of the host Rajputs unlike the Koltas who have to bring their own utensils.[7]

Koltas and Dom are the lowest in the caste hierarchy.

They are not allowed to wear shoes in the localities of the upper caste people.[8]

Kalsi block is administered by the B.D.O who is assisted in his work by five ADOs out of which one ADO is incharge of Tribal Development.

The total geographical area of Kalsi block is 44,962 hectares or 178 sq. miles, out of which cultivated area is 7171.20 hectares. Forest cover is 32,440 hectares and it occupies about 72 per cent of the total area of the block.

On the basis of common problems identified by the villagers, it can be said that accessibility, primary health, education facilities and income generation activities require urgent attention.

**Primitive Tribal Groups in Dehradun District**

The Bhuksa or Buxas, one of the five scheduled tribes of Uttaranchal have been living in this region from remote past mainly in the Bhabhar and Terai regions of central Himalayas. They have been recognized as a primitive tribe and are mainly found in the districts of Dehradun, Nainital and Pauri-Garhwal. They were given the status of scheduled tribe in 1967. Before that, they were placed in the scheduled caste category in 1950. Later they were removed from the list of scheduled caste and placed under the category of backward classes in 1956. As per the 1971 census, the Buxas population of U.P was 23,217. The majority (70 per cent) of the total Buxa population lived in rural areas and the rest inhabited various urban and semi-urban centres.

The Buxas are a patrilineal tribe who presently can be found in the Doiwala and Vikasnagar blocks of Dehradun district. Education has not made much impact upon the Buxa population in general, though modern education is slowly spreading among them. Post-matric scholarships, stipends and book aids are given to the students in the higher classes. Their literacy rate is quite low, it being only 8.71 per cent.

Traditional, this tribe was a forest dwelling community. Later migration took place for a variety of reasons mainly being search for employment. The Buxas being in the main cultivators, also moved out in search of new patches of land, often clearing the jungle by cutting and burning trees.

At present the Buxas are an agricultural community but are mainly dependent on rain as irrigation facities are not adequate. Their economic condition is very poor. Horticulture is practised only by a few families and it is done only for their own consumption, although it has a great potential for income generation. In Doiwala Block, a Buxa youth who had graduated was found pulling Rickshaw as no job was available to him under the State government.

**Development of the Hill Region**

The hill villagers cannot improve their lot because they are poorly educated, do not possess many skills and do not have enough money to invest. As they are cultivating steep slopes without any modern inputs, they continue to get minimal returns. A major difficulty is the inaccessibility of the block officers and the officers of the line departments who rarely visit them. Another difficulty is the inaccessibility to transport facilites, medical centres and communication networks.

As development economists point out, the most productive investment in less developed areas are those that open up the abundant natural resources of the area. The goal of raising income levels should be met by an alternative planning policy in which the basic thrust is on the fullest use of all the resources for the promotion of productive employment and raising productivity[9].

The entire hill region presents a favourable condition for horticulture programme. It will not only help indirect employment generation but also have multiplier effects through backward and forward linkages. The herbs collection and cultivation may also be a profitable venture. 'Floriculture' may be another profitable occupation for the hill people and a replacement of traditional agriculture. A farmer can do this job together with horticulture and herbs cultivation programme.

Despite the importance of livestock to the economy, very little emphasis has been put so far on the livestock development and animal breeding. The apparent risks of increasing number of animals with continued low productivity will further contribute to land and forest degradation. Fisheries are also neglected in the region, largely due to lack of trained manpower and concerted efforts.

The topography of Jaunsar – Bawar is such that all the huts in a village are never situated at the same level. The accessibility to transport facilities, schools, health centres and communication network varies from the better developed Lakhwar to remote Sujau, while Koltas live in separate villages like oli.

**Analysis and Interpretation of Survey Data**

On the basis of the field survey through individual contact with the beneficiaries made by me personally, an attempt is made to depict the socio-economic condition of the selected beneficiaries and their families, the progress in education, financial assistance received so far and income generation done as a resulted of direct financing under the Integrated Tribal Development programmes run by the State government. The field survey was done through a questionnaire which can be seen at Annexure. I also tried to get their views and pereceptions regarding development programmes and behaviour of government officials and the beneficiary's present and future aspirations (Table no.2). It is to be noted that most of the tribals are not literate and have not maintained the bank pass books or kept any account of the loan received, the interest charged or the amount outstanding. They also have no idea of the rate of interest on the amount of loan sanctioned to them. Therefore, data given by them has been memory based and the previous income and the present income has been calculated on the basis of their own assumptions as well as the observations made by me. In some villages like Lakhwar where a branch of State Bank of India is located, the details of loans given and interest charged were obtained from the Bank.

**Results of the Field Survey**

The information was collected through survey schedules by talking directly to the beneficiary or his/her family members and in this way sixty three beneficiaries (38 male and 25 female) belonging to seven villages of the four blocks could be contacted. Others named in the list provided by the district administration were not available due to their being engaged in agricultural operations or fodder collection.

In Lakhwar village of Kalsi Block, an inter-active session was also held where all the beneficiaries who were available in the village during the visit participated and ventilated their grievances freely. This helped in understanding their needs and aspirations.

The main occupation of the ST population in Chakrata Tehsil (Chakrata and Kalsi Block) is cultivation and animal husbandry. As a whole, more than 96 per cent workers are engaged in agriculture and allied activities in the primary sector. On the basis of the field survey, it can be said that development of agriculture, horticulture and animal husbandry linkages are crucial for the over all development of this region.

On the basis of the common problems identified by the villagers, it can be said that primary health facilities and education require urgent attention. Irrigation is scarce and people depend on rains for the agricultural operations. Horticulture, though important to the area, is not getting any incentive as there is no arrangement for fruit and vegetable processing units in the area. Floriculture and cultivation of medicinal plants are thoroughly neglected as no training is provided to the villagers for the scientific cultivation of these herbs and flowers. Lack of consolidation of holdings is another hindrance in the development of horticulture and floriculture.

As pointed out by many writers earlier, (D.N. Majumdar, Nadeem Hasnain etc.) and also found in the present field survey, the Kolta sub-community is the most depressed in the Chakrata region. Special efforts are needed to improve their lot and end the problem of bonded labour as well as the exploitation of women in some pockets of Chakrata.

The survey shows that the tendency of the people to get subsidy without any asset creation and subsequent income generation is widely spread. In Lakhwar and Sujau villages, one person each out of 8 and 9 persons surveyed there, was found to have received subsidy and the loan portion without purchasing the implements or the animal for which it was given. Evidently, there was no addition to his income and his loan burden continues increasing without any means to repay it. He seemed frustrated and resigned to his lot. Because of this 'dependency syndrome' the vocal section of these villages have tried to get the maximum benefits of tribal development programmes, while the Koltas were left out of it. In Sujau village, the beneficiaries chosen in the year 2000-2001 were yet to get their subsidy and loan. A few of them have even visited the State Bank of India Branch at Chakrata but have drawn a blank. The Block officials blame the bank because subsidy portion has been released to them about three months back.

Table 1 given at the end provide the details of the beneficiaries contacted, village wise and gender wise who have been given help under the tribal development programmes.

Table 2 shows the benefits of the financial assistance schemes wherever positively utilised by the beneficiaries and assets created for which subsidy and Bank loan was provided in the seven villages of Chakrata, Kalsi, Vikas Nagar and Doiwala Blocks of Dehradun district. The field visit brought out the following points in vivid detail:

- A total of 58 beneficiaries (34 Male and 24 Female) out of the 63 interviewed (38 Males and 25 Females) have been benefitted in the selected villages. The other five though selected as beneficiary in the year 2000-2001 had yet to receive the financial assistance.
- Subsidy and Bank loan have helped to increase their monthly income and in some cases their income has doubled.
- Out of the 24 female beneficiaries who received assistance, the majority utilised their assets for improving their income, yet few of them who started working right after receiving handloom machine in Kalsi

**Table 1**

**Genderwise Beneficiaries of Income Generating Schemes (under SCA to TSP) in Dehradun District Covering a Total Number of 63 Tribal Beneficiaries in 4 (four) Blocks (Chakrata, Kalsi, Doiwala and Vikas Nagar)**

| *S.N. block* | *Name of the village* | *Name of the beneficiaries* | *Male beneficiaries* | *Female beneficiaries* | *Total no.* | *Remark* |
|---|---|---|---|---|---|---|
| 1. | Kalsi | Lakhwar | 09 | 0 | 09 | Three villages of Kalsi Block |
| 2. | Kalsi | Haripur Bias Nahri | 05 | 02 | 07 | |
| 3. | Kalsi | Kalsi Bazar | 02 | 03 | 05 | |
| 4. | Chakrata | Sujau | 03 | 05 | 08 | Two villages of Chakrata Block |
| 5. | Chakrata | Oli | 07 | 0 | 07 | |
| 6. | Doiwala | Nagal Bulandawala | 10 | 02 | 12 | One village of Doiwala Block |
| 7. | Vikas Nagar | Shahpur | 02 | 13 | 15 | One village of Vikas Nagar Block |
| Total | 4 | 7 | 38 | 25 | 63 | Total seven villages in four Blocks |

Bazar five years back, have abandoned their occupation due to poor earnings.

- In the case of males, one in Lakhwar village (Kalsi Block) and one in Sujau Village (Chakrata Block) did not purchase the asset after getting the money.
- Most of the beneficiaries were unable to tell correctly their increased income, hence it was computed after taking into account their monthly expenditure.
- Some beneficiaries indicated that their income was nil before taking the loan but after getting the subsidy and loan, they have started earning. It was further explained that they were living with their parents and after becoming adults got the financial assistance.
- Some of the beneficiaries were not given the money directly but were provided with assets such as handloom machine (Khaddi), sewing machine and sewing implements.
- Where money was given for house construction and not for income generation purposes, no increase in income was shown.
- In most cases, people did not know the balance amount to be re-paid to Bank, neither did they know about the percentage of interest charged. Some of them showed their pass books but it was not uptodate. Many had misplaced it and had no idea of the amount outstanding.
- In Chakrata, the State Bank of India was yet to disburse loans to the selected beneficiaries of the year 2000-2001 though according to Block officials, subsidy amount had been released to the Bank.
- There was no coordination between the Block and Bank officials and the progress of disbursement after the year 1999-2000 has been extremely tardy.
- There is no follow up visit either by the Bank or Block officials after the amount of loan was disbursed. The officials of Veterinary, agriculture and other line department also did not visit the beneficiaries. The Block officials were too busy in disbursing old age and widow

pensions and hence there was no contact with the beneficiaries. Wherever the beneficiaries were questioned about the visit of Block or other departmental officers, they were not able to recall any such visit. The visit by District and State level officers were so few and far between that it had left no impact.

- The villagers are not aware of the various schemes or programmes run by the State or Central governments and seemed resigned to their fate.
- There is no worthwhile NGO working in the area visited though the presence of one NGO named BAIF which does artificial insemination for a definite charge was mentioned by some people in Lakhwar and Haripur Bias villages in Kalsi Block.
- In Haripur Bias Village (Kalsi Block) where handloom machines were provided and the beneficiaries have created products like shawls, durries etc, there is no arrangement for marketing of these products and hence they keep piling without any worthwhile sale, though private traders sometimes come and purchase.

Table 3 shows the details of the beneficiaries sector-wise of the 4 blocks namely: (1) Kalsi, (2) Chakrata, (3) Doiwala, and (4) Vikas Nagar falling in seven villages namely: (i) Lakhwar, (ii) Haripur Bias Nahri, (iii) Kalsi Bazar, (iv) Sujau, (v) Oli, (vi) Nagal Bulandawala, and (vii) Shahpur, who have been selected for financial assistance. Occupation wise, 33 persons fall in the Primary Sector, 2 in the Secondary Sector and 28 in the Tertiary Sector.

This table shows that the maximum beneficiaries are engaged in the Primary and Tertiary Sector and that the Secondary Sector has very few persons engaged in it. In Primary Sector, most beneficiaries are engaged in agriculture and allied activities like animal husbandry, donkey keeping, land labour and sericulture. Some are engaged in two occupational activities like dhaba work and donkey keeping. Very few persons were found to be engaged in secondary sector i.e. only 2 male workers were engaged in handoom work. There is no female beneficiary in this sector. Many Jaunsaries are engaged in the Tertiary Sector in which males out number the female beneficaries. Among the Buxas, more people were found working in the primary sector than in the Tertiary Sector.

On the basis of this survey, the following observations are made:-

- In Chakrata and Kalsi Blocks, male workers (beneficiaries) are more as compared to females i.e. 72.23 per cent male and 27.77 per cent females.
- In Doiwala and Vikas Nagar Blocks, male workers among Buxas are marginally more than females i.e. 51.85 per cent males and 48.14 per cent females.
- Over all, the number of male workers are more than female workers in the seven villages surveyed (63.49 per cent male and 36.5 per cent females workers).
- Maximum number of male workers are engaged in Tertiary Sector as compared to Primary and Secondary Sectors i.e. 81:48 per cent male and 18.51 per cent female workers are working in Tertiary Sector in all the four tribal Blocks of Dehradun District.
- 52.94 per cent of female workers are engaged in the Primary Sectors as against 47.5 per cent male workers in Chakrata and Kalsi Blocks of Dehradun District.
- Over all the combined strength of male workers in all the three sectors is almost double of the female workers i.e. 63.49 per cent are male workers and 36 per cent are female workers in the tribal blocks studied.
- No female worker was found engaged in the Secondary Sector among those contacted.
- It was observed that in all the three sectors, maximum income is generated by the workers in tertiary sector, followed by primary sector (Agriculture Sector) and Secondary Sector.
- It is also seen that the average monthly income of literate male (Rs. 327.55) is slightly more than the illiterate male worker (Rs. 222.21). But, interestingly,

the monthly average income of illiterate female is slightly more than that of the literate female worker. However, the combined income of literate male and female worker is (Rs. 435.04) slighlty more than illiterate male and female worker (Rs. 411.61).

- Taking over all average income, the male workers earn somewhat more than their counterpart female workers.
- Another remarkable thing is that nobody was found engaged in their traditonal art or craft and handicrafts do not find favour with the tribals of this region. Koltas of Jaunsar-Bawar were mostly landless agricultural workers or road labourers though no body said that he or she was a bonded labour. They lived outside the main village, usually in a hamlet of their own and are the poorest. The economic status of the various castes in Jaunsar-Bawar has a close co-relation with their caste hierachy. Generally, it is the higher castes (Khasas and Brahmins) which are economically well-off. The other castes like Bajgis and Sonar are better off than the Koltas. The Barhai, the Lohar, the Nai and Darzi are the professional castes.

**Education**

Evidence shows that it is the poor who access government schools and SC and ST population are among the poorest. Among the poor, it is the most disadvantaged and those living in remote habitations who opt for government primary school. The raision de etre of a government programme should therefore be to respond to the educational needs of the poor.

The survey showed that tribal population in Dehradun district was way behind their brethren in the district in the matter of literacy specially the female literacy. In Chakrata block, only 32.06 per cent males and 9.55 per cent females were literate as against the district average of 77.95 per cent males and 59.26 per cent females being literate (1991 census figures).

The following table[10] shows the change in the share of ST enrolment by levels of literacy. It also shows that there is more ST population in the low female literacy districts in the country and the share of ST enrolment to total enrolment has increased from 1995-96 to 1998-99.

| Category of District | per cent share of ST enrolment to total enrolment by category | |
|---|---|---|
| | 1995-96 | 1998-99 |
| Very low female literacy | 20.3 | 23.9 |
| Low female literacy | 17.2 | 20.4 |
| Moderate female literacy | 9.3 | 11.7 |
| High female literacy | 3.8 | 3.0 |

Tables 4, 5 and 7 show the literacy and education levels of the persons surveyed. Among the families surveyed in the four blocks of Dehradun District, there are 26 illiterates out of 63 beneficiaries in which 9 are male and 17 female. This clearly shows that illiteracy is higher among females. Number of literate (up to 5th or 5th pass) are 19 in which 15 are Male and 04 are Female beneficaires. Their literacy level is either less than 5th or 5th class pass. Those who fall under education level of 6th standard and above are 18 in number, out of which 14 are Male and 4 are Female. On the basis of the survey, the following points can be made:

- In Chakrata and Kalsi Blocks among the surveyed persons, the literate beneficiaries are more i.e. 61.1 per cent as compared to the illiterate beneficiares who are 38.8 per cent.
- In Doiwala and Vikas Nagar Blocks the literate beneficiaries are 48.14 per cent which is less than illiterate beneficiaries who are 51.85 per cent.
- Taking the beneficiaries of the four blocks as a whole it is found that the number of literates (55.5 per cent) are more than illiterates (44.4 per cent).
- It is interesting to note that in the Jaunsari and Buxa inhabited tribal blocks the number of illiterates are equal, although the sample of Jaunsari beneficiaries was more and among the primitive tribal group of Buxas, the number of illiterates was more.
- Female workers (beneficiaries) in Primary Sector were

mostly illiterate. Male illiteracy in Primary Sector is less as compared to female workers.

- Male workers are mostly below five (-5) literate in Primary sector.
- There are very few female workers in Primary Sector who have passed 5th class (+5).
- Percentage of Male workers in +5 literacy level is more in Primary Sector.
- There are very few illiterate male working in the Primary Sector. On the other hand, very few literate female workers are engaged in the Primary Sector. They are mostly illiterate.
- Maximum literacy is found in male workers of +5 category in Tertiary Sector.
- Male members are more literate in Tertiary Sector as compared to female workers in Tertiary Sector.
- Female illiteracy is the highest among the surveyed persons in Buxa villages of Vikas Nagar and Doiwala Blocks. They are mostly engaged in the primary sector.
- Illiteracy level in Male workers is low in Primary Sector.
- In tertiary Sector the number of illiterates among male and female workers, is virtually the same.
- There is nobody engaged in the Secondary Sector in the surveyed villages.
- +5 literate workers are mostly male in the Tertiary Sector and few female workers are falling in +5 literate category in Tertiary Sector.
- Literacy rate of male workers is higher than female workers in the two Buxa Blocks, although the number of workers (male and female ratio) is marginally the same.
- There is no female worker in Primary Sector who has passed +5 literacy level. All female workers are either illiterate or have read upto Class V but not passed Class V examination.

- Maximum workers (Male and Female) in these blocks are illiterate and those who are literate fall under –5 literacy level.

In this situation, the primary task is to bring about an awakening about education/literacy in the tribal areas and simultaneously improve the quality of the present structure of primary education as well as the availability of teachers. It was heartening to note that the lady teachers of Sujau and Oli primary schools in Chakrata block stayed together in Sujau village and were therefore able to devote their whole time to the education of the village children. But the condition of the Langapokhri girls' residential school will sadden the heart of any visitor. The girls here are forced to fight the vagaries of nature throughout the year, which tells upon adversely on their education and shows in their success rate in examinations, which is rather poor. When I asked a few girls to read from their English study books, they found it difficult to do so.

Though there are government primary schools in most of the villages, the core issue remains that their existence will not automatically extend the education to the whole village and its periphery in the absence of good teachers, text books and safe buildings.

In this context, the quality and delivery of education to the most deprived is of crucial importance. Though there are three Ashram type residential schools at Langapokhri, Lakhamandal and Teuni in Chakrata – two of them for girls, their physical conditions and shortage of teachers is not conducive to a proper atmosphere for study. Langapokhri Ashram school which is located at a distance of 3-4 kms. from Chakrata tehsil and block headquarters and which I visited had been established in the year 1973. It runs classes from class I to X for girls only. Total sanctioned strength of students is 300 whereas 219 were enrolled on the date of the visit. It has a capacity to accommodate only 175 students in its old building, which is used during day time for classes and night time for sleeping. The building is in very poor condition with leaking roof and dirty ambience. Drinking water is scarce and has to be brought from

Chakrata. There is no dining space and the students have to bear the inclemency of weather while eating. There are altogether ten rooms in the building where classes are also held. Total sanctioned strength of teachers for higher Classes (IX and X) are six and four posts are vacant. For the primary section, there is one post of teacher, which is also vacant. For junior classes (VI to VIII), 4 teachers are sanctioned and all were reported to be working.

In admission there is no restriction and all students of Jaunsar Bawer are admitted at the primary stage, but for further education, screening is done after class VI. After class X, only 25 per cent students go to inter college.

It was also found that grant for books per head in Rs. 100/- for junior classes and Rs. 150/- for classes IX and X which is not sufficient for the purchase of books. There is no regular supply of beds, bed sheets and blankets though mattresses were supplied a few days before the visit ($5^{th}$ June, 2002).

There is no playground. Toilets are available but rarely used for want of water. Besides the students, the Principal, the hostel warden, house mother, nurse and four other staff stay in the building. There is no recreation and TV set is not in working condition.

As the present building is totally insufficient for the running of a 300 bed hostel and school, proposals have been sent last year to the State government for the construction of a new building behind the present building where land is available. Besides the school education, adult and vocational education centres are also required in the tribal areas of Chakrata, Kalsi, Vikasnagar and Doiwala. An I.T.I. is going to be opened shortly in Chakrata and its building is ready for occupation. An Ashram type school is also required at Vikasnagar for the Buxas and Koltas, the two most deprived communities of this region. There was an adult education programme being run by an NGO at Shahpur village in Vikasnagar block. But good NGOs are hard to come by, as they are not willing to work in remote and inaccessible areas.

## Health

The National Policy on health (1983) has recommended the primary health care approach. The development of primary health care facilities forms an integral part of the health system and provides a strong base for the overall development of the people.

The hilly regions of Dehradun district face an acute health problem. Despite healthy environment, lower density of population and high altitude, the general health of the people is very poor. Poor nutritional level, socio-cultural customs (i.e. prevalence of polyandry, polygamy and child marriages), widespread smoking and consumption of alcohol is responsible for the poor health of the people of this region[11].

Based on the household survey, common diseases found in the four blocks were fevers, bowel disorders, respiratory diseases, malaria, cholera, diarrhoea etc. The villages visited did not have primary health centres or additional primary health centres. They were located in some other village. Given the inaccessibility of many villages, it would warrant the establishment of more medical centres in the area. There is also need of establishment of more Ayurvedic dispensaries, since the area is rich in growth and availability of a large variety of medicinal plants and herbs about which the local people are quite knowledgeable.

Education and health are the key to development. Better education and better health awareness would create conditions for increase in income and consequent reduction in poverty level. This will also help in changing the unequal social and economic structure in the villages of Chakrata and Kalsi as also elsewhere.

## Socio-economic Characteristic of House-holders

Education level, household income, occupation, health facilities, asset creation, role of NGOs and government officials has been deduced from the survey schedules filled up during the field visits as well as in interaction with the beneficiaries of ITDP programmes during such visits to the seven villages in four Blocks of Dehradun district. All the respondents interviewed were adults and belonged to the age group of 18 to 80 years.

The education variable is the most important barometer for assessing social status of a community. Education has direct bearing on the developmental process. An educated person can be easily persuaded or motivated for effective participation in the developmental process and such person will have his own views and perceptions regarding development programmes and officials engaged in the implementation of such programmes. Moreover, education opens the doors of modernization and social change, though it is another matter that the only graduate Buxa in Nagal Bulandwala village of Doiwala Block was pulling a rickshaw for his livelihood.

It was found during the village visits that the tribals of Dehradun district are low-educated and majority of them are illiterate. The survey data shows that 44.4 per cent respondents were illiterate while 55.6 per cent were literate. Again 30.1 per cent were educated upto primary level only and 7.93 percent had finished high school level. None of the female beneficiaires had finished high school level. The condition of the only graduate among the Buxas – a primitive tribal group has been mentioned earlier. The survey therefore showed that the majority of the respondents were either illiterate or were low-educated.

Significantly, education has a direct bearing on occupation and economic earnings. Table 5 (Aand B) depicts the occupations sector wise – primary, secondary and tertiary. Agriculture is the predominant occupation of the tribals. A sizeable proportion is also engaged in labour. Thus it is clear that agriculture and allied activities including agriculture labour are the main occupations. Most of the households reported that agriculture (26 per cent), petty business (22 per cent) and agriculture labour (24 per cent) are main occupations. Animal husbandry (3 per cent), weaving (3 per cent), sericulture (6 per cent) and tailoring (13 per cent) are the subsidiary occupations of the respondents. It is also worth mentioning that occupation has direct bearing on the income level or the earnings. If the occupation is not economically viable then there will be no sustained source of income or earnings as shown in the case of persons who were given handloom machines (Khaddi) in Kalsi Block.

Family size is an important variable since it decides financial stress of households. If there is a large family, definitely there will be need for more resources to maintain and sustain the family. If the family is small, then the members will have more avenues for growth, education, health care and better food and clothes. The average family size was computed as five members per household.

Monthly income of surveyed households is shown in Table 2. The average annual income per household was found to be Rs. 3104.16. Agriculture constituted 26 percent of total income, while animal husbandry accounted for 3 percent. Business account for high share among the respondents of Lakhwar village, while people engaged in labour dominated in Oli village. The analysis of income pattern also shows that the Koltas and Buxas were very poor and many of them were living below the poverty line. The Jaunsaries were somewhat better in economic terms. They possessed land and were also represented in services.

**Participation in Development Programmes**

Central as well as State governments have initiated various development programmes. In the tribal areas, integrated tribal development programmes as well as special programmes for the primitive tribal groups have been taken up. But the reality is that the tribals are not aware of these programmes and if aware, their participation in these programmes is very low due to their low level of education and poor interaction with the government officials. During the field survey, it was found that the block officials as well as officers from the ITDP or other departments rarely visited these villages. Many times, the respondents did not remember any such visit in either near or distant past. Thus, this lack of awareness of government programmes and interaction with the government functionaries, together with near absence of NGOs in the tribal villages does not ensure active particiption of the beneficiaries. The officals posted at the district and State level hardly get time to visit tribal concentrated areas. This tendency also percolates to officers at the lower levels due to the difficult geographical conditions of the hilly and tribal areas and the constraints in travelling.

The respondents were asked during the survey about the benefits received under the developemnt programmes. Most people interviewed had got benefit either under the IRDP or the ITDP programmes and the PTGs got it under the special programmes.

The purpose for which the financial assistance was received shows that 22 percent households have received assistance for petty business, 29 per cent for agriculture and allied activites, 9 per cent for silk rearing and weaving while 13 percent got for other sundry jobs like tailorng, mule transportetc. Again the number of borrowers who reported receiving assistance between Rs.10-15,000/- were 22 per cent, followed by persons who got Rs. 5-10,000/- (50 per cent). Around one third of the beneficiaries had received assistance upto Rs. 5,000/- only.

**Impact of the Development Programmes**

The tribals were asked about their view perception regarding the impact of development programmes on their life. Most of the respondents stated that the programmes had improved their life to some extent (23 per cent). The percentage of respondents reporting that programmes have largely improved their lives was 52 per cent. Some were of the view that the development programmes have not improved their life (25 percent). The respondents were further asked about the usefulness of the government programmes. A majority of them found it to be useful (75 per cent) with many demanding further help in increasing their income generation. A quarter of the respondents had the perception that the tribal development programmes had not affected their lives (25 per cent). For improving the quality of the programme, the respondents were asked for their suggestions which are shown at Table 2.

Only 57 per cent of the beneficiaries have given their suggestions. Out of total 35 suggestions given by the beneficiaries, first priority was given to loan for the livestock, a total of 9 beneficiaries have suggested it (26 per cent). Second preference was given for housing loan, i.e., 4 beneficiaries have suggested it. Rest all other beneficiaries have demanded loan for miscellaneous work.

## Welfare Programmes for the Primitive Tribals

Most of the Buxas of Dehradun district are small and marginal farmers. There is lack of irrigation and people are burdened with productive and non-productive loans from private sources who charge a high rate of interest. Buxas had no traditional skill except making of mats for local use. The development of infrastructure facility in the area was inadequate. Their educational level is low and majority of them are illiterates. Their main source of sustenance has been reported to be agriculture, though a small number of tribal households is engaged in petty business or rickshaw pulling. Due to this fact, their income is low and most of them are still living below the poverty line. Therefore, government intervention to improve their life, living standards and welfare is called for. The government programmes wherever implemented have made it possible to improve their living conditions and earn a better living.

## Conclusion

Tribal areas, being remote and hilly lack in basic facilities and socio-economic infrastructure. Moreover in agriculture, there is preponderance of small and uneconomic land holdings, leading to low yields. Low investments in agriculture coupled with growing indebtedness have rendered agriculture to subsistence level.

The socio-economic status of the tribals of Dehradun district has been found to be far from satisfactory. The landholdings of tribals are small and marginal. Due to gradual shrinking of land holdings partly due to land alienation and low productivity of crops, the tribals remain in poverty and indebtedness. Again, due to adverse geographical conditions and traditional methods of agriculture, tribal farmers could not get desired returns from growing crops. Due to lack of irrigation, low yielding seeds, less area under commercial crops etc, the tribals cannot grow high value crops.

In the 4 surveyed blocks, villages having undulating terrain, where there is lack of water, or no other irrigation facilities exist, agroforesty promotion, improving quality of livestock, animal husbandry, sericulture and handloom sector could help the inhabitants. This could also provide them with fuel, wood and fodder besides checking severe soil erosion in the area and at the same time it would reduce the pressure on the natural forests.

Awareness of development programmes and apathy of government officials has led to limited interaction and low participation in the development effort. Since, Panchayat elections have not been held for long, the old village Pardhans have also lost interest in pursuing the financial assistance programmes under the ITDP as earlier they were the key functionaries in selecting the beneficiaries. The result is a complete shutdown of the ITDP projects in the district and the absence of a full time project officer for ITDP Chakrata-Kalsi has further receded the prospects of any immediate revival.

It is therefore recommended that the implementation of health, education, infrastructure development and economic programmes should be carried out under the close watch of the tribal welfare department of the State Government in general and the district authority in particular.

## References

1. Report of the Commission for Scheduled Areas and Scheduled Tribes, 1961, Planning Commission, New Delhi.
2. *Ibid.*
3. D.N. Majumdar: Himalayan Polyandry: A field study of Jaunsar-Bawar, Asia Publishing House, New Delhi, 1962, p. 287.
4. S.K. Biswas (ed) Central Himalayan Panorama (Vol. I), Calcutta, 1993, pp. 19.
5. Report of the IAS probationers vist to Chakrata and Kalsi Blocks

published in 'The Administrator' LBSNAA, Mussoorie, Spring 1975, pp. 643-759.

6. *Ibid.*

7. *Ibid.*

8. *Ibid.*

9. Economy of Uttranchal-profile and dynamics of change – P.C. Pandey and others (ed), New Delhi, 2001, pp.74-75.

10. Yash Agarwal: Trends in Access and Retention, a study of Primary Schools in DPEP districts, March 2000.

11. Integrated Area Development Plan for Chakrata Block prepared by the Centre for Micro Planning and Regional Studies, LBSNAA, Mussoorie, p.70.

# 10

# Jharkhand

The tribals, are, by and large, children of nature, their lifestyle being conditioned by their ecosystem. They are spread through the length and breadth of India.

According to the 1991 census, there were thirty tribes in Bihar (Jharkhand). They are: Asur, Baiga, Banjara, Bathudi, Bedia, Bhumij, Binghia, Birhor, Hingia, Chero, Chik Baraik, Gond, Gorait, Ho, Karmali, Kharia, Kharwar, Khand, Kisan, Kora, Korwa, Lohara or Lohra, Mahli, Malpaharia, Munda, Oraon, Parahiya, Santhal, Sauria-Paharia and Savar. Out of these thirty tribes, eight have been identified as the most primitive by applying various indicators of backwardness and their present precarious social existence. They are Asur, Birhor, Birjia, Korwa, Mal Paharia, Paharia, Sauria Paharia and Savar.

These thirty tribes of Jharkhand are largely located in the plateau of Chotanagpur and Santhal Parganas. Agriculturally, they can be divided into settled cultivator and shifting cultivator. Oraon, Munda, Ho and Santhal etc. are settled cultivators whereas Korwa, Paharia, Sauria etc. are shifting cultivators. The problems, which they face, is education, indebtedness, shifting cultivation, migration, unemployment, agricultural labor, special problems of hunting and food gathering, irrigation, power and communication.

Jharkhand as a state has been formed on 15th November 2000 with the bifurcation of Bihar. It consists of 18 districts which formerly came under the Jharkhand Area Autonomous Council. These districts are Palamau, Chatra, Garhwa, Lohardagga, Gumla, Ranchi, West Singhbum, East Singhbum, Dhanbad, Bokaro, Dumka, Pakur, Sahebgunj, Godda, Deoghar, Giridh, Hazaribagh and Kodarma. The whole area was earlier known as the Chotanagpur-Santhal Parganas region. This region has the richest deposit of mineral wealth and forest resources. Important resources are located at Ranchi, Bokaro, Jamshedpur, Sindri, Hazaribagh, Dhanbad and Giridh etc. As per the 1991 census, the total population of Jharkhand was 2,08,16,188 of which the ST population was 59,77,263 which came to 28.71 per cent of the total population. As per 2001 census figures, Jharkhand has a population of 2,69,09,428 and a total territory of 79,714 sq. kms.

The plateau region of Chotanagpur, Santhal Parganas and some parts of West Bengal, MP and Orissa were known as Jharkhand since ancient times. The word 'Jharkhand' consists of Jhar (forests) and khand (land including hills). Since this region was covered with dense forests, it may be assumed that the name is geographically attributed to the virgin forests and hilly tracts of the area.

The name 'Jharkhand' is also found in E.T. Dalton's 'Tribal History of Eastern India' as a place of growing colonies of Kols and the stronghold of the ten chiefs as referred in 'Puranas'. The name Jharkhand is also mentioned in Akbarnama as a place where diamond, ivory or tusks of elephants and silks are abunduntantly available. The place was also inaccessible to the outsiders due to the density of the forest and the warring prowess of the tribals.

Linguistically, there are two groups to which the tribals of Jharkhand belong:

1. Austro-Asiatic - Mundari and other tribes
2. Dravidian-Oraon and Malpaharias

Out of the thirty Scheduled Tribes in Jharkhand, Oraons of Chotanagpur and Sauria Paharia of Santhal Parganas belong to the Dravidian linguistic family and the rest of them, with a few exceptions belong to Austro-Asiatic or Mundari group. The major tribes are Santhal, Oraon, Munda and Ho.

***(a) Mundas:*** The Mundas are also sometimes called 'Kols' and they call themselves 'Horoko' meaning men. They are the earliest aboriginal of the State. It is also suggested that Mundas or Kols occupied jungle lands of the south of the Vindhyan mountains as they were mostly hunters.

Mundas are found in Ranchi, Singhbhum and Hazaribagh districts of Jharkhand. Next to the Santhals and Oraon, Mundas constitute the third largest tribe in Jharkhand. Their highest concentration like the Oraon occurs in Ranchi district.

The word 'Munda' in the Mundari language means a man of prestige and wealth. Mundas decide their disputes as per the direction of the Parha Panchayat consisting of Parha Raja, the Diwan, the Thakur, the Pande, the Karta and the Lal. Comparatively, Mundas are more educated than the other tribes.

They consider themselves to be the original settlers of India and descendants of Sing Borya the Supreme God. They are mainly found in the South of Old Ranchi district. They are one of the well-studied tribal communities and have a language called 'Mundari'. They have produced leaders like Birsa Munda who died a martyr. Of the total scheduled tribes in India, nearly 30 tribes speak the Mundari language. Mundas of Ranchi live in urban surroundings and are getting modernized as they eat food from the market, spend money on jewellery etc. which they never did before. The Mundas were a wandering tribe till they reached Chotanagpur and settled here. When the Mundas entered Chotanagpur, it was a virgin forest. Each family of the settlers made its own clearance of the forest which bcame a 'dika' or a village. The eldest son of the founder became the head of the village in both temporal and religious matters. In times of need, like war etc. several villages united under one man called the 'Manki' who was elected by the headmen of the villages. In the Munda system, the ultimate owner of the land is not headmen or manki but the village as a whole. Cultivation is their primary occupation, while hunting and collection of forest produce are subsidiary occupations. They are mainly nature worshippers and also worship their ancestors.

The Mundas are an endogamous tribe. They do not marry outside the tribal community, not even among the other Kolarian tribes of Chotanagpur. Within the tribe, there are a large number of endogamous clan locally named as "Killi". They believe that all the members of a particular class or Killi are descendants from one common ancestor and therefore marital relations within a clan or a Killi are taboo. The Killis are totemistic.

The Mundas are primarily an agriculturist tribe. Agriculture makes the main bases of their economic life and all their activities are directed towards it throughout the year. They also work on daily wages on construction sites and other industries located in Ranchi. Sale of minor forest produce also supplements their income.

The special feature about the Munda inhabited villages is the land tenure system referred to as "Mundari Khuntkattidari" tenancy. This protects the traditional land and forest rights.

***(b) Santhals :*** The Santhals are the most numerous among the Scheduled tribes of Jharkhand. They now constitute 37.1 per cent of the total tribal population in the state.

The tribe shows a long history of continuous migration from one area to another to keep pace with their increasing number. They have migrated in large numbers from the districts of Jharkhand to West Bengal, Orissa and Assam. Their main concentration is however in the Santhal Parganas.

Initially, the Santhals were hunters who also resorted to shifting cultivation. They preferred to live in jungles or on hill tops. But now they have settled over the plains clearing the jungles and preparing the same for paddy cultivation.

Unlike other tribes, Santhals are quite careful in the construction of their houses with apartments for elders.

Their social life is highly organized. The headman of the village is called 'Manjhi' who collects rent for which he is paid some commission. He is assisted by 'Jog Manjhi' who keeps control over the morale of the people.

The Santhals are known for their cheerfulness, straightforwardness and honesty. Two qualities distinguish them from other tribes. First their capability to convert waste lands into fertile paddy fields and their skill at hunting once in a year when they hunt together killing every bird and beast they come across. The Manjhi is the spokesperson of the village in all matters affecting their temporal life. In the original settlements, it was usual for two or three brothers to start a new village together. The eldest brother always assumed the leading position. Land is conceived of as belonging to the clan. With certain other castes who are cultivators like them, the Santhals claim a special relationship. Chief among them are the Kurmis and the Mahtos who are looked upon as distant kinsfolk. At home they speak the Santhali language, but with others they communicate in Hindi or Bengali. Devnagvi, Bengali and Olchiki scripts are used by them.

***(c) Hos:*** Hos reside in the old Kolhan estate in the Chaibasa Sadar Subdivision of Singhbhum district. They are primarily agriculturists but depend for their livelihood on hunting and minor forest produce.

The Ho settlement area is divided into groups of villages called 'Pira' which is controlled by Manki while the village headman is called Munda. They are assisted by constables called 'Dakuas' appointed by the Manki.

The Hos are the most exclusive tribe. They don't fall prey to outside influence. They are marked by an independent bearing. According to Colonel Dalton, they are physically and morally superior to Mundas, Bhumji and Santhals. The Hos broke off with the Mundas in the Fifth century AD and moved over to Kolhan area of the Singhbhum district, where they lived an independent life. The Hos often fought the British. Their economy is dependent on the Sal and Sagwan trees which are also worshipped by them. Kolhan adivasi area in Singhbhum district was administered under a distinct set of rules. Britishers had made special arrangements to keep them under control and they still claim to be governed by the 'Wilkinson's rule' devised by the British. Like the Mundas, they also have their Munda-Manki system.

***(d) Oraons:*** The Oraons like Santhals also form a large section of tribal population of Jharkhand, West Bengal, Chattisgarh and Orissa. They comprised 17.7 per cent of the total tribal population of Bihar (now Jharkhand) in 1971. Their greatest concentration occurs in Ranchi district and the adjoining Latehar sub-division of Palamau.

Oraons have succeeded in preserving their Mundari language which they speak. They are good agriculturists and are mostly dependent on agriculture for their livelihood. The Oraons generally occupy highest available patch of land in the neighbourhood of their agricultural field and all settlements are close to a spring or well.

The Oraons, a dravidian speaking, short statured,small headed and broad-nosed people mostly live in Ranchi and Palamau districts. They are divided into several clans or gotras. The headman of the Oraon village is called 'Mahto'.

The Oraons employ methods of cultivation which are much advanced as compared to other tribes in Jharkhand. Their most important social institution is the 'dhamkuria' or the boy's dormitory. A number of Oraons are engaged in salaried jobs in government and private organizations.

***(e) Paharias:*** The Paharias are the oldest tribe in India and they mostly reside in Santhal Parganas. Megasthanese, the famous traveler has mentioned in his works the existence of Paharias near the developed Kingdom of Magadh. Paharia language is also known as 'Malto' in the language of their conversation. Paharias are very simple people. Their rituals and festivals have no similarity with other tribes. The most inflential person in Paharia society is 'Jan Guru' whose decision is final and unchallengeable. They worship crops like maize which is their staple food. Drinking water problems and absence of nutritious diet have affected their health.

***(f) Bhumij:*** The Bhumijs are mainly concentrated between the Kasai and Subarnarekha rivers of Singhbhum district, occupying either the banks of the Subarnarekha or the hill ranges. They are mainly agriculturists and work as agricultural labour as well.

The Bhumijs maintain their own tribal panchayats consisting of a headman known as Pradhan whose office is hereditary and whose decision is final.

***(g) Mal Paharias:*** The Mal Paharias or Malers are true Paharias found mainly in Rajmahal hills of Santhal Parganas. They live in the Daman-e-Koh area. Until recently, they were hunters and dependent on Jhum cultivation.

A large Maler village contains about 100 houses with about 500 persons living in them. This village may occupy the summit of a high range of hills. It is usually surrounded by vegetable garden with fences.

A Maler village is controlled by a village council composed of the elders of the village. It is presided over by the Manjhi with the Gorait as his assistant. The Manjhi is the village headman and his post is hereditary alongwith that of the Gorait.

***(h) Birhors:*** Birhors are the smallest but quite an interesting nomadic tribe. They belong to the same racial stock as the Ho and the Munda. They are mostly found in Ranchi and Hazaribagh districts. Birhors are like nomads and live on forest products. They do not possess any permanent home. They change the place of abode with the change of season and convenience, usually four times a year.

They are divided into exogamous clans named mostly after animals and plants. 'Baiga' clan among them is the most powerful.

***(i) Other tribes:*** Other small tribes suffer in neglect and ignorance and apathy of the administration. Due to their stay in remote areas the tribes like Paharias and Birhors are gradually becoming extinct. They are not paid even the minimum wages. The police also brand them as criminal tribes and deal harshly with them. In the areas inhabited by Paharias indebtedness, exploitation, lack of social amenities like schools, dispensaries, drinking water facilities, road and housing are rampant. They are also not getting the benefits of the Government's welfare and rural employment programs. It is therefore not surprising that the population of Paharia tribals in Godda district of Jharkhand, which was 26 lakhs in 1911 has been reduced to only 95,000 in 1981. In Dumka district, their population is only 25,770[1].

**Brief History**

In 1771, the land of Jharkhand came under the jurisdiction of the East India Company after the subjugation of the Raja of Chotanagpur. Since the Britishers were basically interested in revenue collection from the land, they introduced a permanent legal and administrative structure to ensure regular and uninterrupted collection of revenue. The traditional right of the tribals over land and forest (Khuntkatti system) as well as the village council system thus gave way. The Permanent Settlement Act, 1773 legitimized the individual ownership of land which led to the expropriation of tribal lands by the outsiders. That apart, indiscriminate destruction of forests and unplanned mining in the region almost brought the tribal communities to the brink of disaster.

While periodical uprisings against the 'dikus' and the Britishers failed, their violent rebellion under the leadership of Birsa Munda during 1895-1900, forced the British government to pass the Chotanagpur Tenancy Act in 1908 which legalized the 'Khuntikutti' system and arrested further alienation of such lands. But, by that time, nine-tenths of the original 'Khuntikutti' lands had passed into the hands of outsiders.

While the Jharkhand movement among the Mundas and Oraons all along has highlighted the socio-economic disparities between the tribals and non-tribals, the movement amongst the Santhals has veered towards the agrarian problems of the people of Santhal Parganas.

Between 1855 and 1861, Santhal Parganas witnessed agrarian struggles against the moneylenders who used to take possession of tribal lands by lending money to the tribals on exorbitant rates of interest.

The Jharkhand movement was the result of the economic exploitation by the 'dikkus'(outsiders) and it sought to evict them from the Jharkhand which means forest land but the forest wealth attracted more dikkus and industries.

Starting from the movement of Tilka Majhi to santhal rebellion, Bhumji revolt, Sardar Larai, Tana Bhagat movement, the agitation got articulated through major demands for reform. In 1900, Birsa Munda was the first tribal leader to have demanded the establishment of Munda Raj and independence. One hundred years later, in the year of the centennial celebration of his martyrdom, the Jharkhand state has taken shape.

The demand for Jharkhand as a state was first made in 1940. In the early 1940s Shri Jaipal Singh was the most charismatic tribal leader and he established the Jharkhand party on January 1, 1949 as a regional political platform where both tribes and non-tribes could join hands to create a Jharkhand state. It was the strongest party in the region from 1951to 1961. After 1963, following its merger with the congress, the party disintegrated and could not recapture the old heights.

The rise of the Jharkhand Mukti Morcha in 1973, represented a shift in the social base of the Jharkhand movement. The combination of Santhals and Kurmi-Mahatos was a formidable one and it was in ascendancy during the eighties. An ideological dimension was provided by the theory of Jharkhand nationality in the 1970s and 1980s. It brought together various sections, divided by years of hostility, for a joint struggle for a political space. A cultural resurgence began, judged by the output of literature in local dialects and languages.

Chotanagpur and Santhal Parganas were brought under an autonomous area council in the early 1990s. But it fell short of the expectations of the people who demanded nothing less than a full state.

The formation of the Jharkhand state on 15th November 2000 represents the fulfillment of a very old dream-a dream of an order free from exploitation and discrimination, that promises dignity, equality and happiness, deeply cherished by the tribal communities.

**Changing Tribal Identity in Jharkhand**

The term "tribe" denotes those traditional beliefs, arts and practices that an individual acquires as a member of a particular society. It is a homogenous ethnic group with a specific sense of identity based on common language and culture. It is large enough to be a viable group and small enough to be mobilized for common action[2].

The Chotanagpur and Santhal Parganas contain a number of tribes. The term 'Kol' refers to nearly a dozen tribes like the Munda, the Ho, the Santhal and the Bhumij. Unlike the Mundas of Bihar, the Kol of U.P and Madhya Pradesh call themselves Kol without any objection. The name of the other important tribe, the Oraons appears to be derived from 'Uraon'- a Dravidian term which is made of two words- 'ur' meaning village and 'awan' meaning inhabitants. Thus 'Oraons' means those who lived in villages.

The tribe, like any other ethnic group, has its own self image and identity on the basis of which it considers itself historically as well as socio-culturally distinct from other groups.

It is said that the Munda colonized the hilly region of Chotanagpur in successive waves of migration after pushing the Bhumiyas, Savaras and other earlier settlers to still interior hills and forests. Oraons followed them in quick succession. During the period of thousands of years, these tribes split into different groups with the result that now we have as many as 30 Scheduled tribes in Jharkhand[3].

The Chotanagpur plateau ranges from 2000 ft to 3750 ft (Netarhat) above sea level with good climate and scenic beauty. Chotanagpur consists of 14 districts and 3 commissionaries having headquarters at Ranchi (South), Hazaribagh (North) and Daltonganj(Palamau). Santhal Parganas Division consists of four districts.

The tribes of Chotanagpur and Santhal Parganas can be grouped into four basic types: -

(1) *Forest Hunting type*- which consists of Birhor (4,377) and the Korwa (21,940) who are in a stage of hunting and food gathering.

(2) *Plains-Agricultural type*- they consist of Mundas (8,45,887), the Oraon (10,54,066), the Ho (5,36,523), the Santhal Karwar, and others (2,22,758).

(3) *Simple Artisan type*- They consist of the Karmali (38,651) (Ironsmith) (1,69,089), the Mahli, basket makers (91,868) and the chik baraik (weavers) (40,339). They are scattered with the second type of tribals.

(4) *Hill cultivation type*- they consist of the Hill Kharia (10,241), the Asur (7,783) and the Saoria Paharia (39, 269). They live on the hill tops and practice slash and burn agriculture.

Tribes in Jharkhand have a distinct culture and social organizations different from others. Each tribe uses its own dialect for intra-tribal communication. The tribes of Jharkhand range from settled agriculturists like Munda. Oraon, Santhals and Hos to the others like Birhors and Paharias who are mostly food gatherers. This disparity in occupation is also reflected in other indicators like the literacy level. While the literacy rate is highest in the case of Santhals (26.19 per cent), followed by Oraon(24.71 per cent), Munda (18.98 per cent) and Ho (9.62 per cent), it is 3.89 per cent among Kharwars, 3.57 per cent in Kharias and 2.26 per cent in Bhumjis.

While in the erstwhile Bihar State, the tribal population constituted 7.66 per cent of the total population, in the new state of Jharkhand, it comes to 28.71 per cent as per the 1991 census. The issues of deprivation, marginalization, and exploitation of the tribals still remain big issues which remain to be tackled. According to 1991 census, the literacy rate of tribals of Jharkhand was 27.5 per cent as against 41.39 per cent of the general population. The literacy rate of rural tribal women is the lowest, it being only 13.40 per cent. As per the provisional figures of Census 2001, the literacy rate of Jharkhand as a whole is 54.13 per cent with female literacy being 39.38 per cent. The rate of literacy of tribals of Jharkhand has not yet been calculated.

The new State of Jharkhand has very rich mineral resources and it contributed major share of revenue to erstwhile Bihar State. As per the financial statement of 1996-97, the total revenue collection of Bihar was Rs.3100 crores, out of which Rs. 2200 crores was contributed by the Jharkhand area. The forest area as per the 1997 survey comes to 26,668 sq.kms., the percentage of land under forest cover comes to 33.1 per cent in the old Singhbhum district and 33.3 per cent in Giridh, in Ranchi it comes to 16.4 per cent and in the old Santhal Parganas 13.5 per cent.

The Jharkhand State starts with many advantages. It is a state, incredibly rich in resources with the Chotanagpur area having the richest mineral resources. It has red to brown texture of surface soil with vegetation of sal trees. It has a pleasant climate that has attracted the visitors through ages. It also has a tribal ethos marked by egalitarianism and sharing which still survives. Caste does not exist in its vicious and divisive form in the tribal region.

However, the challenges before the people of Jharkhand are daunting. Illiteracy, malnutrition and unemployment are rampant. The tribal population has declined with out - migration and the influx of outsiders. Growth has declined as Bihar as a whole has registered a negative growth rate. Therefore, there is a need for an all encompassing development strategy, that, among other things, should restore the Jhar or Shrub, the green cover, cleanse the polluted rivers, and address the basic problems of poverty and identity. The safeguards for the tribals will have to be further strengthened and enforced in the age of globalization with market forces on the rampage.

**Land Settlement in Jharkhand**

The land in the Chotanagpur and Santhal Parganas is protected under the Chotanagpur Tenancy Act and Santhal Parganas Tenancy Act, 1908. The transfer of raiyati land is restricted under these Acts.

In 1869, the Chotanagpur Tenures Act was passed authorising the appointment of Special Commissioners for the Survey and demarcation of the privileged lands of both the landlords and the tenants. Settlement operations began in the year 1902 and by the end of 1903, sufficient data had been collected by the Settlement officers to justify the introduction of an amending Act. The chief object of the amending Act V of 1903 was to give finality to the record of rights regarding the incidents of Mundari Khuntkatti tenancies. The vexed question of the registration of transfer of, and succession to tenures was settled and all tenures were made saleable for arrears of rent.

The Act, as amended in 1903, remained in force till 1908, by which year, the Settlement operations were nearly completed. The Chotanagpur Tenancy Act came into force from 11th November, 1908. It reproduced with certain modifications the Act V of 1903. The law relating to "settled raiyats" and the procedure for making surveys and record-of-rights with some modifications, were incorporated from the Bengal Tenancy Act. Landlords' privileged lands were defined and provisions was made for a final and conclusive record of their rights.

The Chotanagpur Tenancy Act, however, was not an unqualified success in Ranchi district, particularly in its provisions about transfer in raiyati holdings. In fact, on the whole, it has been a failure as far as preventation of transfer of raiyati lands are concerned. Its chief success has been that it has given the raiyats a greater security of tenure as against their landlords than they had previously. There have been subsequently many amendments in the Chotanagpur Tenancy Act, 1908.

**Survey and Settlement in Ranchi District**

A topographical survey of the district was made in 1860s by Captain Depree. In 1862, a Survey was started in the villages of Barkagarh, Patia and Silam and the work continued for the next ten years. Between 1876-80, a complete Survey and Settlement was carried out by Captain Grey. The total area surveyed, for which record-of-rights was prepared, amounted to 742 square miles. The good effects of this settlement were visible at the time of the Settlement Operations (1902-10) when the agrarian conditions in these villages presented a striking contrast to the conditions prevailing in neighbouring villages, disputes of all kinds in the former being less numerous and less acute.

A revisional Survey and Settlement was undertaken during 1927-35 with a view to make a Survey and an up-to-date record of rights, including matters mentioned in Section 81, of the Chota Nagpur Tenancy Act; of all landlords' privileged lands and of their rights and obligations. It commenced in October 1927 and was concluded in October, 1935.

At the time of the Revisional Survey and Settlement Operations (1927-35) there were 156 villages known as Mundari Khuntkatti villages, where the ancient system of land tenure still survived and the descendants of the original settlers were still the co-proprietors of the land included in the boundaries of the village.

The Mundari Khuntkatti village usually contains three elements, namely-

1. The Khuntkattidars;
2. The parjas or the raiyats, and
3. The subsidiary artisan classes.

The Khuntkattidars are the descendants in the male line of the original founders of the village. They are the owners and are responsible for payment of annual rent to the superior landlord. The duty of collecting the rent rests with the Munda, or civil head of the village community. The villages were also united into groups of ten or twelve known as 'pattis' and at the head of each 'patti' was the Manki, whose duty was like that of the Munda.

**Survey and Settlement Operations in Santhal Parganas**

In Santhal Parganas, there is only one class of ryot, namely the occupancy raiyat. The Santhal Parganas Tenancy Act prohibits creation of under-ryots. The Preamble of Act XXXVII of 1855, by which this district was created removed the entire district from operation of General regulations and Acts of Government in force in the then Presidency of West Bengal.

The first settlement of the district was carried out under the Santhal Parganas Settlement Regulation III of 1872. It barred the action of the Civil courts during the settlement except on special references and in suits valued at more than Rs. 1000 regarding the rights of the zamindars and other proprietors as between themselves. It conferred on the ryots a right of occupancy after 12 years' possession and it fixed the rent for atleast seven years until a fresh settlement was made.

Subsequently, doubts began to be entertained whether the Regulation of 1872 authorized settlement to be made from time to time and it was feared that complications would arise on the expiry of the leases granted by the Settlement officer. It was, therefore, considered necessary, that the government should keep the process of rent enhancement under its own control. Accordingly, the Santhal Parganas Regulation II of 1886 was enacted.

Regulation II of 1886 enabled settlement of rents to be made on the application of ryots, and provided for the recovery by the government of the expenses incurred by it in connection with such proceedings. It did not however, admit of the preparation of a records-of-rights at the same time as the settlement of rents. It was later amended by Regulation III of 1907 which provided for enhancement of rent on account of the improvement made by the Zamindar.

In 1908, Regulation III of 1872 was further amended by Regulation III of 1908, the provision of which embody several important principles. The chief provision among them is the principle emphasized by the settlement, and accepted by the ordinary courts of the Santhal Parganas in the disposal of agrarian cases, that raiyati land cannot be made the subject of transfer. It also affirms the power of the Deputy Commissioner to interfere with illegal alienation of land and generally, to enforce the provisions of the settlement records. The Santhal Parganas Tenancy (Supplementary Provisions) Act, 1949 have placed some of the customary laws of the district in the Statute book, e.g., exchange of raiyati land, subletting of raiyati land under certain circumstances, rate of landlord fees on transfer, rights of raiyats on trees grown by them, etc.

**Present Position**

Due to industrialization, a number of tribal families whose lands were taken away or submerged had to migrate to get work in the tea gardens of Assam and Darjeeling. This has reflected in the declining population of tribals which fell from 10.07 per cent in 1951 to 8.31 per cent in 1981 and 7.66 per cent in 1991. The decline was more pronounced in the case of the Jharkhand region-from 36.81 per cent in 1951 to 30.26 per cent in 1981 and to 28.81 per cent in 1991. This was due to the migration of the tribal population from Jharkhand area and entry of non-tribal people into the region. The extent of poverty and the development of the tribal region could best be understood by an examination of the tribal workers in Jharkhand. The tribal population is by and large engaged in the primary sector. Majority of the tribals are engaged in the cultivation of their own small holdings. A substantial number of the tribals are also engaged as agricultural labor. They are generally landless labourers or have extremely small and uneconomic land holdings. The establishment of large industrial projects in the tribal areas have not benefited the local population and majority of the workers employed in these industries have migrated from the non-tribal areas. The tribals, have thus been unable to enjoy the fruit of modern development due to their low level of education, skill and awareness. The following table gives a picture of the distribution of ST workers.

**Percentage of distribution of ST Workers (1961-81)**

| *S.No.* | *Classification* | *1961* | *1981* |
|---|---|---|---|
| 1. | Cultivators | 78.1 | 63.06 |
| 2. | Agricultural laborer | 9.54 | 23.20 |
| 3. | Mining | 4.29 | 1.80 |
| 4. | Household industry, construction worker, manufacturing, trade, transport and other services | 8.17 | 11.94 |
| | *Total* | *100.00* | *100.00* |

From the above table, it is quite evident that there is a clear trend towards rise in agricultural laborers which increased from 9.54 per cent in 1961 to 23.20 per cent in 1981. There is also an alarming decline in the tribal population engaged in mining and quarrying from 4.29 per cent in 1961 to 1.80 per cent in 1981. There is also a clear trend that a substantial section of the tribal population is moving out of the cultivating class. This may be attributed to the fact that land is passing hands from the tribals to the non-tribal population. These factors are responsible for out-migration of the tribal population from the rural sector in search of employment elsewhere. The process of industrial development undertaken in the course of fifty years of planning has hardly touched the lives of the tribals. Establishment of capital intensive projects like HEC in Ranchi and the Steel Plant in Bokaro have failed to create employment opportunities for the tribals of the region.

A proper enquiry into the causes of poverty of the tribal population in Jharkhand must also take into consideration four other factors as well:

1. Forest and environment
2. Infrastructural facilities for development
3. Employment opportunities in mining and manufacturing industries
4. Rural-urban break-up of the tribal population

## 1. Forest and Environment

Tribals have an intimate relationship with forest, on which they depend for their supply of food, fodder and fuel-wood. They also collect minor forest produce which is an important source of their income. Nearly 75 per cent of the total forest area of erstwhile Bihar state is also concentrated in the six tribal districts of Palamau, Hazaribagh, Ranchi, Singhbhum, Santhal Parganas and Dhanbad which now form part of the State of Jharkhand. Nearly 90 per cent of the total tribal population of erstwhile Bihar state is also concentrated in these six tribal districts. This shows the symbiotic relationship which the tribals have with forest. The major problem of the tribal population is caused by the depletion in forest area. Between 1991 and 1997, there has been a depletion of 144 sq. kms. of forest area in the Jharkhand region as per the report of the Ministry of Forest and Environment of the Government of India.

Deforestation has also affected the geo-ecological balance of the tribal area. It has led to decline in soil fertility and change in climate. Cluster of large capital intensive projects in the area has increased air and water pollution due to emission of hazardous gases and discharge of wastes into the local rivers. The poorer sections of the population and especially the tribals are victims of the environmental degradation.

The forests are one of the main source of economic prosperity to tribals of our country. They also control soil erosion and provide food and fuel. Bihar (now Jharkhand) has a total forest area of 29,232 sq. kms., constituting 16.8 per cent of the State's land area as against the all India percentage of 23 per cent. The per capita forest area is therefore 0.05 hectare as against the all India average of 0.14 hectare.

Forest conservancy began in tribal Bihar (now Jharkhand) in 1946 when an area of 461 sq. km., was demarcated for the first time in Chotanagpur and Santhal Parganas. Forest is closely linked with the life of tribals. The Sal trees are linked to Sarhul and Karma tree with Karma festival. Tribals collect the minor forest produce like mahua flower and seed, sal leaves and branches and fuelwood and fodder from the forests.

According to the National Forest Policy, 1988, environmental stability and ecological balance is to be maintained as they are vital for the sustenance of all life forms.

After the inclusion of forests in the concurrent list through the 42nd Amendment to the Constitution in 1976, the Government issued the Forest (Conservation) ordinance on Oct 25, 1980 prohibiting the state governments from allowing the use of forest lands for any purpose without the approval of the Central government. The ordinance was later passed into an Act No. 69 of 1980.

But the Government was not satisfied with this Act and increased its powers through the Forest (Conservation) Amendment Act of 1988. The amendment forbade the State government to assign by way of lease or otherwise any forestland, or any portion thereof, to any private person or to any authority, corporation or agency without the sanction of the Central Government.

In Chotanagpur area of Jharkhand, 54000 acres of Khuntkatti (original settler clan) forest was taken over by the State in 1947 and no compensation was paid to the tribals. The Government of India Committee on Forest and Tribals reported in 1982 that where the tribals have been allowed to manage their community forests, they have managed the same well. A survey conducted by the ASCI, Hyderabad showed that the income from minor forest produce contributed around 40 per cent of the total income of a tribal household in Central India.

## 2. Infrastructure Facilities for Development

An important determinant of development of any area is the availability of the infrastructural facilities. Development of tribal areas also depend upon the creation and expansion of such facilities. Among the other infrastructural facilities, irrigation assumes great importance in view of the fact that 88 per cent of the tribal population is dependent on agriculture, either as cultivators or as agricultural laborers. The table below gives a picture of the availability of irrigation facilities in the tribal areas of Jharkhand.

| *Undivided districts* | *Percentage of crop irrigated* | | *Total area* | *Cropping intensity* |
|---|---|---|---|---|
| | *1959-62* | *1978-79* | *1978-79* | *1978-79* |
| Santhal Parganas | 12.04 | 7.70 | 41.21 | 1.5 |
| Dhanbad | 0.50 | 30.60 | 26.76 | 1.04 |
| Hazaribagh | 6.18 | 9.51 | 18.29 | 1.17 |
| Palamau | 9.56 | 22.50 | 23.02 | 1.18 |
| Ranchi | 1.46 | 5.40 | 41.44 | 1.06 |
| Singhbhum | 5.62 | 4.20 | 30.58 | 1.03 |

The above table shows that the tribal districts have less than 10 per cent of crop areas irrigated. Only Palamau and Dhanbad had a higher percentage. The districts of Ranchi and Singhbhum which have the highest concentration of tribal population had merely 4.20 per cent and 5.40 per cent irrigated crop area respectively.

The agriculture of the tribals is characterized by:

1. Fragmentation of lands,
2. Land alienation and
3. Excessive pressure of population.

These negative factors get a further fillip due to lack of irrigation facilities and poor and impoverished agricultural workers.

### 3. Employment Opportunities in Mining and Manufacturing Industry

Major mining operations in the state are located in the tribal districts. The districts of Jharkhand have large deposits of coal, iron-ore, mica, copper, limestone, kyrite, bauxite etc. Only in coal, iron-ore and limestone mines, the mining operations and workers are well organized. The employment opportunities in other mining areas are not only limited but also the unscrupulous mining contractors exploit the workers to the maximum extent possible. The worst victims of this exploitation are the tribals.

The situation is similar in the industrial sector also where the tribal labor are not organized and they have not benefited by the establishment of large industrial projects in Jharkhand.

### 4. Urbanization and Rural-Urban Breakup

Urbanization is closely associated with industrialization. The decline of the tribal people in the urban areas of the new state of Jharkhand is on account of lower employment opportunities to them in growing towns and cities. Setting up of big capital-intensive units in the region has caused heavy out-migration of the tribal people to distant areas as their lands have been acquired for establishing large projects. This has reduced the tribal population to a minority in several districts of Jharkhand. In the rural areas also, the percentage of tribal population to the total rural population has gone down. Tribals have also suffered at the hands of the non-tribal landlords and moneylenders who have usurped tribal lands in urban areas.

Chotanagpur plateau in Jharkhand which is part of the great gneissic-schistose plateau of peninsular India, has one of the largest concentration of the tribals in the country. Besides being rich in mineral resources, the 600 meters high Chotanagpur plateau is covered with thick forests which has long sustained the fragile economies of the tribals.

**Panchayati Raj Institutions in Scheduled Areas**

Article 243(M)(1) of the Constitution (73rd amendment) Act 1992 says: "Nothing in this part shall apply to the Scheduled areas referred to in clause (1) and the tribal areas referred to in clause (2) of Article 244"

Article 243(M)(1) of the Act provides:

"Parliament may by law, extend the provisions of this Part to the Scheduled areas and the tribal areas referred to in clause (1) Subject to such exceptions and modifications as may be specified in such law, and no such law shall be deemed to be an amendment of this constitution for the purpose of Article 368."

After the Bhuria Committee recommendations, a bill was introduced in the Parliament and passed on December 19, 1996, which was subsequently assented to by the President on December 24, 1996. This Act called 'The Provisions of the Panchayats (extension to Scheduled Areas) Act 1996 (hereafter referred to as Extension Act)' has extended the Central Act to the Scheduled Areas mentioned under clause (1) of Article 244 of the Constitution. Since the states of A.P., Himachal Pradesh, Maharashtra, Gujarat, M.P., Jharkhand, Orissa and Rajasthan are covered under the Fifth Schedule Areas, it became mandatory on the part of these States to amend their existing panchayat Acts in consonance with the Extension Act within a year i.e. by December 24, 1997. All the above mentioned States have made their own enactments and Jharkhand was the last

State to do so in the year 2001.

The tribal communities in Jharkhand are traditionally well versed in the regulation, control and conduct of their domestic, religious, socio-economic, political and judicial affairs through the combined wisdom of their leaders and village councils. These customary laws, traditional and religious practices differ from tribe to tribe and vary from one village to another.

## References

1. Singh K.S., India's Communities, People of India, National Series Volumes IV to VI (OUP), 1998.
2. Beteille, Andre, "The Definition of Tribe". The Tribe, Caste and Religion in India by Romesh Thapar (ed.), The Macmillan Company of India Ltd., Meerut, 1977, pp. 7-14.
3. Ibid, pp.14.

# 11

# Impact of Tribal Development Programmes on the Condition of Tribals in Jharkhand

## General Situation

According to the provisional population figures as per 2001 census, Jharkhand has a population of 26.9 million. The population growth rate was 23.2 per cent which is much lower than the growth rate of Bihar (28.4 per cent) but much higher than the growth rate for the country as a whole (21.3 per cent). The population density per km is 338 which is less than half of the population density of Bihar (880). As compared with the previous decade, the state registered a slightly lower decadal growth rate (24.0 per cent in 1981-91 and 23.2 per cent in 1991-2001) but a higher population density (274 in 1991 and 338 in 2001). The sex ratio of 934 is close to the all-India average (933). The literacy rate for Jharkhand is 67.9 per cent for males, 39.4 per cent for females and 54.1 per cent for the total population.

According to the National Family, Health Survey (1998-99), 80 per cent of the population of Jharkhand lives in rural areas. Forty per cent of the population is below age 15, and only 3 per cent is age 65 and above.

Housing conditions and the standard of living of household members are generally poor in Jharkhand. 24 per cent of households have electricity compared with 60 per cent in India as a whole. Only one third of the households are within 15 minutes from a safe water supply. Only 14 per cent have piped drinking water.

The disparity in school attendance by sex grows with increasing age of children. While 64 per cent of children age 6-14 are attending school (71 per cent boys and 56 per cent girls), at age 15-17, 64 per cent boys attend school compared with 42 per cent girls.[1]

The economic condition of the tribals in Jharkhand is generally bad. They mostly depend on agriculture which operates on the traditional practices of farming. In spite of efforts by the Missionaries, illiteracy is rampant except for a few oasis like Ranchi and Jamshedpur which have good schools and colleges. Ranchi also has a University, while B.I.T. Mesra near Ranchi is a deemed university. Only one-third of the total area of Chotanagpur is cropped. The cultivable land of this region per head is perhaps one of the smallest units in the agricultural economy of the country. It has been pointed out that in Chotanagpur over 80 per cent of the holding is less than five acres. This indicates that the number of small and marginal farmers is much higher in comparison to All India percentage. The cultivation mainly depends on rainfall.

The Chotanagpur Division contains 69.25 per cent and Santhal Parganas 23.41 per cent of the total tribal population of the state. The highest concentration of tribal people is noticed in Ranchi district; it is inhabited by 30.75 per cent of the tribal population of the state. Further, the tribal males account for nearly 57 per cent and tribal females about 59 per cent of their respective total population in this district. Tribal females outnumber males in Ranchi district. The tribal female population is mostly rural. In Ranchi, only 3.79 per cent tribal females live in urban areas. This low position does not confirm to the popular image of Ranchi as an industrialized city. It suggests, on the other hand that the industrialization- the key to modernization in the Chotanagpur region- has not made any significant impact on the area beyond the fast growing city of Ranchi.

The Indian census defines a worker as a "person whose main activity is participation in any economically productive work by his physical or mental activity. Work involves not only actual work but effective supervision and direction of work". The working population accounts for 55.76 per cent of the tribal males in the state, which means that 44.24 per cent are non-working. The percentage of working to the population of tribal males is the lowest in Ranchi district (53.66) which implies that the percentage of non-workers is the highest (46.34) in this district. This alarming picture of unemployment which has developed among the tribal males of the district needs to be deeply probed by social scientists.

The Indian census has grouped major occupations in ten sectors of employment i.e. cultivation; agricultural labour; livestock; rearing, forestry and fishing, hunting, plantations, orchards etc; mining and quarrying; household industry; other than household industry; construction; trade and lastly the other services. The first four sectors of employment i.e. cultivation; agricultural labour; livestock; rearing, forestry and fishing, hunting, plantations, orchards etc and mining and quarrying may be designated as the primary occupations. The next three sectors of employment i.e. household industry; other than household industry and construction constitutes the secondary occupations. The third category is the tertiary occupation which includes the last three remaining sectors of employment i.e. trade and commerce, transport, storage and other services. These are the sources of livelihood of both tribal and non-tribal people of the region. The tribal people of Jharkhand are, therefore, engaged in all these occupations as well as many other petty activities which are included in the category of "other services".

The most important source of livelihood of the tribes of Jharkhand is cultivation. For the state as a whole, 67.52 per cent of the working tribal males and 39.34 per cent of the females derive their livelihood from this source alone. In Ranchi district, 74.10 per cent of their working males and 51.62 per cent of the females depend on cultivation for their livelihood. This is higher than the other districts of Chotanagpur but slightly less than that of the Santhal Parganas.

Nearly half (50.91 per cent) of the working tribal females in Jharkhand work as agriculture labour, whereas it is only 22.42 per cent in case of the working male population. In effect, about 90 per cent of the tribal families of Ranchi are either engaged in cultivation of their own or work as agricultural labourers on the field of others.

In view of the above discussion, the administration of the tribal development programs in Jharkhand assumes great importance, because the TSP strategy lays greater emphasis on proper implementation of the income generation schemes and development of infrastructures in the region. In this regard, Article 164 of the Constitution is significant, articulating as it does special responsibility of the State for the welfare and development of the tribal population.

Now that the scenario has changed and a new State has been formed, the government has to concentrate on the following issues and also ensure participation of the common tribals in planning and execution processes for the development of its inhabitants. The issues are:

1. Land alienated from them should be restored speedily.
2. Tackle the problems of indebtedness and moneylenders.
3. Problem of education and literacy.
4. Use of indigenous raw material through cottage and small industry.
5. Availability of irrigation, power, seeds and fertilizers for agriculture.
6. Availability of employment and promotion of self-employment measures.
7. Proper utilization of the natural resources and its marketing.
8. Improvement of health conditions and drinking water needs of the tribals.

According to Statistics collected in Sept 1994, Bihar's share in All India Production of Principal Minerals was 14.6

per cent which was highest in the country whereas the people living in these areas were the tribals who were facing difficulty in even getting two square meals a day. The issue of poverty and development is therefore of primary concern to the Indian policy makers. Failure to improve the lot of tribals in Jharkhand so far, has been the result of the complex inter-play of economic and political forces and the maladies in the administrative machinery.

Almost all the big industries like TISCO, TELCO, Tinplate, HEC, Bokaro Steel etc. are based in cities like Jamshedpur, Adityapur, Chaibasa, Ghatsila, Chakardharpur, Ranchi, Bokaro and Dhanbad. This has resulted in displacement of tribal people from their homeland without providing re-settlement services and adequate compensation.

The major mining centers also fall within Jharkhand. The iron ore, copper, mica, limestone, kyanite, bauxite, uranium, asbestos, manganese etc. are the major minerals besides coal.

Due to large-scale industrialization in the tribal area around Hatia and Ranchi, there has been large-scale socio-cultural disintegration of pre-existing culture. It has been established that this large scale industrialization is without much conscious effort to benefit the local tribal and semi-tribal communities. It has resulted in social disruption and the tribals have been adversely affected. The result to the uprooted tribals is loss of traditional occupation, land, house, traditional way of life and unemployment, making them compete with the migrants in the local markets. They form the fifth category and their frustrations result in unrest and agitation in the tribal areas. The natural wealth of this area contrasts vividly with the desperate poverty of the people who inhabit it. They have a distinct culture and identity which they are determined to preserve. Further, their identity and culture is rooted to their land and they are sensitive towards it.

In Jharkhand, the tribals are fast losing content of their traditional autonomous system of tribal administration like in Daimn-I-Koh in Santhal Parganas and Kolhan in

Singhbhum granted to them hundreds of years ago. The Panchayati Raj system has also created some complications with the adhyaksha of Zila Parishad emerging as co-sharer of powers with the deputy-commissioner.

The Chotanagpur Tenancy Act 1908 came into force from 11 November 1908. However it was not an unqualified success, particularly in its provisions about transfers in Ryoti holdings. Its chief success was that it gave the raiyats a greater security of tenure as against their landlords than they had previously.

There have been several amendments in the Chotanagpur Tenancy Act. In the year 1921-22, the Tana Bhagats under the influence of the non-cooperation movement adopted an attitude that was antagonistic to landlords and distrustful of government leading to non-payment of rent.

After independence, the Land Reforms Act was enacted in 1950 which ended the permanent settlement made in 1793 by Lord Cornwallis and established a direct link between the state and the tenants. Provision was made in the Bihar Land reforms (Amendment) Act, 1953 for taking over all estates and tenures within a particular area by issue of a single notification. Thus the entire intermediary interests except the Mundari Khuntkatti tenancy within the meaning of Chotanagpur Tenancy Act, 1908 and the Bhuinhari tenure were vested in the state.

**Tribal Development in Jharkhand**

The tribal sub-plan area in Jharkhand comprises of 112 blocks. To give a boost to development, 14 integrated tribal development projects were conceived. For the achievement of their goals, the priority has been given to land, agriculture and forests. Other programs include education and power projects, social welfare, education, health and rural development.

During the Sixth Five year plan, Modified Area Development Approach (MADA) was adopted to cover small pockets of tribal concentration having 10,000 population. In this, 50 per cent or more were to be tribals. At present 48

MADA pockets comprising of 484 villages in Jharkhand has been taken up for development. Under MADA, programs concerning agriculture, land reforms, minor irrigation, drinking water, animal husbandry, forestry, education, cooperatives, fishery and cottage industry are implemented.

The Tribes of Jharkhand are predominantly rural in character with 93 per cent living in the rural areas. Therefore the development intervention invariably has to be rural oriented.

According to the estimation of the National Commission for Scheduled Castes and Scheduled Tribes about 85 per cent tribal population of Jharkhand is compelled to live below the poverty line. The sizable tribal population is in want of basic amenities of life like safe drinking water, nutritive food, education, medical care and adequate housing. It is therefore essential that any strategy of tribal development in Jharkhand should provide for these essential amenities to every tribal individual.

The best measure of tribal development is the change in the quality of life of the tribal community. It is also important to have comprehensive time bound plans of tribal development but its success will depend largely on the extent of the involvement of the tribal people themselves. Experience of the working of the Panchayati Raj institutions has shown that the Gram Sabhas have not been successful in achieving their goals due to lack of public participation and proper guidance by the government officials. Another result of this has been that the tribal development programs so far implemented have had only partial success.

This therefore calls for measures to introduce comprehensive planning in all the integrated tribal development areas of Jharkhand. Needs of the local people and their economy should get the highest priority. The Chotanagpur region is full of forests, therefore forest based economy is suitable for the region. To promote this concept emphasis should be given to sericulture, lac cultivation, pisciculture, dairy farming, animal husbandry and bee-keeping etc. This will engage tribals in their traditional occupations leading to income generation which will help them in crossing the poverty line. The tribal should also have full right on minor forest produce. They should be given a participation in the marketing of their produce through the cooperatives.

Presently the tribals in Jharkhand have an average income of Rs. 250-300 per capita per month and quite a good number of them are in debt. To improve this, attention is to be focused on their educational development, skill promotion and socio-economic conditions. A positive step would be to encourage the traditional craft and forest based industries. This will provide employment and also bring economic stability.

Tribal areas of Jharkhand are potentially rich in minor forest produce items like Kendu leaf, sal seed, mahua, kusum, kranj, plas, harra, bahera, amla, neem, honey and wax, lac, gum, tamarind and mahua flowers.

Collection, processing and marketing of MFPs have a direct bearing on the income of the tribals living in that region. Presently, the TCDC and the forest development corporations are selling most of the MFP items without processing, either through forward sale basis or through tender basis. Thus most of the MFPs are exported from the tribal areas in raw form which does not give a good price to the collectors of these MFPs. There is immense need of first stage processing of MFPs and value addition at the tribal household level. Forest based industries, therefore, should be located in the tribal areas for generating employment.

## Education

Education like other resource base leads one to power. Power is concevied as the ability to control resources both physical and human to enhance one's own interest. The role of education in pre-democratic era was to work under social stratification which in turn collaborated with a non-democratic State. Now, there has been a complete change with the State taking up primary education as a basic task and the right to education becoming a fundamental right.

In the tribal sub-plan area of Jharkhand, there are 45 (+2) schools. Further, in the whole state, there are five hundred nine nationalised high schools and twenty three Government High Schools, imparting secondary education.

But on analysis of data from the 1991 census, it has been found that only 9 per cent blocks in Jharkhand have a literacy rate of 31 per cent or more. In Santhal Parganas division, out of 42 blocks, only one block has a literacy rate of this level. Even in south Chotanagpur area where educational activities increased due to missionaries, only 13 block out of 100 have this literacy level. Majority of the tribals (76 per cent) never get enrolled at a school and those who do get enrolled, drop-out of the school later. In the survey, it was found that out of 237 students enrolled only 111 attended the classes and 123 of them discontinued study by the end of the school. The enrollment of tribal children is adversely affected by low parental education, occupation and socio-economic conditions of their families.

**Health**

The National Family Health Survey in 1993 conducted by the International Institute of Population Sciences, Mumbai had collected health related data of the tribals in Jharkhand. This include IMR, U5MR, antenatal care, pregnant women receiving tetanus injections and use of iron tablets etc. It has been found that the STs have higher rates of IMR, U5MR, as compared with the general population. Majority of the ST women (79 per cent) do not get antenatal care and 82 per cent do not receive tetanus injection during pregnancy. Similarly, majority of ST women (82 per cent) do not receive iron tablets. Majority of ST children (57 per cent) do not receive any immunization and are malnourished as measured by weight for age (62 per cent) and height for age (63 per cent). The conclusion is that the health condition of the tribals of Jharkhand is very low because of their illiteracy, poverty, rural background and non-access to health facilities.

The second National Family Health Survey (NFHS-2) conducted in 1998-99, provides information on fertility, mortality, family planning and other important aspects of health, nutrition and health care in Jharkhand.

This report says that most households in Jharkhand

(70 per cent) use private doctors or private hospitals or clinics for treatment when a family member is ill. Only 19 per cent normally use the public medical sector.

NFHS-2 has also collected information on selected lifestyle indicators for household members. According to household respondents, 17 per cent of adult men and 3 per cent of adult women smoke, 29 per cent of adult men and 12 per cent of adult women drink alcohol, and 49 per cent of adult men and 11 per cent of adult women chew paan masala or tabacoo.[2]

## Agriculture

Despite being endowed with rich minerals, the economy of Jharkhand is predominantly agricultural with 71 per cent of its population being dependent on it for its livelihood with 43 per cent of the income being obtained from agriculture. Agriculture in this region is characterized by low productivity and stagnated growth. The region has suffered due to low investment in the rural infrastructure like irrigation, rural roads, rural electrification and market improvement etc. A large portion of its plateau region has undulating land surface causing problems of social erosion. About 60 per cent of the cultivable area is tand land and the remaining 40 per cent is don land. Paddy is the major crop with 61 per cent of the total crop area. The other crops are maize, marua and wheat. Pulses cover 7 per cent of the crop area. The yields of almost all crops are low in the Jharkhand region as compared to the national average.

The reason of this backwardness is the small increase in the use of modern inputs like HYV seeds, fertilizer, pesticides and farm implements. There is also dearth of irrigation facility in the region as the net irrigated area formed only 7.68 per cent of the total net sown area. This compares very poorly with the national average of 31 per cent.

Due to its dependence on rainfall, agriculture is seasonal, concentrated from mid June to December. Only a small area which has the benefit of irrigation is brought under Rabi crops and vegetables. The farmworkers of this region also faced the problem of unemployment or underemployment in the off-season period and therefore migrate to other areas in search of jobs.

Despite these geo-physical conditions there exists a good potential of raising crop-yields and agricultural diversification in this region. This area has a ground water potential of 482 crore cubic meters per year but only 4.1 per cent of it has been exploited so far for irrigation. Presently, the farmers have mostly got dug-wells.

**Rural Credit**

Rural credit happens to be an important input for promoting growth and equity in the rural sector of the economy. Rural credit, however suffers from the twin problems of inadequacy and unsuitability. This problem is present in a more intense form in the tribal areas.

Formerly, Taccavi loan was given to farmers by the government but it suffered from several defects like delay in distribution and inadequate supervision. Government, took initiative in promoting credit-societies known as Primary agricultural cooperative credit society (pacs) in the non-tribal areas and large area multipurpose cooperative societies (LAMPS) in the tribal areas. In 1970-71 these societies met 20 per cent of the credit needs of rural India. In 1976, regional rural banks were established to provide credits to rural people. Most of these regional banks have now become sick.

Subsidised IRDP loan has been the most important form of credit in the rural areas of Jharkhand for the tribals with milch cattle and drought animals being the most sought after items of loan from the banks. It has been found that very few of the tribals have access to institutional or cooperative credit. Only 13 per cent of the tribals have taken loans from institutional sources.

**Land Alienation**

Land alienation is one of the most important issue in Jharkhand. The tribals have witnessed continued alienation and encroachment of their land both by the individuals and the government. The urbanization and industrialization in the area has resulted in considerable influx of outsiders, putting pressure on the land and the natural resources of the tribals living on the periphery of such urban centers.

The issue of tribal land alienation has attracted considerable attention in the past. Most of the illegal transfer of land takes place because of the widespread indebtedness among the tribals. After independence, the acquisition of land for public purpose has been the major factor responsible for tribal land alienation. The continued deforestation has also added to the agony of the tribals.

One study conducted by the Ministry of Rural Development (Deptt. of Land Reforms), Govt. of India in the late eighties on the problem, extent and remedies of the land alienation of the tribals of Chotanagpur and Santhal Parganas, showed that 18 per cent of the tribal families had alienated land in one form or the other. Sale (49.56 per cent), mortgages (35.11 per cent) and encroachment (4.89 per cent) were observed to be the major causes of alienation. The study also pointed out the dismal performance in the field of restoration of land to the tribals.[3]

Tribal land alienation can only be arrested with the proper implementation of the Chotanagpur Tenancy Act and the Santhal Parganas Tenancy Act as well as by having the social security measures for the tribals in the region. The silver lining is that the tribals have become more conscious and are fighting against land alienation. It is also worth noting that the Gram Sabhas under the new Panchayati Raj Act can play an important role in arresting land alienation.

**Land use**

The total land area in Jharkhand is around 7.70 million hectares, out of which around 2.39 million hectares is under cultivation which is approximately 22.54 per cent of the total area. The forest area is around 2.30 million hectares while barren non-agricultural land is around 0.55 million hectares, agricultural barren land is around 0.29 million hectares, tree and fruits are planted on 0.1 million hectares, fallow land account for 0.78 million hectares, current fallow land are 1.14 million hectares. Around 77.46 per cent of the area is not fit for cultivation either due to forests or other uses or being fallow land. Around 2.19 million hectares is rain-fed areas while irrigation is available in only 0.2 million hectares.

Forest happens to be a very important resource in the area. The area is very rich in bio-diversity with a large range of flora and fauna available in the area. The forest cover percentage varies from 11.27 per cent in Dumka to 43.67 per cent in Hazaribagh, 21 per cent in Ranchi, 28.87 per cent in Lohardaga, 15.05 per cent in Gumla, 22.06 per cent in East Singhbhum, 40.43 per cent in West Singhbhum and 43.23 per cent in Palamau.

However, there has been a continuous decrease in forest cover in recent past. This decline in forest has a serious implication for the tribals residing in the area. It has not only endangered their food security but also increased the drudgery of the people who collect the forest produce. Most of the tribals collect forest produce for their own consumption and very few of them sell it in the market. While 69.5 per cent of the tribals collect forest produce, 75.9 per cent of them consume it themselves and only 11.1 per cent of them sell it in the open market.

This region is also rich in mineral resources. It has substantial deposits of coal, bauxite, copper, iron-ore, dolomite, graphite and limestone etc. In 1993-94, the Jharkhand area contributed around 13.4 per cent of the mineral production in value terms.

**Economic condition**

Though the tribals of Jharkhand live in a resource abundant area, they suffer from economic deprivation of scarcity in the continued fall in their means of sustenance because of forest legislations, alienation of their land, development of substitutes for some of their products like lac and fragmentation of their land because of growth in their population. The new opportunities of improving their well being in the form of education and skill development, jobs and expansion of existing resources, are not available to most of them. Judged from any index of development, they are at the lowest ladder. They also suffer from various forms of exploitation.

The monthly per capita expenditure, which is an indicator of the well being of a person is very low among the tribals. 58 per cent of the tribals in Jharkhand are below poverty line and their monthly per capita expenditure has been found to be less than Rs.125 by the 44$^{th}$ round of the National Sample Survey. The condition of the Ho is the worse among them. 72 per cent of the Ho live below poverty line. They are followed by Santhals(68.8 per cent), Oraon (57.6 per cent) and Munda (50.5 per cent).

Most of the tribals who reside in rural areas have very poor living conditions. Though most of the tribals participate in economic activities, they do not have access to highly productive livelihood. So they remain poor, deprived and exploited.

Settled cultivation is the main occupation of tribals in Jharkhand as 49.4 per cent of them depend on it. Agriculture plantation labor is another important occupation. 25.3 per cent of the tribals are dependent on it. Very few of the tribals are engaged in primitive occupations like hunting, trapping and gathering of minor or major forest produce. Only 5 per cent of the tribals get their livelihood from such occupations. Livestock and poultry raising activity has attracted very few families. Only 1.7 per cent of the tribals depend on it for their livelihood.

Most of the tribals have some land. Only 3.4 per cent are landless. The incidence of landlessness is highest among the primitive tribes (7.9 per cent).

Most of the tribals are small and marginal land-holders. 57.4 per cent of them own 1 hectare or less land and 14.4 per cent have less than 0.2 hectares. Even these 57.4 per cent of the tribals own only 12.7 per cent of the land with 3.8 per cent of the large land holding tribals having more than 10 acres of land owning 24 per cent of the land. Most of them sell the product of their land directly to the consumer. Only

7.1 per cent sell their products to the traders. Only 3/5$^{th}$ of the vegetable production and 15 per cent of paddy is marketed. The variety of forest produce as well as livestock are sold in the village market.

Market has been a source of exploitation of the tribals. To mitigate it, the government started Tribal Cooperative Marketing Fedration of India (TRIFED) and encouraged the State Tribal Cooperative Development Corporations (TCDC) and other cooperatives to directly purchase minor forest produce from the sellers. The role of LAMPS in marketing inputs and outputs of tribals has been quite limited. Vegetable cooperatives and cooperatives for stone quarrying have met with only limited success. The outside traders continued to dominate the market in the tribal areas.

Access of tribals to PDS facility is also very low. Very few of them are able to get grains from the public distribution shops as these shops do not exist in remote areas.

**Special Central Assistance to Tribal Sub-plan**

The state government receives Special Central Assistance to the Tribal Sub-plan for the welfare of tribals. However, these funds are sometimes diverted for other purposes. The concerned departments fail to furnish the utilization report of the funds given earlier or identify the actual beneficiaries and it has been so admitted in the Bihar Tribal Sub-plan document of the year 1994-95 (p. XIV).

The government development programs have been broadly providing infrastructure like irrigation-minor, medium and left irrigation, giving wells at subsidized rate to tribals, distribution of subsidized seeds and fertilizers, giving assets and loan under IRDP, training under TRYSEM, houses under Indira Awas Yojana and schemes under JRY and employment assurance scheme. Presently, they have been merged in one scheme namely Swarn Jayanti Gramin Swarozgar Yojana. For the primitive tribes, special schemes have been initiated and efforts have been made to settle them by providing land and dwelling places. For this purpose Gair Mazrua government land has been settled with the landless at many places.

Most of the irrigation projects have remained incomplete for many years. However, wherever they have been completed, tribals and others have taken advantage of it and raised their production level. Majority of the beneficiaries of wells and pump sets have increased the cultivation of vegetables. However the beneficiaries looked dissatisfied in the mode of selection of beneficiaries, delay in sanction of loans and poor quality of the pump sets. It appears that the selection of beneficiaries as well as the choice of assets has not been done in a participative manner. The loans appear to have been forced upon the beneficiaries without consulting them and the subsidy has been shared by the block office, local leaders and the banks. The majority of tribals did not know about the ITDP schemes and in the absence of follow up by the officials, TRYSEM met only with moderate success as the training was given without assessing the absorption capacity of the vocations chosen.

**Role of NGOs**

The NGOs action programs have been more participative than the government programs. This was evident in the integrated development of adopted villages (KGVK, Rukka) and the training and skill development of tribals by the SRI, Ranchi besides the programs conducted by the Ramakrishna Mission. But the NGOs have a limited area coverage and their dependence on government funding hampers the continuity of the programs.

People's reaction to NGOs have been quite favourable and they feel that their performance has been good. As the NGOs work with people, they gain better confidence of the tribals.

**Traditional Social Institutions of Tribals of Jharkhand**

The tribals of Jharkhand have their traditional social institutions, consisting of village councils and inter- village councils. The different tribal groups have different names for the head of the village and inter- village councils. Manki-Munda system is prevalent among the Mundas. A cluster of villages make a parha and its chief is Manki. The Oraons, call him their Parha Raja. In Santhal Parganas, he is called

Manjhi.

The traditional tribal institutions share the following characteristics:

- They administer customary laws and settle inter-personal and inter-village disputes.
- The posts are hereditary.
- The women are excluded from the village councils.

The traditional institutions vary in their effectiveness. The Hos of Kolhan area have the most effective traditional institutions. In general, with the introduction of Panchayati Raj, the traditional institutions have weakened.[3]

**Panchayati Raj in Jharkhand**

The 73rd constitutional amendment together with the Extension to Scheduled Areas Act in 1996, is a landmark in the direction of the empowerment of the tribal people. Jharkhand Panchayati Raj Act 2001 paves the way for tribal self-rule.

The practice of tribal self-rule in India is nothing new. There are evidences of it in the form of traditional village administration and tribal socio-political system. Tribal system of government was disturbed by the Britishers. The changes initiated by them had a far-reaching impact on tribal social organization, economy and polity. The tribals of Jharkhand reacted to this interference in the form of violent rebellions and these struggles can be seen as aspects of their desire and aspirations for equality and liberty.

Tribal self-rule can become a reality if the Extension of Panchayats Act 1996 and the Jharkhand Panchayat Raj Act 2001 address the issues of land alienation, indebtedness, poverty, drinking, illiteracy, housing, deforestation, unemployment, migration, exploitation and industrialization etc. These Acts have many positive features in that the Gram Sabha has been made supreme and endowed with power to control water, minor minerals, minor forest produce, land alienation, drinking, indebtedness and marketing etc.

The provisions of the Panchayats (Extensions to the

Scheduled Areas) Act 1996 was enacted keeping in mind the distinct traditions and customs of the tribal people on one hand and their special needs and problems on the other. The Jharkhand Panchayat Raj Act was passed in 2001 to bring about confirmity with the provisions of the Extension Act of 1996. The number of total panchayats in Jharkhand is 3753. About 50 per cent of seats are reserved for STs in the Scheduled Areas. $1/3^{rd}$ of the seats is reserved for women in both tribal and non-tribal area but the new act of Jharkhand is faced with problems at two levels viz. the level of policy and the level of implementation.

When we compare Jharkhand Panchayati Raj Act 2001 with the provisions of the Panchayats Act 1996, there are many instances of the watering down of the spirit of self-rule. The spirit of the traditional tribal village organizations like the parha, Munda-Manki or Parganait is absent in the Act of 2001. There is also a limited space for participatory democracy in it though there is definitely a paradigm shift in the approach of the government towards safeguarding tribal interests through Gram Sabhas.

There are also problems for Gram Sabha not from outside but from within their own community like the tribal elite. This is aggravated because most of the tribals are illiterate and ignorant. They are not aware of their rights and duties. Hence, they are vulnerable to exploitation by their elite.

The tussle is also likely to take place between the politicians, officials and Gram Sabha for control over resources like minor forest produce, minerals, water and forest etc. and their management.

There are many positive elements in the Act of 2001. The Act endows Gram Sabha with powers to make its own plan and budget. In an ideal situation, the intervention of Gram Sabha should facilitate prosperity, progress, harmony and unity. But given the complexity of social relationships in a village where both tribal and non-tribals reside, it is going to be an uphill task to accomplish the objectives set out in the act.

To give special governmental protection to the tribals, the tribal areas have been covered by Fifth and Sixth

Schedules. The tribals of Jharkhand are covered by the Fifth Schedule where the Governor of the state is required to submit an annual report to the President of India on their welfare and development. Fifth Schedule also has relevance to the implementation of Panchayati Raj in Jharkhand state as the post of the head of the Panchayat will be reserved for the tribals. but there are six districts in Jharkhand which are non-scheduled areas and they will not be covered by this Act. These districts are Godda, Dhanbad, Bokaro, Girdih, Hazaribagh and Palamau. In these districts non-tribals will be heading the Panchayats. Increased tribal participation in the Panchayati Raj has occurred with the presence of large number of tribals in the various offices of the Panchayati Raj. No conflict or tension was either observed or reported between the traditional and the statuary Panchayat. Being capable of rendering certain positive services in the field of material benefit to the tribals, the Statuary Panchayats secured the cooperation of the tribals since its inception. The degree of this cooperation went on increasing slowly and gradually and never received a setback. The tribals now feel that the Statuary Panchayat has become popular due to its manifold developmental activities.

It has been observed in Ranchi district that the tribal Mukhiyas are clear about their role in developing their panchayats. They do understand the functions of Panchayats. The tribals now attach the same importance to their offices as to those of the village headman, parha Raja etc. This shows the increase in the level of their participation in the Panchayati Raj.

**Ranchi**

Ranchi originated as a small tribal town in 1834 and has attained its present size within a century and half. Before industrial development, the environs of Ranchi were endowed with attractive natural landscape. Ranchi has now become the center of political, administrative, educational and industrial functions and is the capital of the newly created state of Jharkhand.

Ranchi covers roughly an area of 55.24 sq.kms. It extends

from Kanke in the north, Hotwar in the east, Dhurwa in the south and Pandra in the west. It is part of the Chotanagpur plateau which resembles a tableland with a few inselbergs. The inselbergs locally called 'Tongaris' ranging in elevation from a few meters to over 200-300 meters from the plateau level are of two types :

1. The gneissic formations and
2. A softer earthly rock known as Khondalite.

In pre-Wilkinson period, the villages of Ranchi may have been an ordinary settlement inhabited predominantly by the Munda and Oraon tribes and depending on the surrounding agricultural lands and forests. The original settlement was Purani Ranchi, a hamlet at the base of the Ranchi hill which is still the most important landmark in the city. Formerly, Ranchi was administered from Chatra, a small town near Hazaribagh. Selection of Ranchi as a regional administrative center in 1934 was dictated by geographical and strategic considerations. Ranchi was raised to the status of the headquarters of a Deputy Commissioner in 1943. It became the headquarters of Chotanagpur Division in 1954 and also the summer capital of Bihar.[4] The district is dividend in two subdivisions namely Ranchi Sadar and Khunti with 11 and 9 Blocks respectively.

**Results of the Field Survey**

The detailed information was collected through interview schedules by talking directly to the beneficiary and by this method 51 ST beneficiaries belonging to seven (7) tolas of the two chosen Blocks of Ranchi district namely Murhu and Ormanjhi were contacted individually and the survey schedules were filled up in their presence. In all 25 households were chosen from each village following the procedure of simple random sampling.

In Guttigarha village of Murhu Block in Khunti sub-division of Ranchi district, an interactive session was also held where the villagers expressed their opinion freely and fearlessly. It is to be noted that there were no female beneficiaries under ITDP schemes in the seven tolas of the two Blocks surveyed and 76.47 per cent of the male beneficiaries were found literate as compared to 55.6 per cent literate beneficiaries (both male and female) found in Chakrata-Kalsi area of Dehradun district of Uttaranchal.

The main occupation of the people in the surveyed villages is agriculture and more than 96 per cent people are engaged in agriculature either as cultivators or as agricultural labourers. Thus development of agriculture, irrigation and animal husbandry is crucial to the overall development of the region.

The people who participated in the inter-active session complained about lack of irrigation and wanted food processing facilities in the area around Ranchi as it is known for its fruit and vegetable production. Development of horticulture is also urgently required.

Earlier in 1991, the IAS Officer-trainees of the Lal Bahadur Shastri National Academy of Administration, Mussoorie had visited some districts of Chotanagpur for village study purposes. They found that Land and Forest have been the twin pillars of tribal economy. The tribals have been the best reclaimers of land but the forest laws have been insensitive to their customs and traditions.[5]

The socio-economic survey of the fifty one (51) tribal households which was done in the month of Decvember 2002 in the Murhu and Ormanjhi tribal blocks of Ranchi district has corrborated this. All the beneficiaries turned out to be tribal males. There were no female beneficiaries in these villages and tolas.

Table 1 which is given below gives an idea of the total number of beneficiaries contacted during the field survey.

The important points which emerged out of the field study are given here,

They are :

(1) The educational status of Surveyed family members reveal that 76.47 per cent are literate and 32 per cent have read upto primary level, 27.45 per cent upto middle level and 17.64 per cent upto secondary level. This comapres favourably with the literacy rate of Jharkhand which is only 67.9 per cent for males.

| S.N. | Name of the Block | Name of village and Tola | Male benef-icia-ries | Female benef-icia-ries | Total no. of benef-iciaries | Remarks |
|---|---|---|---|---|---|---|
| 1. | Murhu | Gutigarha (Piritola) | 02 | Nil | 02 | During field survey, 25 Beneficiaries of village Gutigarha of Murhu Block were contacted. |
| 2. | Murhu | Gutigarha (Daugara) | 16 | Nil | 16 | During field survey, 26 Beneficiaries of village Rukka of Ormanjhi Block were contacted.The visits were done without prior notice. |
| 3. | Murhu | Gutigarha | 07 | Nil | 07 | |
| | | (Daugara) | | | | |
| 4. | Ormanjhi | Rukka | 02 | Nil | 02 | |
| | | Pahantoli) | | | | |
| 5. | Ormanjhi | Rukka (Rukka Seeya) | 02 | Nil | 02 | |
| 6. | Ormanjhi | Rukka (Rukka Tungri) | 16 | Nil | 16 | |
| 7. | Ormanjhi | Rukka | 05 | Nil | 05 | |
| 8. | Ormanjhi | Rukka (Mutha Toli) | 01 | Nil | 01 | |
| | | Total | 51 | Nil | 51 | 2 Blocks and 2 Villages conaining 7 Tolas |

(2) The crops grown are dependent on the rains. The irrigation network is very poor and the only source of irrigation are dug wells.

(3) Land holding of the average household is 1-2 hectares. All families have homestead land of their own.

(4) There is a trend of single crop subsistence farming.

Paddy is the chief crop grown on the 'Don' lands. In the 'Tanr' land millets and pulses are grown in rotation.

(5) Most of the tribals have some livestock. Nearly all of them have a bullock, some cows, hens, pig etc. Both the villages have also got tractors through group loan but while the tractor given to Guttigaraha village is being used for cultivation, the tractor in Rukka village is lying disused under a tree for want of some minor repairs.

(6) The collection and sale of minor forest produce is also a source of income for the tribals. They collect these MFPs and sell at the local 'hat' or bazar.

(7) There were no cases of land alienations in the villages visited as it was a predominantly tribal area. Gutigarha village of Murhu Block is inhabited mainly by Mundas and they have a village elder who acts as their leader and spokesman. The villagers meet occasionally in the village community hall and discuss matters of common interest.

(8) In Rukka village (Ormanjhi Block), there is the parha panchayat of Oraons which meets regularly and disposes of the matters brought before it. This customary body is still alive and throbbing inspite of the establishment of Panchayati Raj institutions in Ranchi district.

(9) Most of the tribals complained of grovernment apathy towards their plight. Many of them had received pump sets, improved varieties of seeds and fertilizer under the IRDP/ITDP programmes. Most of them know about these programmes and apply for loan and subsidy provided under these programmes.

(10) The benefits of extension work have reached the tribals in this area and some NGOs are also working in the area especially the one in Rukka village which is doing remarkable extension work in agriculture, horticulture and animal husbandry.

Table 2 shows the benefits of financial assistance given under the various schemes being run by the Government of India through the State governments and the assets created by the beneficiaries alongwith the suggestions given by them. The salient features of the this table are given here:

1. A total of 51 beneficiaries were surveyed and individually contacted during the field survey programme but there were no female beneficiaries in the villages visited and only the male beneficiaries were available.
2. Subsidy and loan provided by the government through banks have helped the beneficiaries and their incomes have increased though a few did not admit of any increase or were not able to give their monthly or annual income at the time of the interview.
3. Most of the tribal beneficaries in Guttigarha village had Bank pass books though many were not updated. The position was similar in Rukka village of Ormanjhi Block.
4. The visits of Block/Bank officials to the villages were few and far between. Many did not remember any such visit. Similar was the case of Animal Husbandry/ Agriculture department officials who rarely went to the villages.
5. The villagers are also not aware of the various programmes being run by the welfare or the Tribal welfare Department.

Tables 3 and 6 give the details of beneficiaries occupation wise. It shows that 47 out of 51 beneficiaries are engaged in the primary sector and only 4 (four) fall in the tertiary sector. There is no beneficiary who is engaged in the Secondary Sector. The classification of main workers by sectors (primary, secondary and tertiary) has been made on the basis of the 1991 census report classification. There are no female workers as mentioned in earlier pages.

Monthly per capita income varies from Rs. 150/- to Rs. 6,240/- among the tribals of Guttigarha village while in Rukka village, it varies from Rs. 200/- to Rs. 2000/.

Nobody was found engaged in the traditional art or craft. People either cultivated their land or worked on other's lands. Most of them also kept bullocks, cows, hens, pigs etc. Bee-keeping was attempted in Guttigarha village but some large insects attacked the bees and ate up the queen bee. So the programme was alandoned.

Tables 4, 5 and 7 show the Block wise literacy and education levels of the surveyed persons in the two Blocks. Out of 51 persons surveyed, 12 were illiterate, 16 had studied upto primary level and 14 had studied upto secondary level while 7 had passed the Matric examination while 2 were intermediate pass. The illiterates were evenly distributed in the two villages and those who had studied upto class V and above were also in the same proprtion.

Nobody has studied beyond intermediate level in these two villages and seven tolas which shows the backwardness of the area and the poverty of the residents of these villages and tolas.

Therefore, there is an urgent need to bring about an awakening about the benefits of educaton/literacy in the tribal areas of Ranchi district.

Table 8 gives the average monthly income and annual income of an illiterate beneficiary and a literate beneficary which is marginally more. Monthly income of an illiterate person comes to Rs. 926/- while that of a literate person is Rs. 1022/-.

All the persons interviewed were adult males. Significantly, education has a direct bearing on occupation and economic earnings.

Family size is also an important variable since it decides financial stress of households.

The tribals were asked about their views and suggestions about the development programmes being implemented by the Block/ITDP. There were demands for development of infrastructure items like making the village roads Pucca and also providing rural electrification. There were other demands like pump sets, irrigation wells and putting a lift in the irrigation well already constructed. As irrigation is the basic requirement for agriculture, there were also suggestions for providing canal irrigation and also lift irrigation particularly in the Rukka village of Ormanjhi Block. There were also demands for Indira Awas and opening of a middle school in village Rukka. A suggestion was also given for the opening of fruit and vegetable processing units in the area.

Low literacy level of these villages and low income has also led to people being engaged only in the primary sector. There is no business activity though from the suggestions received, it is apparent that people want to increase their income by diversifying their occupations like going for food processing work, handloom items or work in the tertiary sector etc. The lack of female beneficiaries is also a sad commentary on the efforts made by the Block/ITDP/MADA officals of Jharkhand and it compares unfavourably with that of Uttaranchal where among the total surveyed, one third were female beneficiaries.

## References

1. National Family Health Survey of Jharkhand State (NFHS-2), 1998-99, published by the International Institute for population sciences, Mumbai (February 2002), pp. 3-10.
2. *Ibid.*
3. Annual Report of the Ministry of Rural Development (Deptt. Of Land Reforms), Govt. of India, New Delhi, 2000.
4. Nadeem Hasnain – Tribal India Today, 1983, Harnam Publications, New Delhi, pp.73-114.
5. Report on Tribal and Forest question in Bihar (1991) prepared by Land Reforms Unit of Lal Bahadur Shastri National Academy of Adminitration, Mussoorie.

# 12

# Comparative Study of the Position of Tribals in Jharkhand and Uttaranchal

A Comparative study of the tribal beneficiaries in the above two States has been attempted here on the basis of important indicators like literacy, education, health, occupation in Primary, Secondary and Tertiary Sectors, success of Income generating Schemes of rural development and tribal development programmes being implemented through the five-year plans and development of infrastructure, the details of which are available in Chapters IX and XI.

The field study was first conducted in four blocks of Dehradun district in Uttaranchal namely Chakrata, Kalsi, Doiwala and Vikasnagar in June-July 2002. In December 2002, another field study was undertaken in the two Blocks of Ranchi district in Jharkhand namely Murhu and Ormanjhi.

In all seven villages in the four Blocks of Dehradun district were taken up for field survey while seven tolas in the two Blocks of Ranchi district were covered during the survey. The names of the villages, tolas and the number of persons covered during the field survey (both male and female) can be seen in Tables I relating to Uttaranchal and Jharkhand. In short, 63 persons were contacted during the field survey in Uttaranchal while 51 persons were covered during the field study in Jharkhand.

In Jharkhand, all the 51 beneficiaries were males while in Uttaranchal, 40 males and 23 females were contacted during the field study. In Uttaranchal, the age of beneficiaries varied from 18 years to 65 years and in Jharkhand, it varied from 21 years to 65 years.

The questionnaire which was filled up in the presence of the beneficiaries of IRDP/ITDP schemes gives interesting information and it can be seen at Table 2. The period in which the loan and subsidy was given to the tribal beneficiaries ranges from years 1996-97 to 2000-2001 in Uttaranchal and from the year 1984-85 to 2002-2003 in the case of Jharkhand.

In Jharkhand, the maximum amount given as individual loan is Rs. 28,660/- given to Shri Sukhlal Munda of Rukka village for house construction while the lowest is Rs. 2000/- given to Shri Bhaiya Ram Munda of Daugarha tola, Guttigarha village as agricultural loan. The maximum amount given as group loan is Rs. 3,25,000/- for the purchase of a tractor in both these villages. The difference is that while the tractor purchased by the beneficiaries of Guttigarha village is being used by them and also earning income, the tractor purchased in Rukka village is lying disused under a tree for want of some minor repair. The better position in Guttigarha vilage is due to the leadership of Shri Samu Munda who has a hold on the villagers and who takes active interest in helping his fellow villagers in taking benefit of the income generating programmes.

In Uttaranchal, the lowest amount of individual loan is Rs. 2500/- given to Smt. Kanchan Devi of Kalsi Bazar in Dehradun district for purchase of handloom machine while the highest amount given as loan comes to Rs. 22,000/- given to two beneficiaries each namely Shri Shasasku of Oli village in Chakrata Block and Shri Bhagwan Singh of Nagal Bulandawala in Doiwala Block. These loans were provided for construction of house. No group loans for tractor etc have been given in the four Blocks of Dehradun district probably due to the hilly terrain. Here small loans have been provided for purchase of donkeys, Rickshaws, cow, bulls, buffaloes, sewing machine, silk rearing, handloom, carpentary tools and petty business.

In Ranchi district loans have been given mostly for pump sets and house construction purposes with a few also getting finance for purchase of rickshaws, cows or for seeds and fertiliser. Though some of the beneficiaries in this district got assistance in the period 1984-85 to 1989-90, they were mostly for pump sets as irrigation is a crying need of the area. Those who got assistance between the years 1994-95 to 1998-99 also purchased pumsets. Those who got loan in the years 2001-2002 and 2002-2003 include loan for purchase of seed and fertiliser, though in earlier years, the predominant number belonged to those who purchased pump sets for irrigation.

The field survey in Jharkhand also threw up an interesting point that hard work and preservience helped the beneficiary to take good advantage of the financial assistance schemes and they could generate sufficient amount of money to repay the Bank loan and also give their family a better life. One such example is of Shri Ramay Munda of Guttigarha village who got a loan of Rs.14,800/- in the year 2002-2003 and was able to raise his income by Rs. 20,000/- in a year. This is because he possesses some skill in repair of pump sets and machines which he used to good advantage. This brings us to the need of the spread of education and vocational training among the poor tribals so that he/she becomes aware of the government programmes and takes a lead in getting his due.

In Uttaranchal, the beneficiaries belong to the years 1996-97 to 2001-2002 and belong to both genders as compared to Jharkhand where there are only male beneficiaries. Here also there are some success stories like the case of Shri Jaipal Singh of Lakhwar village who got a loan of Rs. 6000/- in the year 1996-97 and now has an income of Rs. 4000/- per month from running a dhaba. Among female beneficiaries also, the increase in income in one year has been quite good as is the case of Smt. Leela Devi of village Haripur Bias Nahri in Kalsi Block who got Rs. 6000/- in the year 2000-2001 and now has an income of Rs. 1200/- per month, thus netting an increase of Rs. 700/- per month by rearing two buffaloes.

There has been some benefit of income generating schemes in all cases as we find in the four blocks of Uttaranchal; an increase in the per capita income of Rs. 800/ per month in a period of four years while in Jharkhand, the maximum increase comes to Rs. 6240/-. But there are quite a few households whose per capita income is as low as Rs. 100/- per month only like the case of Shri Undar of village Shahpur in Vikasnagar Block of Dehradun district. In Jharkhand, the minimum per capita income was Rs. 150/ - per month in the case of Shri Samu Munda of Dongda Tola in Murhu Block.

An analysis of the help given under IRDP/ITDP schemes shows that in Uttaranchal, beneficiaries took loan for the purchase of cows, bullock, buffaloes, mules and donkeys while many in Doiwala Block took loan for Rickshaws. In fact the only graduate Buxa tribal in Doiwala Block has been forced to ply a Rickshaw as he did not get any other job. In Vikasnagar Block, many female beneficiaries have got loan for handloom machine (Khaddi) but they are lying disused. In Lakhwar village, loans given for dhaba and donkeys have earned good income. The ladies who got sewing machines in Kishanpur Grant village in Doiwala Block are also able to earn some money though it is quite meagre.

In Jharkhand also, there has been funding for diverse purposes but mostly relating to agriculture. While pump sets have been quite in demand, house construction is another activity for which loan is eagerly sought. Some persons have also taken loan for animal husbandry and seeds and fertilizer. There are also many persons who have not created any asset inspite of getting the loans. In fact, out of the 50 beneficiaries, as many as 15 persons i.e. 30 per cent of the total beneficiaries interviewed have not been able to create any asset. This is a sad state of affairs.

In contrast, out of the 63 beneficiaries in Uttaranchal, 61 had created some asset while 2 persons had not been able to do so. This comes to 3 per cent of the total beneficiaries. In this state, there have been both male and female beneficiaries and 56 per cent of them are literate while 44 per cent are illiterate.

In Jharkhand, all the beneficiaries were male and their literacy rate came to 76.47 per cent while 23.53 per cent were illiterate.

54 per cent of total workers in Uttaranchal were engaged in primary sector while 3 per cent were engaged in the secondary sector and 43 per cent in the tertiary sector. In Jharkhand, 92 per cent were engaged in the primary sector, nil in the secondary sector and only 8 per cent in the tertiary sector. These figures speak for themselves and reflect the state of the economy of the respective regions.

During the PRA exercises (Participatory Rural Appraisal) done at the respective villages and also during the individual interaction with the beneficiaries, many suggestions were given by them which are summarised as follows:

**Uttaranchal**

1. Loans (by the Government and the Banks) should be provided at low rates of interest (4 per cent).
2. Amount of loan should be increased as it was insufficient for the purchase of two donkeys or two cows or buffaloes.
3. In Kalsi Block, the handlooms were lying unused due to shortage of raw materials. Hence it should be provided by the government at cheaper rates.
4. Many people who had taken loans in earlier years wanted fresh loans to increase their business.
5. In Chakrata Block, many tribals were not provided loan inspite of sanction and the matter was lying unattended between the Bank and the Block. After it was pointed out to the higher authorities, the loan amounts were released, but after a lapse of one year.
6. Loans should be given for purchase of livestock, like cow, buffalo, goat etc. 19 per cent beneficaries in Dehradun district asked for it.

**Jharkhand**

1. Villages should be electrified.
2. Irrigation should be provided to the fields through canal/ lift irrigation.

3. Indira Awas (Housing loan) be provided to those who do not have a house.
4. Pucca road should be built to connect the tolas. Roads should be repaired.
5. Pumsets should be energised.
6. More loan for purchase of tools and implements.
7. Construction of irrigation wells (15' diameter).
8. Pass books should be issued by Banks.
9. Middle school should be opened in the village.
10. Processing units (for fruits and vegetables) should be started.
11. Government programmes should be properly implemented and monitored.

The suggestions given by the beneficiaries in these newly formed states give an idea of the requirements and aspirations of the tribal people residing there. While in Uttaranchal, the economy of a hill area compels them to ask for smaller things like livestock, petty business etc, the tribals of Ranchi district being nearer to a big city like Ranchi demand development of infrastructure like roads, electricity, irrigation, food processing industries besides housing. Since everybody has some land and depends on agriculture, the demand for pumpsets and irrigation wells can be better understood.

## Blockwise and Genderwise Comparision of Sectoral Beneficiaries of both the States (Uttaranchal and Jharkhand)

### *Uttaranchal (Dehradun District)*

According to sectoral classification made by the Census of India 1991, there are three main occupations viz. (i) Primary Sector, (ii) Secondary Sector and (iii) Tertiary Sector. In the two hilly Blocks of Uttranchal namely Kalsi and Chakrata, there is predominance of the Agricultural sector or Primary sector i.e. Agriculture and Animal Husbandry. There are a total 17 (27 per cent) beneficiaries involved in it out of 63 (100 per cent) total beneficiaries, of which 9 (14.28 per cent) beneficiaries are male and 8 (13 per cent) are female.

In the two Blocks namely Doiwala and Vikasnagar, a total of 16 (25.39 per cent) beneficiaries; 7 males (11.11 per cent) and 9 females (14.28 per cent) are engaged in Primarv Sector.

When we combine the beneficiaries of all the 4 Blocks of Uttaranchal namely (i) Kalsi, (ii) Chakrata, (iii) Doiwala, (iv) Vikasnagar, then the total comes to 16 Male beneficiaires and 17 female beneficiaries who are involved in the Primary Sector or Agricultural Sector.

In Secondary Sector only 02 (3.17 per cent) beneficiaries are involved in Handloom work, who are all male. There are no female beneficiaries in this sector.

The Tertiary sector is further sub-divided in categories such as (a) Shopkeeper, (b) Carpentry, (c) Small Hotel (Dhaba), (d) Mule rearing, (e) Domestic work, (f) Tailoring, (g) Anganwadi helper, (h) Road labour, (i) Road Mistry etc.

There are a total 15 (24 per cent) male and 02 female (3.17 per cent) beneficiaires in this sector making a total 17 (27 per cent) male and female beneficiaries.

There are a few beneficiaries who are engaged in both the sectors (having two occupations) i.e. Agriculture in Primary Sector and Shopkeeping (Parchoon shop) in Tertiary sector.

There are altogether 39 male beneficiaries (62 per cent) and 24 female beneficiaries (38 per cent) who are engaged in different economic activities in the four blocks of Dehradun district.

***Jharkhand (Ranchi District)***

In the two Blocks of Murhu and Ormanjhi, 51 beneficiares have been occupationally divided in the three main sectors of occupation (a) Primary Sector, (b) Secondary Sector and (c) Tertiary Sector in the same way as earlier done in the case of Uttranchal.

- The analysis shows that 47 (75 per cent) beneficiaries are involved in Primary or Agricultural sector out of which

24 (47.5 per cent) belong to Murhu Block and 23 (45.9 per cent) beneficiaries belong to Ormanjhi Block.

- There are no female beneficiaries and nobody is engaged in activities relating to Secondary Sector.
- There is only 1 (2 per cent) beneficiary in Tertiary Sector in Murhu Block. The beneficiaries in this Block are of Munda tribe.
- There are 26 beneficiaries (51 per cent) in Ormanjhi Block but there is no female (0 per cent) beneficiary.
- There are only 3 (6 per cent) beneficiaries in the Tertiary Sector mainly working as tractor driver or in other service. Here also there is no (0 per cent) female beneficiary.

When we combine all these sectors and both the Blocks of Murhu and Ormanjhi, we find that 47 male (75 per cent) beneficiaries are engaged in Agriculture or Primary Sector as compared to 39 (62 per cent) involved in Primary or Agricultural Sector in Uttaranchal.

This clearly indicates that in Jharkhand 13 per cent more tribal male beneficiaries are engaged in Primary Sector. Secondly, Secondary sector has been completely neglected.

Jharkhand's share in tertiary sector is also low as compared to Uttaranchal. Here only 4 (8 per cent) out of 51 (100 per cent) total beneficiaries are engaged in Tertiary sector, whereas in the four Blocks of Uttaranchal, there are 28 (44.44 per cent) beneficiaries out of the total 63 (100 per cent) male and female beneficiaries who were involved in the Tertiary sector. This shows that agriculture is the main occupation in Jharkhand while people in Uttranchal are engaged in other occupations also besides agriculture.

Occupational details of the tribal beneficiaries in Jharkhand which is exclusively male and mainly agricultural, show that the other occupations of Primary sector do not hold much appeal such as, Animal husbandry, horticulture and Sericulture etc which are more favoured in Uttranchal's tribal blocks.

In Uttranchal where 28 (44.44 per cent) male and female tribal beneficiaries are involved in tertiary sector, the total number of occupations are thirteen (13), whereas there are only three (3) activities in Jharkhand. This indicates that the Tertiary sector is more developed in Uttaranchal. One reason can be that in Doiwala Block there are 12 (19.4 per cent) beneficiaries {10 male (16 per cent) and 2 female (3.17 per cent)} who are land less and therefore they go for occupations included in the Tertiary Sector. On the other hand most of the tribal beneficiaries in Jharkhand have got some land for cultivation and therefore prefer to engage in agriculture.

It is also observed in both the States of Uttranchal and Jharkhand that Government schemes and programmes which have been made for the social and economic development of STs are not being properly implemented at grassroot level. It is because community participation is minimal inspite of the introduction of "Panchayati Raj Institutions". The programmes have shown more impact wherever the local leaders have taken the lead like in Guttigarha village of Murhu Block in Jharkhand.

If Government agencies at Block level and Gram Panchayats at village level effectively inform the general masses about the benefits of Government schemes, the tribals can take benefit of them. Otherwise village people remain unaware of such programmes and become victim of the lethargy and insensitivity of the local tribal development administration.

If Panchayati Raj Institutions function properly, then the village people specially illiterate, STs/SCs and female beneficiaries can take more advantage of the various income generating schemes as well as other schemes for the development of infrastructure in tribal and Scheduled Areas.

# 13

# Observations, Conclusion and Suggestions

The approach to development of Scheduled Tribes was initially laid by the First Prime Minister of India in his 'Tribal Panchsheel' which found revalidation in the Dhebar Commission (1961) and Shilu Ao Committee (1969) reports.

The various plan documents have subsequently reviewed the performance of the tribal development programmes and they have highlighted three fields where performance has been found to be deficient. They are: inability on the part of the States to prepare project reports for integrated tribal developemnt projects (ITDPs), absence of coordination among different agencies engaged in the development and welfare programmes for the tribal and the non-participation of tribal representatives and traditional tribal institutions in the development and production sectors.

We talk of tribal development without spelling out what it means, particularly in the tribal context. In the first instance, we need to remind ourselves that the tribal communities have been living autonomously almost in isolation in remote far-flung areas of the country, mostly hills and forests. Their contact with outside world has been of recent origin dating back to a century or two. Each tribal community in the course of its separate autonomous existence, has developed its own economic systems, socio-political organisation, material culture, language etc. As such, we should accept the cardinal principle that each tribal society is unique in its make up. Presently, we find that the different tribal communities spread over the length and breadth of the country are in different stages of development and exhibit disparities in income, education and social conditions. Form this, one can draw the inference that the conventional socio-economic development process may suit the elite strata of the tribal communities, but may not be much helpful to the general mass of the tribal people. For example, technical education may be a prized attainment for a Mizo or Meena youth, but may not be attractive to a member of Shompen, Bonda or Birhor society.

It is also noteworthy that all the tribal communities do not live in environments of identical resource edowments. Some may be better placed but contemporaneously most live in impoverished degraded and sparse surroundings. As a result, they are deeply mired in penury and want.

Inadquacy of income and accumulated wealth leads to deprivation in quality of tribal life leading to poor education, poor health etc. The tribal people have the lowest average incomes and a larger population of people are in the lower income classes.

**Incidence and Intensity of Poverty**

Using the poverty line as consumption of Rs. 2,444/- per person per year, the assumption that for tribal people, income and consumption patterns coincide, the head count ratio is that 50 per cent of the tribal people are below the poverty level. This poverty index is based on calorie-intake and ignores shelter, clothing and medicines which are essential for survival. For other people, it is only 26 per cent.

**Literacy and Education**

For a better quality of life, knowledge, values, skills and attitudes are very important and education being a social resource, helps in reducing inequality.

The definition of a literate followed during the 1961, 1971 and 1981 census is as follows:

"A person who can both read and write with understanding in any language is to be taken as literate" The literacy rates given below have been worked out by

**Population and literates of Scheduled Tribes population 1961-1981 (India as a whole)**

| | | *Population* | | | *Literates* | | |
|---|---|---|---|---|---|---|---|
| | | *Persons* | *Males* | *Females* | *Persons* | *Males* | *Females* |
| 1961 | Total | 28,965,543 | 14,554,425 | 14,411,118 | 2,313,402 | 1,897,528 | 415,874 |
| | Rural | 28,199,882 | 14,151,058 | 14,048,824 | 2,143,657 | 1,775,993 | 367,664 |
| | Urban | 765,661 | 403,367 | 362,294 | 169,745 | 121,535 | 48,210 |
| 1971 | Total | 36,408,514 | 18,361,797 | 18,046,717 | 3,964,647 | 3,138,484 | 826,163 |
| | Rural | 35,128,288 | 17,687,622 | 17,440,666 | 3,600,010 | 2,891,116 | 708,894 |
| | Urban | 1,280,226 | 674,175 | 606,051 | 364,637 | 247,368 | 117,269 |
| 1981 | Total | 51,628,638 | 26,038,535 | 25,590,103 | 8,441,477 | 6,384,931 | 2,056,546 |
| | Rural | 48,427,604 | 24,364,350 | 24,063,254 | 7,221,458 | 5,588,070 | 1,639,388 |
| | Urban | 3,201,034 | 1,674,185 | 1,526,849 | 1,21,019 | 796,861 | 417,158 |

*Source* : Census of India Handbooks.

dividing literates by the population of the district, state or country.

The above table shows that sex differentials exist in literacy rates, but these are narrowing with the passage of time, as indicated by a rising trend in the ratio of the female literacy rate to the male literacy rate. During the two decades of 1961-1981, the literacy rate increased by 36 percentage points for the total ST population as agains 12-28 percentage points for the total population.

The Rural-Urban ratio also shows a slight movement towards urban areas. While in 1961, as many as 97.36 per cent of the total ST population lived in villages, their percentage declined marginally to 96.48 per cent in 1971 and it further moved down to 93.80 per cent in the 1981 census.[1]

Literacy among tribal people has increased at a slower rate with literacy among females increasing at a rate faster than males. However, effective literacy rates among tribals are low at 40.8 per cent as against 53.5 per cent of all Indians. The level of disparity is about 76.3 per cent. It has been estimated that non-attendance rate among tribals is higher as also the school discontinuance rate. There is also evidence to suggest that the percentage of tribal students completing beyond middle level school amd matriculation, is lower than that of all-India students.[2]

**Health Care**

The estimated percentage of tribal villages without adequate health care facilities is higher than that of other villages (Table 2.6). The immunisation rates (Table 2.7) for tribal mothers and tribal children (Table 2.8) are the lowest. The tables show that the quality of tribal life is still the poorest in the country. They lack nutritious food and are prone to debilitating diseases.[3]

**Tribal Development and Five year Plans**

The three main objectives of development, as envisaged by Michael Todaro, an eminent devlopment economist are:-

(i) the ability to provide the basic necessities of life,

**Table 2.6**

**Health care facilities by type of villages in Rural India 1994 (Percentage of Villages)**

| *Type of villages* | *Sub centre within village* | *No. of sub-centre Hospital with 5 Kms* | *Pharmacy within the village* | *Anganwadi within the village* |
|---|---|---|---|---|
| SC villages | 18.2 | 65.2 | 25.8 | 56.1 |
| ST villages | 11.3 | 75 | 12.5 | 48.8 |
| SC/ST villages | 25 | 60.4 | 31.3 | 52.5 |
| All villages | 21.5 | 58.1 | 28.5 | 52.8 |

*Source:* Estimated from data collected in NCAER Survey, 1994.

**Table 2.7**

**Percentage of perspective mothers immunised by social groups in Rural India, 1994**

| *Type of immunistion* | *SCs* | *STs* | *All* |
|---|---|---|---|
| T.T. immunisation | 52.5 | 39.4 | 53 |
| Iron tablets | 35 | 29.6 | 34.2 |
| B.P. Check ups | 24.3 | 12.8 | 26.6 |

*Source:* Estimated from data collected in NCAER, Survey 1994.

Table 2.8

**Percentage of children Aged 12-23 months immunised by social groups in Rural India, 1994**

| *Type of immunisation* | *SCs* | *STs* | *All* |
|---|---|---|---|
| DPT (3 doses) | 53.6 | 46.4 | 37.5 |
| Polio (3 doses) | 54.6 | 46.6 | 58.1 |
| BCG (1 dose) | 62.6 | 54.2 | 64.3 |
| Measles (1 dose) | 48.9 | 42.1 | 52.9 |
| All (8 doses) | 42.6 | 39.5 | 48.5 |

*Source: Estimated from data collected in NCAER Survey, 1994.*

(ii) to be a person with self-esteem, and

(iii) freedom of choice.

The development process, must therefore, aim at eliminating deprivation and restoring dignity and self-confidence in the tribal people. It should also ensure them command over the local resources.

It is noteworthy that since independence many high-powered committees have been formed to study the problems of the tribal people and several working groups have been set up by the planning commission as an exercise to the formulation of five year plans. In 2002 the government of India has also set up the second Scheduled Areas and Scheduled Tribes Commission under Article 339 (1) to study the problems of tribals and implementation of the tribal development programmes under the Chairmanship of Shri Dilip Singh Bhuria. The first such commission was set up in 1960 under the Chairmanship of Shri U.N. Dhebar.

The Central and State governments have allocated large funds for tribal development over the years so as to sustain their development through economic activities. But most of these programmes are not self-sustaining and if funding dries up, most of these programmes die a natural death. It has also been found that 80-85 per cent of the funds allocated for tribal development are actually spent on meeting the cost of administration of these programmes.[4]

The developmental programmes aim at achieving the twin objectives of (i) area development in terms of provision of essential infrastructure like irrigation facilities, communication, health, promotion of education, development of horticulture and soil conservation, strengthening rural credit delivery structures, rural electrification, drinking water supply etc, and (ii) economic upliftment of individual tribal families by providing them income-generating durable assets under the Integrated Rural Development Programme (IRDP), Integrated Tribal Development Programme (ITDP) supplemented by Special Central Assistance to Tribal Sub-plan and special programmes for the development of primitive tribal groups and various sectors of the state plan.

As mentioned in earlier chapters, the Constitution has given certain safeguards to those groups that are included in the list of Scheduled Tribes. The safeguards are of two types: (1) protective safeguards and (2) developmental safeguards. The protective safeguards are manifest in the reservation in educational institutions and posts and services for the Scheduled Tribes. These safeguards have helped the tribals to get admission in educational institutions, particularly in the technical and professional institutions. The reservations in services have benefited the tribals by helping them enter into government services. The reservations in Panchayati Raj institutions, State legislatures and Parliament have provided them with opportunities to raise the problems of the oppressed in these institutions of democracy.

The thrust of our argument is that the tribals today have covered a large distance with the help of planned development. There has been extension of education. There are facilities of irrigation in the tribal areas. A number of rural development programs have been initiated which have also enabled the tribals in income generation. The community beneficiary programs have provided infrastructure to the tribal villages. In fact, the planned development of the tribals consists of a package of benefits to raise their standard of living. The extension of educational facilities, transport, irrigation and the working of non-governmental organizations (NGOs) have gone a long way in creating an awakening among the tribal masses.

In tribal areas, food, fuel, fodder, water and other bio-mass play a crucial role in meeting daily survival needs. The environmental degradations in the tribal areas are the combination of the problems that have risen from low level of development, as well as impacts of recent industrial developments. Poverty is both a cause and effect of environmental degradation.

The economists make a distinction between growth and development. According to them, development is a gradual unfolding of evolution while growth is an increase in capital. When sociologists employ the term development, they generally refer to social development, social justice and humanism. Economists, imply quantitative progress, that is, increased capital for defining growth. In simple words, development is progressive and growth is quantitative. Amaratya Sen has analyzed the differentiation between economic development and economic growth in the following words:

"Growth is not the same thing as development and the difference between the two has been brought out by a number of recent contributions to development economics. But it can scarcely be denied that economic growth is one aspect of economic development."[5]

The term of reference in economic growth is invariably the GNP. The economic development refers to social factors like life expectancy, literacy, health, education etc as given in the World Development Reports and Human Development Index. Thus in a nutshell, the difference between development and growth are qualitative and quantitative. Actually, economic development is nothing but an expansion of people's entitlement and capabilities enhanced by the use of entitlements. Amaratya Sen has provided a definition of entitlement thus: "It refers to the bundle of commodities over any of which a person can establish command, by using the rules of acquirement that govern his circumstances."[6] The State or its institution provide entitlements to the people in the form of medical service, health, education, provident fund, maternity leave, pension etc. The development of tribals is also an entitlement to the tribals given by the Constitution. Viewed in this perspective, the growth of GNP per head is a simple version of the growth approach.

Development is a complex of many forces. It is well directed investment in various sectors. It is an arrangement in which economic and political power is redistributed and readjusted.

The experiments in development started with the community development programs in 1958. Thereafter came the Tribal Sub-plan area approach (1974) and Modified Area approach. Masses of tribal people have witnessed and in some respects, participated in the process of development. What is their comprehension of the perception of development? Susana Devalle has studied the problem in Jharkhand area and she says in her book 'Discourses of Ethnicity': "In the course of interviews, adivasis from across the political spectrum criticized the present pattern of development in Jharkhand. Development has variously been called 'civilization' and 'progress' and was not necessarily considered to be positive. In many instances, it was perceived as an autonomous force with as much of an 'evil' content as a plague that has befallen upon the adivasis. This view, was however, balanced with realistic remarks. For instance, 'we are victims of progress:' 'civilization has not been good for the tribes.' 50 lakhs of families have been uprooted in 33 years. Jharkhand is very important in minerals and forests. These big and industrial projects are colonial-oriented, exploitative, not for the benefit of common man; under-privileged people always take the trash of civilization and later on realize that they have lost 'civilization'.[7]

The above views of Devalle have also been corroborated by other anthropologists who have worked among the tribals of Jharkhand. S.Jones, for instance, remarked about the illusory nature of development in Jharkhand where industries have remained small modern non-tribal enclaves in the middle of large areas of rural, tribal underdevelopment.[8] The fact that development has not been translated into concrete benefits for the people of Jharkhand but has resulted in further pauperization and extraction of resources, has also been understood by the people of the area. This is evidenced by their rejection of several development schemes. Further, the development process has thrown up problems of gigantic dimensions in Uttaranchal. Unscientific exploitation of forests has given rise to movements like the 'Chipko' movement which is a manifestation of the simmering discontent of the people with the planning process as it functions in the hilly and tribal areas of the country. The ecosystem of the region has been endangered by deforestation for both commercial and non-commercial purposes.[9]

Similar is the conclusion of Jan Breman with reference to the villages of Surat in South Gujarat. He establishes that development has made the tribals migrants and paupers. There has started a process of de-peasantization. The entry of non-tribals in the tribal hinterland has made the tribals into subordinates. Actually, the result of development has made the tribals dependent upon the State and the non-tribals.[10] In Southwest Gujarat, most of the laborers and daily wage earners are tribals. Thus the old saying that the tribals are immobile has now become a thing of the past.

Despite a plethora of legislative measures, special safeguards and other developmental efforts, tribal rights in land and forest, reversion from peasantry class to labour, large scale displacement, increasing inequality and poverty, degraded social status, loss of identity and lack of confidence have emerged as baffling problems for the tribals as well as policy makers. Some Constitutional measures were undertaken earlier like the Fifth Schedule for the tribals of plain area and Sixth Schedule for North-eastern region besides granting them reservation in both the Parliament and State legislatures.

Pandit Nehru's 'Tribal Panchsheel' is rarely kept in view while formulating schemes and programs for the development of Scheduled Tribes. It is therefore, necessary to formulate a comprehensive tribal policy which will lay the guidelines for their integration with the mainstream, preservation of their way of life and promotion of their arts and crafts, their relationship with their land and the forests, their institutions of self-management, their displacement and rehabilitation under big projects etc, so that their assimilation and development could be smooth and keeping in with their culture.

Tribals do feel that the last 50 years of development strategy has created several problems like identity crisis and marginalization. What has been done to counter these feelings? The government and the planners have changed strategies in successive five year plans. We have come from CDB to TDB, TDA, ITDP, MADA and TSP (Tribal Sub-Plan).

Lately to provide control over resources and better planning for tribal development, the government has created separate states of Jharkhand, Uttaranchal and Chattisgarh.

The basic development strategy should be to provide all tribals food and shelter first. It can be a one point program- to strengthen their economy. Rest of the development will follow.

Secondly, other development programs could also utilize the knowledge available with the tribals and raw materials found in the area. For example, the food for work program can be used for constructing unmetalled road connecting each village to the metalled road. The houses should be built with the local raw materials, which can be repaired by them.

Lastly the strategy should have the flexibility to change according to the need and situation of the place. There cannot be one development program to suit all the tribals. The development policy and planning should follow the need strategy to be expressed through the Gram Sabhas, rather than being guided from the Central or State headquarters.

Today globalization has made the world smaller and the growing use of science and technology makes the process singular. All the Societies of the world are following this model. It is only the stages, which makes countries/ areas/ communities developed or underdeveloped.

Now emphasis is being laid on participatory management of development measures of the government. Attention is being given to generate more opportunities of employment, improve quality of life, to provide nutritive food to tribal children and mothers, minimize regional imbalances etc. It is planned to provide basic education, housing, health facilities and safe drinking water to everyone. The tribal people can now take part in self-governance through Panchayati Raj.

The World Development Report (2000-2001) with its focal theme on 'Attacking Poverty' recognizes three major strategies for removing poverty. They are promoting opportunity, facilitating empowerment and enhancing security for poor people as the key to reduce poverty.

Who are poor? They are the people who lack adequate food and shelter, who lack education and health, people who face extreme vulnerability to ill health, economic dislocation and natural disasters. In essence, one can define poor people as those who experience multiple deprivations. The Planning Commission in 1993 had attempted to define poverty on these lines and included education, health and nutrition as important indicators. Education is considered as an important opportunity for the development of human capital or human capabilities, the deprivation of which in itself, represents poverty. Further, the mutually reinforcing relationship between poverty of education and income poverty suggests that education, as a principal factor, can contribute to income poverty. Income poverty may pull children from out of the school system, thus denying them the opportunity of participating in school education, even at the basic level. In India, as per the latest records of the planning Commission (1999) more than one third of the country's population is still living below poverty line. Thus the connection between income, poverty and education becomes more significant.

Planning Commission has constituted a working group on the empowerment of Scheduled Tribes during Tenth Five year plan to review the existing approach, strategies, priorities etc and to suggest effective intra-sectoral convergence. One of the important items for review is the manner of utilization of Special Central Assistance to TSP and grant-in-aid under Article 275(1) of the Constitution. The present study also attempts to find out the benefits accruing out of these programs to the Scheduled Tribes in the newly created states of Jharkhand and Uttaranchal. On the basis of impressions gathered from the field study as well as the data collected from various sources, it has been found that there is need for a shift in approach in the process of empowerment of Scheduled Tribes and efforts should be made to create an environment which is conducive for them and enables them to lead a life of self-confidence with dignity. The approach towards empowering them should be holistic in nature so as to accomplish all round development of these weaker sections with an intra-sectoral approach with inputs both from the government and non-governmental organizations. Efforts should continue to extend all assistance to STs to ensure speedy socio-economic development through qualitative and quantitative efforts. The aim is to bring about equitable distribution of material goods and growth with social justice.

There is an urgent need to ensure effective implementation of funds earmarked under the SCA to TSP and Article 275(1) of the Constitution. It has been recommended by the Ministry of Tribal Affairs that funds under TSP should be put under a separate head in the State budget to be operated by the Department concerned with tribal welfare. In case of TSP funds of States/UTs, it should be used for integrated development of the tribal block under the supervision of Tribal Welfare Commissioner.

About 50 years back, the renowned expert on Tribal Affairs, Mr. Verrier Elwin, had mentioned in his autobiography the points which are necessary for tribal development. They are:

1. That their land should be guaranteed to them and that any further alienation of it to outsiders should be stopped.
2. That their rights in forests should be respected and that an entirely new attitude should be taken towards them by the forest authorities throughout India.
3. That the problem of indebtedness should be solved without delay, partly by legislation and partly by a great intensification of the cooperative movement and the availability of easy credit from official sources.
4. That the problem of industrialization of the tribal areas must be regarded much more seriously and that where the tribal people are dispossessed of their lands and settled elsewhere, intelligent and generous measures should be taken to compensate them.
5. That the long isolation of the tribes should come to an end, and they should be welcomed everywhere and on equal terms. It is necessary to avoid creating a sense of inferiority in the tribal people."[11]

The above issues and problems are crucial to the welfare

and development of Scheduled Tribes in India and their relevance has not diminished with the passage of time.

When we analyze the strategies of development of tribals in the last fifty years, we get the same result. The general population had developed a system of social mobility, which allowed majority of Indian communities to change. But the 582 odd tribal communities have continued with their lives in socio-economic independence, each one sticking to their traditions. This was an additional challenge before the unified development process created after independence.

To begin with, the area/community has to be provided with the facilities of road, electricity, irrigation, proper housing and sanitation, basic education and health measures. It is also a fact that the approach to tribal development has been criticized on the line of multiplicity of schemes. The life-patterns of the tribals did not allow them to participate in all the schemes together rather it had worked as barrier.

Further the development process is a part of the welfare of the people depending on subsidies, as the tribal people's poverty did not allow them to contribute any share. This created the wrong impression in that the tribals considered the house, cattle etc. provided by the government not as their property and thus did not take proper care of these assets.

Planned change is an ongoing process, requiring constant attention, desire, stamina and acceptability. There is no optimum, no limit of development. As per our understanding, the tribal villages have not been able to take part in the process of development. The two basic parameters of the quality of life- health and education remain abysmal even after fifty years of planning. The majority of tribals have still not been able to grasp the benefits of education. The human development indices of the STs are still at a much lower level and the gap vis-à-vis the others is on increase. Tribal economic development will be a reality if the desire for change is felt as the need of the entire community. Here it may be relevant to quote from the India Development Report, 2002 which says that even after fifty years of independence, a large number of Indians are illiterate. In fact, with 321 million illiterates as per the 2001 census, the number of illiterates today exceeds the population of the country at independence. The main problem with primary schooling is high drop-out rates and teacher accountability. High drop-out rate reflects on the poor quality of schools because there is evidence that there is demand for schooling. Again health is important for welfare. The health policy goals should be to : (a) reduce infant mortality from 72 per 1000 live births to the level in Kerala that is 12 per 1000 live births, over a period of five years, and (b) reduce all-India child mortality (age1-5) to keral a level.

To attain these goals, we need to do the following :

1. Expand programme of immunisation and ante-natal care for pregnant mothers to attain 90 per cent coverage.
2. Ensure in five years immunisation of all infants and children of age 1-2 years.
3. Expand the coverage of Integrated Child Development Services (ICDS) and improve it as per the Tamilnadu Integrated Nutrition Programme phase II.
4. Mobilise NGOs and media in a national campaign.
5. Assure supply of clean drinking water both in urban and rural areas.[12]

**Conclusion**

We may conclude by quoting from the evaluation of the tribal development programs made by the Working Group for the empowerment of the Scheduled Tribes in Tenth Five year plan (2001), which says that development has suffered at three levels:

(a) Policy

(b) Implementation; and

(c) Recruitment and training of personnel.[13]

Therefore, any strategy for the development of the tribals should aim at:

(a) Removal of disparities between one tribal group and

another, and

(b) Minimizing the gap between the tribals and the non-tribals.[14]

Our tribal development programs, so far, have been largely target-oriented plans that look only into the disbursement of a given amount of funds for the tribal development schemes in a given year. They are not need-based programs. The problem of the tribals differ in the various regions of the country and also in different areas of those regions. They need micro-level analysis and local solutions.

Unfortunately, many good plans have failed at the implementation level because persons concerned with implementation are generally unsympathetic to them. There is no rapport with the tribals and their values and sentiments. Unless this rapport is established by understanding their life and culture, the development programs, however useful and good cannot give fruitful results. For development to be substantial and lasting there is no alternative to the active participation of the tribals in their development process.

The approach towards empowering STs in the Tenth Five Year plan tends to be holistic in nature so as to accomplish all round development of the weaker sections with an inter-sectoral approach and inputs from both the governmental and non- governmental agencies.[15]

**Suggestions**

1. At the national level, there is an urgent need to adopt a comprehensive national policy for the empowerment of tribals with definite goals and targets to be achieved within a specific time frame. The policy so adopted should be able to provide a perspective which ensures that the status of the tribal population is raised to that of the rest of the society and they get their due share of benefit from development programs.
2. For effective implementation of the above policy, a National Plan of action also needs to be formulated by taking into consideration all the tribal specific issues,

namely high rates of literacy, health and nutritional deficiencies, lack of employment and income generation opportunities; lack of basic amenities like housing, drinking water, sanitation, communication linkages, land-alienation; indebtedness; social exploitation through debt bondage (bonded labor), migrant labor, displacement etc. The National Plan of action should also specify clearly the sector-wise action points, along with allocations required, agencies responsible, the time frame set, mechanisms for implementation and monitoring etc.

3. The National Policy for rehabilitation of the displaced persons needs to be finalized expeditiously. This policy should have a special focus on the rehabilitation of the displaced tribals. It should not only ensure that no deterioration takes place in the living conditions of tribals that existed prior to displacement but should also provide for betterment. The thrust of such rehabilitation should center around provision of "land for land" lost in acquisition etc.

4. As the primitive tribal groups are struggling for their survival, there is an immediate need for the preparation of a National Action Plan for survival, protection and development of primitive tribal groups. Keeping in view their socio-cultural conditions and special needs, the proposed action plan should have an in-built flexibility to cater to the specific need of each such tribe and its environment besides ensuring the basic minimum services of food security, nutrition, drinking water supply, primary health care, primary education and housing.

5. There should be a definite personnel policy for the tribal areas to ensure that;

   (i) All the officers and staff who are interested in the task of handling welfare/development work of STs should undergo sensitization program as a pre-requisite;

   (ii) Officers working for the welfare/development of STs should not be disturbed before completion of a minimum two or three years, unless their conduct is detrimental to the interests of the STs.

6. Keeping in view the special commitments made by a national policy of education 1986 for raising the educational status of STs at par with others, action needs to be initiated not only for strengthening the ongoing programs, but also for taking additional steps to tackle persistent problems of low literacy, high dropout rates through easy access to residential schools and other facilities like hostels, scholarships, free books, uniforms, mid-day meals etc. Vocationalization of education at middle/high school levels and promotion of employment oriented courses may also be taken up.

7. The health policy for the tribal areas should include the following:

   (i) Extension of primary health infrastructure to cover inaccessible areas;

   (ii) Evolving the new strategy of combining the indigenous tribal medicine with that of the Indian system of medicines, so as to reach the health care to interior tribal areas;

   (iii) Improving health education and health awareness amongst the tribals to improve access and utilization of health services; and

   (iv) Starting specially focussed sub-programs on Malaria, Leprosy, Blindness control, T.B and HIV in respect of tribals.

8. Food and nutrition security is of vital importance to tribals, especially to PTGs, as some of them are getting extinct due to starvation and malnutrition. Therefore special efforts are to be made to reach the nutritional programs for far-flung tribal areas. Large scale opening of village Anganwadis and expansion of village grain bank scheme may be taken up.

9. Employment and income generating opportunities through wage/self-employment for 300 days in a year need to be ensured. Efforts may also be made to extend

micro-credit for self-employment ventures and consumption credit when no work opportunities are available.

10. There is an urgent need to expand agriculture extension programs in the tribal areas and train the tribal youth in the application of modern methods and techniques towards achieving more production.
11. Irrigation is a major problem in tribal areas and therefore water management techniques need to be adopted on a wider scale. Rainwater harvesting and micro-irrigation systems need to be developed.
12. The legal provisions for prevention of alienation and restoration of tribal land should be extended to the entire state and should not be restricted to Scheduled and notified areas alone.
13. States need to be persuaded to bring forth necessary amendments in their existing laws and regulations concerning sale of tribal lands to non-tribals.
14. Alienation normally takes place on account of severe indebtedness. Hence provisions of debt redemption act, moneylender's act, bonded labor abolition act and such other legislations should be rigorously implemented.
15. There should be an exclusive administrative machinery for restoration of tribal land to tribals at the ITDP level. Monitoring and evaluation of the entire process should be entrusted to the commissioner of tribal welfare at the state level.
16. The respective state governments should document the customary tribal rights in forest and other concessions/ privileges enjoyed by the tribals in the forest/Scheduled areas with the consultation of Gram Sabhas. Further these documents should be made available to all the Gram Sabhas and Gram Panchayats in the Scheduled areas.
17. The problem of tribals residing in forest areas, which are not recognized as revenue villages, should be resolved expeditiously so that these tribals are not denied the

benefits of development schemes.

18. There is a need to clearly define rights of tribals in joint forest management and community/social forestry schemes. Besides, tribal Panchayats may be involved in processing of minor forest produce to give them benefit of added value.

19. There is an urgent need to provide legal and constitutional framework for recognizing and acknowledging the intellectual property rights of the tribal communities to such resources and traditional knowledge.

20. NGOs have an important role in promoting tribal empowerment. However, there should be rigorous screening of NGOs working in tribal areas to ensure their good track record. Critical activities should be identified for each state where NGO's involvement is to be encouraged. There should be arrangement for proper monitoring and evaluation of such NGO run programs to see whether their work is benefiting the tribals.

21. For the TSP strategy to succeed, it is necessary to see whether the programs being implemented by the ITDPs were formulated in accordance with the needs of the people. The concept of planning from below needs to be given a concrete shape.

22. It is essential for all the states/UTs to adopt a separate budget mechanism for TSP. Preferably, the Maharashtra model should be adopted by all TSP states. This means earmarking a fixed percentage at the state level for tribal development schemes and placing these funds under the nodal department of tribal welfare for prioritization.

23. The ITDP project officer should be assigned a key role in planning, administration and implementation of tribal development programs. ITDP should be taken as a unit of planning and the officers of the line department should report to the ITDP project officer.

24. More funds should be allocated to those areas where deprivation of tribals is quite high like in education and health. Today most of the states have been allocating

insufficient resources to these sectors. As a result, the physical infrastructure is inadequate and the quality of service delivery system leaves much to be desired.

25. Resource allocation is only a necessary condition, but not sufficient for improvement in the quality of services. Here too, the involvement of beneficiaries themselves and of other voluntary organizations must be ensured.

26. The funds under Article 275(1) of the Constitution should mostly be used for infrastructure development and for integrated development of a tribal block.

27. Public Distribution System is poor in many of the ITDP blocks and needs to be strengthened.

28. It has been noted that the intended benefits of tribal development programs are not fully reaching the tribals because of gaps in implementation and delivery systems. The tribal development programs cannot be effectively implemented without the active participation of the tribals. Mobilization of tribals through the Gram Sabhas is essential for the effective utilization of the funds for tribal development.

29. The provisions of the Panchayati Raj Extension Act, 1996 should be implemented by all the state governments and release of plan funds every year to the state governments by the Planning Commission should be made contingent upon the state certifying that they are implementing the provisions of this act.

30. The Gram Sabha should function as a guiding organization in the Scheduled areas and their recommendation must be made mandatory for the Gram Panchayats.

31. Advanced planning needs to be undertaken at the ITDP or Block level for formulating enough number of specific schemes based on a socio-economic profile of the target groups so that utilization should not be hindered for want of schemes.

32. As some income generating schemes are already covered by the Swarnjayanti Gramin Swarozgar Yojana, there is a need to increase the ratio of funds for development of infrastructure in the TSP areas and it

may be kept at 80% while 20% of funds may be allocated for family-oriented income generation programs.

33. There is an urgent need to operationalize the existing rights, directions and provisions relating to STs in the Constitution including the Fifth and Sixth Schedules.

## References

1. O.P. Sharma – Scheduled Tribes –Population and literacy, New Delhi 1991, p. 27.
2. Report of the NCAER, Survey, 1994.
3. *Ibid.*
4. The Silenced Drums: A review of Tribal economic development by K.G. Karmakar, New Delhi, 2002, pp. 72-77.
5. Amartya Sen, Resources, Values and Development, Oxford University press, 1985.
6. *Ibid.*
7. Susana Devalle- 'Discourses of Ethnicity', New Delhi, 1989, p.101.
8. S.Jones- Tribal Underdevelopment in India, Development and Change, 1978, IX, pp. 84-85.
9. The Central Himalayan Panorama (Vol.I) by S.K. Biswas (ed), Calcutta, 1993, p.9.
10. P.C.Jain- Planned Development among tribals, Rawat Publications, New Delhi, 1999, pp. 84-85.
11. Verrier Elwin- The Tribal World of Verrier Elwin- an autobiography, Oxford University Press, Delhi, 1992, pp. 302-303.
12. India Development Report 2002, Oxford University Press, New Delhi, pp. 15-16.
13. Report of the Working Group on the empowerment of the Scheduled tribes during the Tenth Five year plan, Planning Commission, New Delhi (2001).
14. *Ibid.*
15. *Ibid.*

# Annexure-I

FIGURES AT A GLANCE

(Progress Made)

| INDICATORS (Selective) | 1961 Total | 1961 STs | 1991 Total | 1991 STs |
|---|---|---|---|---|
| - Population (in Million) | 439.2 | 30.1 | 846.3 | 67.8 |
| - Sex Ratio (Fenales/1003 Males) | 941 | 937 | 927 | 972 |
| - Literacy Rate | | | | |
| Total | 24.0 | 8.5 | 52.2 | 29.6 |
| Female | 12.9 | 3.2 | 39.3 | 18.2 |
| - Work Participation Rate | 42.9 | 56.9 | 37.5 | 49.3 |
| - No. in Govt. Services (in lakhs) (1984 & 1994) | 30.0 | 1.5 | 35.7 | 1.9 |
| - Below Poverty Line (Rural-%) (1977-78 & 1993-94) | 53.1 | 72.4 | 37.3 | 51.9 |

| INDICATORS (Latest) | Total | STs | % |
|---|---|---|---|
| - Population (in Million-1991) | 846.3 | 67.8 | 8.1 |
| - Sex Ratio (1991) | 927 | 972 | - |
| - Literacy Rate (1991) | 52.2 | 29.6 | - |
| - Enrolment Ratios (1997-98) | | | |
| I-V Classes | 89.7 | 90.7 | - |
| VI-VIII Classes | 58.5 | 43.2 | - |
| - School Drop-out Rates (1993-94) | | | |
| I-VIII Classes | 52.3 | 77.7 | - |
| - Health and Child Care | | | |
| Primary Health Centres (1996) | 21853 | 3258 | 14.9 |

| | | | |
|---|---|---|---|
| Health Sub-Centres (1996) | 132773 | 20355 | 15.3 |
| ICDS Projects (1998-99) | 4200 | 750 | 17.8 |
| - Work Participate Rate ( % 1991) | 37.5 | 49.3 | - |
| - Below Poverty Line (Rural-% 1993-94) | 37.3 | 51.9 | |
| - Members of Parliament (Lok Sabha-1999) | 545 | 41 | 7.5 |
| - Members of legislative Assemblies-(1999) | 4072 | 539 | 13.2 |
| - Members in PRis (1991-1997) | 1792332 | 225090 | 12.6 |
| - No. in I.A.S. (As on 1.3.2000) | 5227 | 253 | 4.9 |
| - No. in IRS. (AS on 1.11.1999) | 3207 | 231 | 7.2 |
| - Displaced Persons (in lakhs:1951-1990) | 213.0 | 65.4 | 40.1 |
| - Resettled Persons (in lakhs:1951-1990) | 53.8 | 21.2 | 39.4 |
| - Land alienation (As of January 1999) | | | |
| Area alienated (Area in Acres) | NA | 917590 | - |
| Area Restored (Area in Acres) | NA | 537610 | - |
| - Crime Rate (Actual Number:1998) | 1779111 | 4276 | 0.2 |

# Annexure-II

QUESTIONNAIRE FOR INDIVIDUAL BENEFICIARY FOR ALL THE SCHEME

**IMPLEMENTED BY MINISTRY OF TRIBAL AFFAIRS.**

**(A) PART IDENTIFICATION**

1. Name of the Beneficiary.
2. Father's Name.
3. Male/Female.
4. Caste/sub-Group.
5. Age.
6. Educational Qualification.
7. Name of the Village/Block/Panchayat & District.
8. Occupation.

**(B) PART DETAILED INFORMATION OF BENEFICIARIES WITH RESPECT TO DIFFERENT SCHEMES -**

1. Total amount received, both subsidy and loan availed for income generatingscheme out of SCA to TSP. (Indicate the name of Income Generating Schemes. (Since 1996-97 year-wise)
2. Subsidy amount under SCA to TSP for income generating scheme since 1996-97, yearwise. (please indicated the income generating scheme for which subsidy is availed)
3. Amount loan availed against the Sdussidy for income generating scheme since year-wise. ( Please indicate the scheme against which loan is availed by the beneficiary).
4. Bank loans against, the scheme availed by the -beneficiary
5. Rate of interest
6. Amount of interest paid
7. Total amount repaid to the Bank Institute against the loan.
8. What is the income before availing the subsidy and loan.
9. What is the per-capita income after getting the subsidy or loan.
10. Difficulties faced in taking subsidy and loan.
11. Is there any asset created after availing these bene fits.

If' any. details there of -

12. Any Officer of Tribal Development Department -from Community Development Bl Sub-Division/District has visited the village.
13. Date of the last visit of the officer may be indicated.
14. Any other officer from other Sectoral Department has visited the village.
15. Name of 'the scheme funded out of SCA to TSP or any other scheme, may be indicated.
16. Suggestions, if any:

**(C) PART OTHER CENTRAL SECTOR/ CENTRALLY SPONSORED SCHEMES:**

1. Name of the Scheme (Girls'/Boys' Hostel, Educational Complex, VTI/Residential School under Article 275(1) of the Constitution).
2. Class/Trade.
3. Criteria for admission.
4. Material provided by the Hostel/Institution/Ashram Schools

   (a)Dress (b) Shoes (c) Stationery (d) Bed (e) Bed Cot (f) Almirah (g) dining arrangements etc.
5. Facilities available such as toilet/latrine/bathroom/ library/electricity etc.
6. Whether the meals/lunch provided in time and its quality.
7. Medical facility.
8. Administrative (whether Warden reside in campus).
9. Role of' Principal/Headmistress/Trade incharge.
10. Any stipend received.
11. Rema rk s/op i n l on o f the beneficiary.

**(D) PART THIS IS ONLY FOR NGO based scheme :**

1. Name of the NG 0 (For scheme Complex/Grants to NGO, Development of PTGs and Vocational raining Centre)
2. Name of NGO (Where the feneficiaries received the benefits)

   (a) Nature of work

   (b) Admission date

(c) Criteria for admission
(d) Material received (Raw material)
(e) Stationery
(f) Stipend
(g) Any problem
(h) Suggestions

3. DEVELOPMENT OF PTGS:

1. Name of the NGO
2. Awareness about the scheme
3. Whether any Seminar/Awareness programme organised by the NGO
4. Status of Drinking Water/Nutrition/Health facility
5. Others Suggestions

ANY OTHER ITEMS

**Table 1**

**Genderwise Beneficiaries of Income Generating Schemes (Under SCA to TSP ) in Dehradun District Covering a Total Number of 63 Tribal Beneficiaries in 4 (four) Blocks (Chakrata, Kalsi, Doiwala and Vikas Nagar)**

| *S.N.* | *Name of the block* | *Name of the Village* | *Male beneficiaries* | *Female beneficiaries* | *Total no. of beneficiaries* | *Remarks* |
|---|---|---|---|---|---|---|
| 1. | Kalsi | Lakhwar | 09 | 0 | 09 | |
| 2. | Kalsi | Haripur Bias | 05 | 02 | 07 | Three villages of Kalsi Block |
| | | Nahri | | | | |
| 3. | Kalsi | Kalsi Bazar | 02 | 03 | 05 | |
| 4. | Chakrata | Sujau | 03 | 05 | 08 | Two villages of Chakrata Block |
| 5. | Chakrata | Oli | 07 | 0 | 07 | |
| 6. | Doiwala | Nagal | 10 | 02 | 12 | One village of Doiwala Block |
| | | Bulandawala | | | | |
| 7. | Vikas Nagar | Shahpur | 02 | 13 | 15 | One village of Vikas Nagar Block |
| Total | 4 | 7 | 38 | 25 | 63 | Total seven villages in four Block |

**Table 2. Blockwise and Villagewise Income of the Beneficiaries before Sub-plan in Dehradun**

| S. N. | Name of the Tribal Block and village (in brackets) | Name of the Beneficiary | Age (yrs) | Amount of financial assistance provided (Rs.) | Family income before available the subsidy and loan (Rs.) | Family income after getting subsidy and the loan (Rs.) |
|---|---|---|---|---|---|---|
| 1. | Kalsi (Lakhwar) | Shri Surendra Pratap Singh | 46 | 12,000/- | 700/-pm | 1200/-pm |
| 2. | | Shri Ajit Singh | 31 | 12,000/- | 800/-pm | 1200/-pm |
| 3. | | Shri Kripal Singh | 42 | 6000/- | 500/-pm | 800/-pm |
| 4. | | Shri Narayan Singh | 53 | 18,000/- | 800/-pm | 1200/-pm |
| 5. | | Shri Pradip | 27 | 6000/- | 700/-pm | 1200/-pm |
| 6. | | ShrMohinder Singh | 55 | 6000/- | 1500/-pm | 2000/-pm |
| 7. | | Shri Janak Singh | 51 | 16,000/- | 600/-pm | 3000/-pm |
| 8. | | Shri Jaipal Singh | 32 | 6,000/- | Nil | 4000/-pm |
| 9. | | Shri Chatar Singh | 42 | 16000/- | 800/-pm | 1300/-pm |
| 10. | Kalsi (Haripur Bias Nahri) | Smt. Leela Devi | 45 | 6000/- | 500/-pm | 1200/-pm |
| 11. | | Shri Dil Chand | 55 | 2500/- | 700/-pm | 1500/-pm |
| 12. | | Shri Lachi Ram | 60 | 2500/- | 1200/-pm | 1800/-pm |
| 13. | | Shri Prem Singh | 60 | 2500/- | 2000/-pm | 2500/-pm |
| 14. | | Shri Mahanand | 40 | 2500/- | 1500/-pm | 2500/-pm |
| 15. | | Shri Ram Singh | 80 | 2500/- | 1500/-pm | 3000/-pm |
| 16. | | Smt. Kamla Devi | 45 | 6,000/- | 700/-pm | 1200/-pm |
| 17. | Kalsi (Kalsi Bazar) | Smt. Roshni Devi | 40 | 2500/- | 1000/-pm | 2000/-pm |
| 18. | | Shri Shyam Singh | 40 | 6,000/- | 1000/-pm | 1500/-pm |
| 19. | | Smt. Kanchan Devi | 35 | 2500/- | 700/-pm | |
| 20. | | Smt. Gyaro Devi | 55 | 2500/- | | |

**and after availing the subsidy and bank loan under the schemes of Tribal District (Uttaranchal)**

| *Loan Sanction in the year* | *Increase in income* Rs. | *Monthly per capita income* Rs. | *Assets created by beneficiaries* | *Suggestions given by the beneficiaries* |
|---|---|---|---|---|
| 1996-97 | 500/- | 240/- | Petty business (Parchoon shop) | Loan should be provided at low rate of interest. |
| 1996-97 | 400/- | 240/- | Petty business (Parchoon shop) | Nil |
| 1996-97 | 300/- | 160/- | A Pair of bulls | Nil |
| 1996-97 | 400/- | 240/- | Buffaloes | Nil |
| 1996-97 | 500/- | 240/- | Carpentry tools purchased | Nil |
| 1996-97 | 500/- | 400/- | Constructed Dhaba (purchased utensils and other items) | Nil |
| 1996-97 | 2400/- | 600/- | Purchased two donkeys | The amount of loan is insufficient for two donkeys |
| 1996-97 | 4000/- | 800/- | Constructed Dhaba (Purchased utensils and other items) | Rate of inmerest should be lowered (4%) |
| 1996-97 | 500/- | 260/- | Two donkeys | |
| 2000-01 | 700/- | 240/- | Two buffaloes | Loan for mini dairy farm required |
| 2000-01 | 500/- | 300/- | Three handloom Machine (two purchased out of his own money) | Raw material required for handloom |
| 2000-01 | 600/- | 360/- | Handloom Machine | Old age pension sought |
| 1999-2000 | 500/- | 500/- | He got a sewing machine and sewing implement | He wants to increase his business through ready made shop |
| 1999-2000 | 1000/- | 500/- | One Sewing Machine and implements | Wants to do ready made business |
| 1996-97 | 1500/- | 600/- | One Sewing Machine | He requires more loan to expand |
| 1999-2000 | 500/- | 240/- | One cow | Loan for livestock (Cow) |
| 1999-2000 | 1000/- | 400/- | Handloom Machine(Khaddi) | |
| 1999-2000 | 500/- | 300/- | Opened shop (Dhaba) | Wants to increase his Hotel business |
| 1996-97 | - | 260/- | She works as an Anganwadi Workers. Handloom machine | Barber shop (Beauty Palour) desired |
| 1996-97 | - | - | Handloom Machine | Nil |

*Contd.*

| S. N. | Name of the Tribal Block and village (in brackets) | Name of the Beneficiary | Age (yrs) | Amount of financial assistance provided (Rs.) | Family income before available the subsidy and loan (Rs.) | Familyincome after getting subsidy and the loan (Rs.) |
|---|---|---|---|---|---|---|
| 21. | | Shri Sasku | 31 | 18,000/- | 800/-pm | 1000/-pm |
| 22. | Chakrata (Sujau) | Shri Muna Ram | 35 | 18,000/- | Since loan has not yet been provided it cannot be computed | He has gone to SBI Chakrata many times but told that his Subsidy has not been received |
| 23. | | Smt. Sumani Devi | 50 | 17,750/- | 5000/-pm | -do- |
| 24. | | Smt. Suro Devi | 30 | 17,750/- | Nil | Nil |
| 25. | | Shrimati Libba | 50 | 3000/- | 500/-pm | 800/-pm |
| 26. | | Shri Dhannu | 55 | 5000/- | 300/-pm | 1000/-pm |
| 27. | | Smt. JagooKali | 45 | 17,750/- | 300/-pm | 1000/-pm |
| 28. | | Shri Panch Ram | 45 | 16,000/- | 800/-pm | 3000/-pm |
| 29. | | Smt. Mossam-at Thetchki | 50 | 17750/- | 400/-pm | 1500/-pm |
| 30. | Chakrata (Oli) | Shri Shasasku | 28 | 22,000/- | 2000/-pm | The loan and subsidy is yet to be given |
| 31. | | Shri Sabal Singh | 25 | 11,000/- | Nil | Nil |
| 32. | | Shri Mangat Ram | 25 | 8,000/- | 1000/-pm | 3000/-pm |
| 33. | | Shri Dhayanu | 32 | 14,000/- | 800/-pm | 2000/-pm |
| 34. | | Shri Asoju | 40 | 9,000/- | 500/-pm | 1200/-pm |
| 35. | | Shri Munna | 28 | 8,000/- | 1000/-pm | 2500/-pm |
| 36. | | Shri Tota Ram | 35 | 4,500/- | 800/-pm | 1200/-pm |

| *Loan Sanction in the year* | *Increase in income* Rs. | *Monthly per capita* income Rs. | *Assets created by beneficiaries* | *Suggestions given by the beneficiaries* |
|---|---|---|---|---|
| 1996-97 | 200/- | 200/- | Two donkey purchased in 1998-99. One died and one was sold two years back. | |
| 1996-97 | | | Since loan has not yet been provided it cannot be computed | The matter was discussed with PD, DRDA Dehradun and BDO/ADO Chakrata who have promised to get it released. |
| 1996-97 | | | Subsidy has not been received | The matter was referred to BDO/ADO and Director Tribal Welfare Dehradun and PD, DRDA Dehradun for speedy redressal |
| 1996-97 | Nil | Nil | The beneficiary was unable to tell | The matter has benn reported to BDO Chakrata /SBI Chakrata and officers at Dehradun who have promised to look into the matter. |
| 2000-01 | 300/- | 160/- | A pair of Bullock | Nil |
| 1996-97 | 700/- | 200/- | Carpentry tools purchased | Does not require any further loan |
| 1996-97 | 700/- | 200/- | One buffalo and calf | Nil |
| 1996-97 | 2200/- | 600/- | Two mules purchased | Nil |
| 2000-01 | 1100/- | 300/- | One buffalo, which died later | Nil |
| 2000-01 | | | The loan and subsidy is yet to be given | Nil |
| 2000-01 | There is no increase in income as the money given was for house construction. | | There is no increase in income as the money given was for house construction. | Nil |
| 1996-97 | 2000/- | 600/- | Two Donkeys | Nil |
| 2000-01 | 1200/- | 400/- | A pair of bullocks | Nil |
| 2000-01 | 700/- | 240/- | One donkey | Nil |
| 2000-01 | 1500/- | 500/- | Loan for two donkeys taken but not purchased | Nil |
| 2000-01 | 400/- | 240/- | One buffalo, which died later | Animal husbandry should be promoted in the area |

| *S. N.* | *Name of the Tribal Block and village (in brackets)* | *Name of the Beneficiary* | *Age (yrs)* | *Amount of financial assistance provided (Rs)* | *Family income before available the subsidy and loan (Rs)* | *Family income after getting subsidy and the loan (Rs)* |
|---|---|---|---|---|---|---|
| 1. | Doiwala (Nagal Bulandawala) | Shri Atma Ram | 38 | 6000/- | 1000/pm | 1900/pm |
| 2. | Doiwala (Kishanpur Grant) | Shri Lal Singh | 32 | 6000/- | 1500/-pm | 3000/-pm |
| 3. | Doiwala (Nagal Bulandawala) | Shri Ratan Singh | 25 | 5000/- | 1000/-pm | 1500/-pm |
| 4. | | Shri Leela Ram | 42 | 5000/- | 500/-pm | 1500/-pm |
| 5. | | Shri Hari Ram | 35 | 5000/- | 1800/-pm | 2500/-pm |
| 6. | | Shri Devendu Singh | 28 | 5000/- | 700/-pm | 3500/-pm |
| 7. | | Shri Tilak Ram | 40 | 5000/- | 1500/-pm | 3000/-pm |
| 8. | Doiwala (Nagal Bulandawala) | Shri Krishna Lal | 45 | 5000/- | 500/-pm | 900/-pm |
| 9. | Doiwala (Kishanpur Grant) | Smt. Radha Rani | 45 | 6000/- | 150/-pm | 500/-pm |
| 10. | Doiwala (Kishanpur Grant) | Smt. Shakuntla Devi | 35 | 6000/- | 500/-pm | 900/-pm |
| 11. | Doiwala (Nagal Bulandawala) | Shri Bhagwan Singh | 45 | 22,000/- | 1000/-pm | Could not be ascertained |
| 12. | Doiwala (Kishanpur Grant) | Shri Sunder Lal | 53 | 6000/- | 1200/-pm | 1500/-pm |

| *Loan Sanction in the year* | *Increase in income Rs.* | *Monthly per capita income Rs.* | *Assets created by beneficiaries* | *Suggestions given by the beneficiaries* |
|---|---|---|---|---|
| 2000-01 | 900/- | 380/- | Two Cows | Transport loan may be provided |
| 2001-02 | 1500/- | 600/- | A pair of bullock | Housing loan required as he is homeless |
| 2001-02 | 500/- | 300/- | One Rickshaw (He pulls his own rickshaw) | Housing loan and loan for small business desired |
| 2000-01 | 1000/- | 300/- | One Rickshaw | Required loan for marriege of daughter |
| 1999-00 | 700/- | 140/- | One Rickshaw | Housing loan required |
| 2001-02 | 2800/- | 500/- | One Rickshaw | Housing loan required |
| 2001-02 | 1500/- | 700/- | One Rickshaw | Housing loan required |
| 2001-02 | 400/- | 180/- | One Rickshaw | Housing loan required |
| 2000-01 | 350/- | 100/- | One sewing machine (60 mts of clothes scissors, buttons etc) | Nil |
| 2000-01 | 400/- | 180/- | One sewing machine (60 mts of clothesscissors, buttons etc) | Loan for livestock (specially for cows) |
| 2000-01 | - | - | Constructionof house | Grant for livestock (for buffaloes) |
| 1999-00 | 300/- | 300/- | Constructedhouse of two rooms | Nil |

| *S. N.* | *Name of the Tribal Block and village (in brackets)* | *Name of the Beneficiary* | *Age (yrs)* | *Amount of financial assistance provided (Rs)* | *Family income before available the subsidy and loan (Rs)* | *Family income after getting subsidy and the loan (Rs)* |
|---|---|---|---|---|---|---|
| 1. | Vikas Nagar (Shahpur) | Shri Ram Kumar | 35 | 22,000/- | Nil | Nil |
| 2. | | Smt. Leela Devi | 25 | 4,800/- | 1500/-pm | 1900/-pm |
| 3. | | Km. Premvati | 18 | 4,800/- | Nil | Nil |
| 4. | | Smt. Angoori | 30 | 6,000/- | Nil | Nil |
| 5. | | Smt. Shyama Devi | 35 | 6,000/- | 1000/-pm | 1400/-pm |
| 6. | | Km. Usha Devi | 19 | 6,000/- | Nil | Nil |
| 7. | | Km. Guddi Devi | 18 | 4,800/- | 400/-pm | 700/-pm |
| 8. | | Smt. Shakuntla | 26 | 4,800/- | 800/-pm | 1300/-pm |
| 9. | | Shri Undar | 40 | 6,000/- | 300/-pm | 500/-pm |
| 10. | | Smt. Premila | 30 | 6,000/- | 1500/-pm | 1500/-pm |
| 11. | | Smt. Sulochana | 25 | 6,000/- | 500/-pm | 1200/-pm |
| 12. | | Smt. Vimla | 40 | 6,000/- | 400/-pm | 1400/-pm |
| 13. | | Smt. Gendi Devi | 65 | 6,000/- | Nil | 1500/-pm |
| 14. | | Km. Kamla | 25 | 6,000/- | Nil | 600/-pm |
| 15 | | Km. Urmila | 17 | 6,000/- | Nil | Nil |

| *Loan Sanction in the year* | *Increase in income Rs* | *Monthly per capita income Rs.* | *Assets created by beneficiaries* | *Suggestions given by the beneficiaries* |
|---|---|---|---|---|
| 2000-01 | Nil | Nil | The subsidy is given for construction of house under PTG scheme with 20 % own share. (Constructed one room tenement) | Assistance for livestock (Goats) and Sericulture required |
| 2000-01 | 400/- | 380/- | One sewing machine+ 30 mts clothes | Assistance for livestock (Goats) |
| 2000-01 | Nil | Nil | Loan for one sewing machine under PTG scheme (one sewing machine+ 44 mts clothes) | Nil |
| 1996-97 | Nil | Nil | For silk rearing.(10 trays + net) | Assistance for livestock (Cows, Goats etc.) |
| 1996-97 | 400/- | 280/- | 10 trays for silk rearing | Loan for livestock (for buffalo) |
| 1996-97 | Nil | Nil | Sewing machine given in May 2002 (One sewing machine+ 30 mts of cloth) | Nil |
| 1996-97 | 300/- | 140/- | Sewing machine | Nil |
| 1996-97 | 500/- | 260/- | Sewing machine | Loan for livestock (for Goats) |
| 1996-97 | 200/- | 100/- | Shed construction, 10 trays+ Jali (Net) | Nil |
| 1996-97 | Nil | Nil | For silk rearing. (12 trays + Jali ) | Nil |
| 1996-97 | 700 | 240/- | Nil | Loan for Livestock (for goats) |
| 1998-99 | 1000/- | 280/- | Nil | Nil |
| 1996-97 | 1500/- | 300 | 15 trays +Jali for silk rearing | Nil |
| 1996-97 | 600/- | 120 | One sewing machine + 60 mts clothes | Loan for livestock (for goats) |
| 1998-99 | Nil | Nil | One Sewing machine | Loan for Sericulture |

**Table 3**

**Blockwise and Genderwise Sectoral (Primary, Secondary and Tertiary Sector)* Occupations of the Beneficiaries of Kalsi and Chakrata in Tribal Blocks in Dehradun District**

| *S.N.* | *Blocks* | *Villages* | *Occupations* | *Male* | *Female* | *Total* | *Remarks* |
|---|---|---|---|---|---|---|---|
| 1. | Kalsi and Chakrata (Janunsari who are Scheduled Tribes | (i) Lakhwar | (i) Primary Sector | | | | |
| | | (ii) Haripur Bias Nahri | Agriculture | 8 | 7 | 15 | |
| | | | Animal keeping and Agriculture | - | 1 | 1 | Two occupations |
| | | (iii) Kalsi Bazar | Animal Husbandry | 1 | - | 1 | (Primary and Tertiary |
| | | (iv) Sujau | | | | | |
| | | (v) Oli | (ii) Secondary | | | | |
| | | | Handloom work | 2 | - | 2 | |
| | | | (iii) Tertiary Sector | | | | |
| | | | Shopkeeper (Parchoon) | 2 | - | 2 | Two Occupations |
| | | | Carpentry and Agriculture | 2 | - | 2 | (Primary and Tertiary |
| | | | Small hotel (Dhaba) | 3 | - | 3 | |
| | | | Mule rearing | 1 | - | 1 | |
| | | | Domestic work | - | 1 | 1 | |
| | | | Tailoring | 3 | - | 3 | |

*(Contd.)*

| S.N. | Blocks | Villages | Occupations | Male | Female | Total | Remarks |
|---|---|---|---|---|---|---|---|
| | | | Anganwadi Helper | - | 1 | 1 | |
| | | | Labour and Road Labour | 3 | - | 3 | |
| | | | Road Mistry | 1 | - | 1 | |
| | | | Grand Total | 26 | 10 | 36 | |

* According to the classification of main workers by sectors (Primary, Secondary and (Tertiary).

The Primary Census Abstract (PCA) gives the classification of workers by nine fold industrial categories. For a more meaningful economic analysis, workers can be grouped into Primary, Secondary and Tertiary Sectors. Workers in Primary Sector would include all those who are working in industrial categories I,II, III and IV, i.e. all those who are classified as cultivators; agricultural labourers; workers in livestock, forestry, fishing, hunting and plantations and other activities allied to agriculture; and those working in mining and quarrying. Secondary sector would include workers who have been classified under industrial categories V and VI, i.e., manufacturing, processing etc. servicing and repairs have been separately calssified into those working in household industries and those working in non-household industries.

Tertiary sector would include workers classified under industrial categories VII, VIII and IX, i.e., those working in trade and commerce; transport, storage and communications; and other services.

*Source* : Final population totals paper-2 of 1992 Census of India 1991, series 1, India.

**Table 3**

**Blockwise and Genderwise Sectoral (Primary, Secondary and Tertiary Sector) occupations of the beneficiaries of Doiwala and Nagar Block in Dehradun District**

| S.N. | Blocks | Villages | Occupations | Male | Female | Total | Remarks |
|---|---|---|---|---|---|---|---|
| 1. | Doiwala and Vikas Nagar ( Buxas who are among the primitive tribal groups | (i) Nagal Bulandawala<br>(ii) Shahpur | (i) Primary Sector | | | | |
| | | | Land Labourer | 5 | - | 5 | |
| | | | Land Labour and Agriculture | 1 | 6 | 7 | Two occupations |
| | | | Sericulture | 1 | 3 | 4 | (Both Primary) |
| | | | (ii) Tertiary Sector | | | | |
| | | | Rickshaw Pulling | 2 | - | 2 | |
| | | | Cycle Repair | 1 | - | 1 | |
| | | | Labour | 2 | 1 | 3 | |
| | | | Tailoring | - | 1 | 1 | |
| | | | Tailoring and Agriculture | - | 3 | 3 | Two Occupations ( Primary and Tertiary) |
| | | | Sewing | 1 | - | 1 | |
| | | Grand Total | | 13 | 14 | 27 | |

**Table 4**

**Blockwise and Genderwise Literacy and Education Level in two Blocks (Kalsi and Chakrata) of Dehradun District**

| *S.N.* | *Name of the Block* | *Name of the Village* | *Details of Male Literacy* | | | *Details of Female Literacy* | | |
|---|---|---|---|---|---|---|---|---|
| | | | Illiterate | Literate upto 5th Pass | VI and above | Illiterate | Literate upto 5th Pass | VI and Above |
| 1. | Kalsi | Lakhwar | - | - | MA.B.Ed | - | - | - |
| 2. | " | " | - | - | 12th pass | - | - | - |
| 3. | " | " | - | 5th pass | - | - | - | - |
| 4. | " | " | - | - | 10th pass | - | - | - |
| 5. | " | " | - | - | 7th pass | - | - | - |
| 6. | " | " | - | - | 8th pass | - | - | - |
| 7.. | " | " | - | 4th pass | - | Illiterate | - | - |
| 8. | " | " | - | - | 12th pass | - | - | - |
| 9. | " | Haripur Bias Nahri | - | - | 8th pass | - | - | - |
| 10. | " | " | - | - | - | - | - | - |
| 11. | " | " | Illiterate | - | - | - | - | - - |
| 12. | " | " | Illiterate | - | - | - | - | - - |
| 13. | " | " | - | 5th pass | - | - | - | - |
| 14. | " | " | - | - | 8th pass | - | - | - |
| 15. | " | " | - | 1st pass | - | - | - | - |
| 16. | " | " | - | - | - | Illiterate | - | - |

*(Contd.)*

| S.N. | Name of the Block | Name of the Village | Details of Male Literacy | | | Details of Female Literacy | | |
|---|---|---|---|---|---|---|---|---|
| 17. | " | Kalsi Bazar | - | - | - | Illiterate | - | - |
| 18. | " | " | Illiterate | - | - | - | - | - |
| 19. | " | " | - | - | - | - | - | - |
| 20. | " | " | - | - | - | Illiterate | - | - |
| 21. | Chakrata | " | - | - | 12th pass | - | - | - |
| 22. | " | Sujau | - | Literate | - | - | - | - |
| 23. | " | " | - | - | - | Illiterate | - | - |
| 24. | " | " | - | - | - | Illiterate | - | - |
| 25. | " | " | - | - | - | Illiterate | - | - |
| 26. | " | " | Illiterate | - | - | - | - | - |
| 27. | " | " | - | - | - | - | 5th pass | - |
| 28. | " | " | - | Literate | - | - | - | - |
| 29. | " | " | - | - | - | Illiterate | - | - |
| 30. | " | Oli | Illiterate | - | - | - | - | - |
| 31. | " | " | - | Literate | - | - | - | - |
| 32. | " | " | - | Literate | - | - | - | - |
| 33. | " | " | Illiterate | - | - | - | - | - |
| 34. | " | " | - | Literate | - | - | - | - |
| 35. | " | " | - | Literate | - | - | - | - |
| 36. | " | " | - | Literate | - | - | - | - |
| | | Total | 6 | 11 | 9 | 8 | 1 | 1 |

**Blockwise and Genderwise Literacy and Education Level in tow Blocks (Doiwala and Vikas Nagar) of Dehradun District**

| *S.N.* | *Name of the Block* | *Name of the village* | *Details of Male Literacy* | | | *Details of female literacy* | | |
|---|---|---|---|---|---|---|---|---|
| | | | Illiterate | Literate upto 5th Pass | VI and above | Illiterate | Literate upto 5th Pass | VI and Above |
| 1. | Doiwala | Nagal Bulandawala | - | Literate | - | - | - | - |
| 2. | " | Krishanpur Grant | - | - | 8th Pass | - | - | - |
| 3. | " | " | - | - | BA Pass | - | - | - |
| 4. | " | " | Illiterate | - | 6th pass | - | - | - |
| 5. | " | " | - | - | - | - | - | - |
| 6. | " | " | - | 8th Pass | - | - | - | - |
| 7.. | " | " | - | - | 8th Pass | - | - | - |
| 8. | " | " | - | Literate | - | - | - | - |
| 9. | " | " | - | - | - | - | 5th Pass | - |
| 10. | " | Krishanpur Grant | - | - | - | - | 5th Pass | - |
| 11. | " | Nagal Bulandawala | Illiterate | - | - | - | - | - |
| 12. | " | Krishanpur Grant | Illiterate | - | - | - | - | - |
| 13. | Vikas Nagar | Shahpur | - | Literate | - | - | - | - |
| 14. | " | " | - | - | - | Illiterate | - | - |
| 15. | " | " | - | - | - | Illiterate | - | - |
| 16. | " | " | - | - | - | Illiterate | - | - |

*(Contd.)*

| *S.N.* | *Name of the Block* | *Name of the village* | *Details of Male Literacy* | | | *Details of female literacy* | | |
|---|---|---|---|---|---|---|---|---|
| 17. | " | " | - | - | - | Illiterate | - | - |
| 18. | " | " | - | - | - | - | - | - |
| 19. | " | " | - | - | - | Illiterable | - | - |
| 20. | " | " | - | - | - | Illiterate | - | - |
| 21. | " | " | - | 2nd Pass | - | - | - | 6th Pass |
| 22. | " | " | - | - | - | - | Literate | - |
| 23. | " | " | - | - | - | Illiterate | - | - |
| 24. | " | " | - | - | - | Illiterate | - | - |
| 25. | " | " | - | - | - | Illiterate | - | - |
| 26. | " | " | - | - | - | - | - | 8th Pass |
| 27. | " | " | - | - | - | - | - | 8th Pass |
| | | Total | 3 | 4 | 5 | 9 | 3 | 3 |

**Table 5 (A)**

**Blockwise and Genderwise Literacy Levels of Jaunsari (ST) Beneficiaries in Two Hilly Blocks (Chakrata and Kalsi ) and their Occupational Details**

| *Block Chakrata and Kalsi* | *Illiterates* | | *-5* | | *+5* | | | | *Total* |
|---|---|---|---|---|---|---|---|---|---|
| | *M* | *F* | *M* | *F* | *M* | *F* | *M* | *F* | |
| Primary Sector | | | | | | | | | |
| Village : | 1 | 7 | 6 | - | 3 | 1 | 10 | 8 | 18 |
| 1. Lakhwar | | | | | | | | | |
| 2. Sujau | | | | | | | | | |
| 3. Oli | | | | | | | | | |
| 4. Kalsi Bazar | | | | | | | | | |
| 5. Haripur Bias Nahri | | | | | | | | | |
| Secondry Sector | 2 | - | - | - | - | - | 2 | - | 2 |
| Tertiary Sector | 3 | 1 | 3 | - | 8 | 1 | 14 | 2 | 16 |
| Grand Total | 6 | 8 | 9 | Nil | 11 | 2 | 26 | 10 | 36 |

**Table 5 (B)**
**Blockwise and Genderwise Literacy Levels of Jaunsari (ST) Beneficiaries in Two Hilly Blocks Doiwala and Vikas Nagar and their Occupational Details**

| *Block Doiwal and Vikas* | *Illiterates* | | *-5* | | *+5* | | *Total* | | |
|---|---|---|---|---|---|---|---|---|---|
| *Nagar* | *M* | *F* | *M* | *F* | *M* | *F* | *M* | *F* | |
| Primary Sector | | | | | | | | | |
| Village : | 2 | 10 | 4 | - | - | - | 6 | 10 | 16 |
| 1. Shahpur | | | | | | | | | |
| 2. Kishanpur Grant | | | | | | | | | |
| 3. Nagal Bulandawala | | | | | | | | | |
| Secondary Sector | - | - | - | - | - | - | - | . | Nil |
| Tertiary Sector | 1 | 1 | 2 | - | 5 | 2 | 8 | 3 | 11 |
| Grand Total | 3 | 11 | 6 | - | 5 | 2 | 14 | 13 | 27 |

**Table 6**

**Occupations of the Beneficiaries (Genderwise) in the 7 villages namely: (i) Lakhwar, (ii) Haripur Bias Nahri, (iii) Kalsi Bazar, (iv) Sujau, (v) Oli, (vi) Nagal Bulandawala and (vii) Shahpur in Kalsi, Chakrata, Doiwala and Vikas Nagar Blocks of Dehradun District Respectively**

| *S.N.* | *Occupations* | *Male* | *Female* | *Total* | *Remarks* |
|---|---|---|---|---|---|
| 1. | Primary Sector | | | | |
| | (i) Agriculture | 8 | 7 | 14 | |
| | (ii) Animal Husbandry and Agriculture | 1 | - | 1 | Two occupations (both Primary) |
| | (iii) Animal keeping and Agriculture | - | 1 | 1 | Two occupations (both Primary) |
| | (iv) Land Labour and Agriculture | 6 | 6 | 12 | Two occupations (both Primary) |
| | (v) Sericulture | 1 | 3 | 4 | |
| | Sub Total | 16 | 17 | 33 | |
| 2. | Secondary Sector | | | | |
| | (i) Handloom work | 2 | - | 2 | |
| | Sub Total | 2 | Nil | 2 | |
| 3. | Tertiary Sector | | | | |
| | (i) Shopkeeper (Parchoon) | 2 | | 2 | |

(Contd.)

| *S.N.* | *Occupations* | *Male* | *Female* | *Total* | *Remarks* |
|---|---|---|---|---|---|
| | (ii) Carpentry and Agriculture | 2 | - | 2 | Two occupations (Tertiary and Primary) |
| | (iii) Hotel (Dhaba) | 3 | - | 3 | |
| | (iv) Mule rearing | 1 | - | 1 | |
| | (v) Road Mistry | 1 | - | 1 | |
| | (vi) Road labour/Other labour | 5 | 1 | 6 | |
| | (vii) Rickshaw Puller | 2 | - | 2 | |
| | (viii) Tailoring and Agriculture | - | 4 | 4 | Two occupations (Tertiary and Primary) |
| | (ix) Sewing | - | 1 | 1 | |
| | (x) Cycle Repair | 1 | - | 1 | |
| | (xi) Tailoring | 3 | - | 3 | |
| | (xii) Anganwadi Helper | - | 1 | 1 | |
| | (xiii) Domestic work | - | 1 | 1 | |
| | Sub Total | 20 | 8 | 28 | |
| | Grand Total | 38 | 25 | 63 | |

**Blockwise and Genderwise Ocupations of all the Beneficiaries in Tribal Blocks in District Dehradun**

| S.N. | Blocks | Villages | Occupations | Male | Female | Total | Remarks |
|---|---|---|---|---|---|---|---|
| 1. | Kalsi | (vi) Lakhwar | Agriculture | 3 | 3 | 3 | |
| | | (vii) Haripur Bias | Shopkeeper Parchoon | 2 | - | 2 | |
| | | Nahri | Carpentry | 1 | - | 1 | |
| | | (viii) Kalsi Bazar | Small hotel/ Dhaba | 2 | - | 2 | |
| | | | Mule rearing | 1 | - | 1 | |
| | | | Domestic work | 0 | 1 | 1 | |
| | | | Tailoring | 3 | - | - | |
| | | | Handloom work | 2 | - | 2 | |
| | | | Anganwadi Helper | - | 1 | 1 | |
| | | | Labour | 1 | - | - | |
| | | | | 16 | 05 | 21 | |
| 2. | Chakrata | Sujau and Oli | Animal Husbandry and Agriculture | 1 | - | | Two occupations |
| | | | Agriculture | 5 | 4 | | (Primary and Secondary) |
| | | | Animal Keeping and | - | 1 | | Two occupations (Son in service) |

(Contd)

| *S.N.* | *Blocks* | *Villages* | *Occupations* | *Male* | *Female* | *Total* | *Remarks* |
|---|---|---|---|---|---|---|---|
| | | | Agriculture | | | | |
| | | | Carpentry and Agriculture | 1 | - | | |
| | | | Road Labour | 2 | - | | |
| | | | Road Mistry | 1 | - | | |
| | | | | 10 | 05 | 15 | |
| 3. | Doiwala | Nagal Bulandawala | Land Labour | 5 | - | | |
| | | | Rickshaw Pulling | 2 | - | | Landless |
| | | | Cycle repair | 1 | - | | |
| | | | Labour | 2 | 1 | | |
| | | | Tailoring | - | 1 | | |
| | | | | 10 | 2 | 12 | |
| 4. | Vikas Nagar | Shahpur | Land Labour and Agriculture | 1 | 6 | | Two occupations |
| | | | Agriculture and Tailoring | - | 3 | | |
| | | | Secriculture | 1 | 3 | | |
| | | | Sewing | - | 1 | | |
| | | | | 2 | 13 | 15 | |
| 5. | | | Grand Total | | | 63 | Beneficiaries of all the four blocks |

**Genderwise Occupations of all Beneficiaries in all the 5 Villages Namely: (i) Lakhwar, (ii) Haripur Bias Nahri, (iii) Kalsi Bazar, (iv) Sujau, (v) Oli, (vi) Nagal Bulandawala and (vii) Shahpur in Kalsi, Chakrata, Doiwala and Vikas Nagar Blocks of Dehradun District Respectively**

| *S.N.* | *Occupations* | *Male* | *Female* | *Total* | *Remarks* |
|---|---|---|---|---|---|
| 1. | Agriculture | 08 | 07 | 15 | Only Agriculture |
| 2. | Shopkeeper Parchoon | 02 | - | 02 | Parchoon shops |
| 3. | Carpentry and Agriculture | 02 | - | 02 | Two occupations Primary and Secondary, 1st Carpentry and 2nd Agriculture |
| 4. | Hotel (Dhaba) | 03 | - | 02 | Animal Husbandry |
| 5. | Mule rearing | 01 | - | 01 | Two occupations, 1st Primary and 2nd Secondary |
| 6. | Animal Husbandry and Agriculture | 01 | - | 01 | |
| 7. | Animal Keeping and Agriculture | - | 01 | 01 | |
| 8. | Road Mistry | 01 | - | 01 | |
| 9. | Land Labour and Agricultue, Road Labour also another labour | 11 | 07 | 17 | There are three types of labour, 1st land Labour and Agriculture, 2nd Road Labour and 3rd Other labour |
| 10. | Rickshaw Puller | 02 | - | 02 | |
| 11. | Tailoring and Agriculture | - | 04 | 04 | Two occupations |

*(Contd.)*

*(Contd.)*

| S.N. | Occupations | Male | Female | Total | Remarks |
|---|---|---|---|---|---|
| 12. | Sericulture | 01 | 03 | 04 | |
| 13. | Sewing | - | 01 | 01 | |
| 14. | Cycle repair | 01 | - | 01 | |
| 15. | Tailoring | 03 | - | | |
| 16. | Handloom work | 02 | - | | |
| 17. | Anganwadi Helper | - | 01 | | |
| 18. | Domestic work | - | 01 | | |
| | Total | 38 | 25 | 63 | |

**Table 7 (a)**
**Literacy Position of Surveyed Households**

| *Bolcks* | *Literate* | *Illiterate* | *Total* |
|---|---|---|---|
| Chakrata and Kalsi Blocks inhabited by Jaunsaries (ST) | 22 (35%) | 14 (22.22 %) | 36 (57.14%) |
| Doiwala and Vikas Nagar Blocks inhabited by Buxas (PTG) | 13 (21%) | 14 (22.22 %) | 27 (43 %) |
| Total | 35 (55.6 %) | 28 (44.4 %) | 63( 100%) |

**Table 7 (b)**
**Male and Female Position of Surveyed Households**

| *Blocks's* | *Male* | *Female* | *Total* |
|---|---|---|---|
| Jaunsari blocks (Chakrata and Kalsi) | 26 (41.26 %) | 10 (16 %) | 36 (57.14 %) |
| Buxa block (Doiwala and Vikas Nagar) | 14 (22.22 %) | 13 (21 %) | 27 (43 %) |
| Grand total | 40 (63.49 %) | 23 ( 37 %) | 63 ( 100 % ) |

**Table 7 (c)**
**Sectorwise Classification of Main Workers**

| *Sectors* | *Male Workers* | *Female Workers* | *Total Workers* |
|---|---|---|---|
| Primary Sector | 16 (25 %) | 18 (28.5 %) | 34 (54 %) |
| Secondary Sector | 02 (3%) | Nil | 02 ( 3 %) |
| Tertiary Sector | 22 (35 %) | 05 (8%) | 27 (43%) |
| Total | 40 (63 % ) | 23 ( 36.5 %) | 63 (100 %) |

**Table 8 : Income Generated by the Beneficiaries in the Blocks of Chakrata, Kalsi, Doiwala and Vikas Nagar in Dehradun District**

| *S. N.* | *Income of different categories of beneficiaries* | *Amount (Rs.)* |
|---|---|---|
| 1. | Average monthly income of an illiterate male beneficiary | 222.21 |
| 2. | Average yearly income of an illiterate male beneficiary | 2666.62 |
| 3. | Average monthly income of an illiterate female beneficiary | 189.40 |
| 4. | Average yearly income of an illiterate female beneficiary | 2272.9 |
| 5. | Average monthly income of a literate male beneficiary | 327.55 |
| 6. | Average yearly income of a literate male beneficiary | 3930.69 |
| 7. | Average monthly income of a literate female beneficiary | 107.49 |
| 8. | Average yearly income of a literate female beneficiary | 1289.97 |
| 9. | Total monthly income of all the beneficiaries engaged in the Primary Sector | 7720.00 |
| 10. | Total monthly income of all the beneficiaries engaged in the Secondary Sector | 666.00 |
| 11. | Total monthly income of all the beneficiaries engaged in the Tertiary Sector | 7920.00 |
| 12. | Total monthly income generated by all the beneficiaries engaged in all the three sectors | 16,300.00 |
| 13. | Average monthly income of a beneficiary engaged in Primary Sector | 227.05 |
| 14. | Average monthly income of a beneficiary engaged in Secondary Sector | 330.00 |
| 15. | Average monthiy income of a beneficiary engaged in Primary Sector | 293.33 |
| 16. | Average monthly income of a beneficiary combining all the three Sectors | 258.73 |
| 17. | Average yearly income of a beneficiary combining in all the three Sectors | 3104.76 |

**Table 1**

**Genderwise Beneficiaries of Income Generating Schemes (Under SCA to TSP ) in Ranchi District Covering a Total Number of 51 Tribal Beneficiaries 25 of Village Gutigarha Daugara and 26 of Village Rukka of Jharkhand State**

| *S.N.* | *Name of the block* | *Name of the Village and Tola* | *Male beneficiaries* | *Female beneficiaries* | *Total no. of beneficiaries* | *Remarks* |
|---|---|---|---|---|---|---|
| 1. | Murhu | Gutigarha (Piritola) | 02 | Nil | 02 | During field survey, 25 |
| 2. | Murhu | Gutigarha ( Daugara) | 16 | Nil | 16 | Benficiaries of village |
| | | | | | | Gutigarha of Murhu Block. |
| 3. | Murhu | Gutigarha ( Daugara) | 07 | Nil | 07 | were contacted |
| 4. | Omanjhi | Rukka (Pahantoli) | 02 | Nil | 02 | During field survey, 26 Benefi- |
| 5. | Omanjhi | Rukka (Rukka Seeya) | 02 | Nil | 02 | ciaries of village Rukka of |
| 6. | Omanjhi | Rukka (Rukka Tungri) | 16 | Nil | 16 | Ormanjhi Block were contacted. |
| 7. | Omanjhi | Rukka | 05 | Nil | 05 | The visit was done without prior |
| 8 | Omanjhi | Rukka (Mutha Toli) | 01 | Nil | 01 | notice. |
| | Total | | 51 | Nil | 51 | 2 Blocks and 2 Villages and 7 Tolas |

**Table 2. Blockwise and Villagewise Income of the Beneficiaries Before Tribal Sub-plan in Ranchi**

| S. N. | Name of the Tribal Block and village (in brackets) | Name of the Beneficiary | Age (yrs) | Amount of financial assistance provided (Rs) | Family income before available the subsidy and loan (Rs) | Family income after getting subsidy and the loan (Rs) |
|---|---|---|---|---|---|---|
| 1. | (Murhu) Guttigara TolaPiritola | Shri Raghu Nath Munda | 30 | 12,700/- | 4,000/- | Total 6 members infamilyIncome not given |
| 2. | -Do- | Shri Sunil Munda | 38 | 12,700/- | 5,000/- | Total 9 members infamily.Income not given |
| 3. | 'Murhu' Daugara | Shri Panda Munda | - | 12,700/- | 6,664/- | Total 8 members infamily. Income not given |
| 4. | -Do- | Shri Aitwa Munda | 30 | 12,700/- | 5,000/- | Total 10 members family. Income not given |
| 5. | -Do- | Shri Prau Munda | 40 | 12,700/- | 3,000/- | 5000/- |
| 6. | -Do- | Shri Bisa Munda | 41 | 12,210/- | 4,000/- | 12,480/- |
| 7. | (Murhu) Guttigara | Shri Sanik Munda | 40 | 10,000/- | 3,000/- | 8,160/- |
| 8. | -Do- | Shri Putti Munda | 45 | 12,200/- | 5,000/- | 22,500/- |
| 9. | -Do- | Shri Hathi Rami Munda | 60 | 14,000/- | 4,800/- | 15,000/- |
| 10. | -Do- | Shri Sama Munda | 28 | 11,667/- | 6,000/- | 74,880/- |
| 11. | -Do- | Shri Bodoi Munda | 30 | 6,700/- | 6,000/- | 14,000/- |
| 12. | (Murhu) Guttigarha Gola | Shri Paran Munda | 26 | 6,700/- | 7,000/- | 11,000/- |
| 13. | -Do- | Shri Galu Munda | 27 | 6,700/- | 5,000/- | 6,000/- |
| 14. | -Do- | Shri Lomba Munda | 40 | 6,700/- | 5,000/- | 6,000/- |
| 15. | -Do- | Shri Ram Munda | 25 | - | - | 2,000/- |

**and After Availing the Subsidy and Bank Loan Under the Schemes of District of Jharkhand State**

| *Loan Sanction in the year* | *Increase in income* Rs. | *Monthly per capita income* Rs. | *Assets created by beneficiaries* | *Suggestions given by the beneficiaries* |
|---|---|---|---|---|
| 1996-97 | Could not be ascertained | 667/- | IRDP Pump set and Rikshaw | Nil |
| 1996-97 | -Do- | 556/- | Nil | Nil |
| 1996-97 | -Do- | 555/- | Rikshaw | Nil |
| 1994-95 | -Do- | 500/- | Nil | Nil |
| 1995-96 | 2,000/- | 278/- | Pump Set | Nil |
| 1995-96 | 8,480/- | 1,040/- | Pump set and House Construction | Pucca road approach |
| 1997-98 | 5,160/- | 680/- | Pump set and House construction in 2001 | 1. Village electrification 2. Pucca road approach |
| 1997-98 | 17,500/- | 1,875/- | Pump set | -Do- |
| 1998-99 | 10,200/- | 1250/- | House repairing and Pump set | -Do- |
| 1997-98 | 68,880/- | 6,240/- | House construction | -Do- |
| 1994-95 | 8,000/- | 1,167/- | Nil | Nil |
| 1994-95 | 4,000/- | 4,583/- | Nil | Nil |
| 1994-95 | 1,000/- | 500/- | Nil | Nil |
| 1994-95 | 1,000/- | 500/- | Nil | Nil |
| 1996-97 | - | - | - | He is not a beneficiary |

*(Contd.)*

| S. N. | Name of the Tribal Block and village (in brackets) | Name of the Beneficiary | Age (yrs) | Amount of financial assistance provided (Rs.) | Family income before available the subsidy and loan (Rs.) | Family income after getting subsidy and the loan (Rs.) |
|---|---|---|---|---|---|---|
| 16. | (Murhu) Guttigara Dogada | Shri Kurchu Munda | 45 | 11,000/- | 12,000/- | 24,000/- |
| 17. | (Murhu) Guttigara | Shri Ramay Munda | 25 | 14,800/- | 10,000/- | 30,000/- |
| 18. | Murhu Tola Dongda | Shri Samu Munda | 50 | 14,400/- | 667/- | 750/- |
| 19 | -Do- | Shri Panda Munda | 39 | 7,000/- | 5,000/- | 10,000/- |
| 20. | -Do- | Shri Deyal Singh Munda | 27 | 16,000/- | 8,000/- | 24,000/- |
| 21. | -Do- | Shri Ramai Munda | 40 | Rickshaw (100 %) Subsidy | 600/- | 800/- |
| 22. | -Do- | Shri Mangau Rami Munda | 26 | 3,25,00/- (Group Loan) | Nil | 1,250/- |
| 23. | (Murhu) Daugarha | Shri Sagar Munda | 46 | 12,210/- | 8,000/- | 30,000/- |
| 24. | -Do- | Shri Bhaiya Ram Munda | 21 | 2,000/- | 900/- | No increase |
| 25. | -Do- | Shri Lodo Munda | 22 | 14,900/- | 6,000/- | 7,000/- |
| 26. | (Ormanjhi) Chakla Village, Rukka | Shri Lodo Oraon | 50 | 15,500/- | 12,000/- | 12,200/- |
| 27. | -Do- | Shri Uday Oraon | 35 | 10,000 | 5 Man Dhaan | 5 Man Daan and Vegetables |
| 28. | (Oramanjhi) Tola tungri | Shri Suresh Oraon | 40 | | 10 Man Dhaan | 15 Man Dhan and growing vegetables |

| *Loan Sanction in the year* | *Increase in income* *Rs.* | *Monthly per capita income* *Rs.* | *Assets created by beneficiaries* | *Suggestions given by the beneficiaries* |
|---|---|---|---|---|
| 1995-96 | 12,000/- | 2,400/- | - | No knowledge or information regarding the schemes |
| 2002-03 | 20,000/- | 2,500/- | | For repairing the machiines, tools and impliment are not sufficient |
| 1988-89 | 83/- | 150/- | Nil | Nil |
| 1997-98<br>2001-2002 | 5,000/- | 833/- | Pump set, repair of old house | Wants a well in his field |
| 1998-99<br>2001-02 | 16,000/- | 2,667/- | Purchased motor cycle | After getting the loan, pass book is not given by the bank |
| 1997-98 | 200/- | 200/- | Got Rickshaw | Nil |
| 1998-99 | 15,20/- | 1250/- | Box for bee keeping etc | Nil |
| 1995-96 | 22,000/- | 1,188/- | Pump set the irrigation well | He wants to install lift in |
| 2002-03 | - | - | Seeds, manure (fertilizer) | Sanctioned loan on 10.10.2002 |
| 1997-98 | 1,000/- | 15,70/- | Pump set | Does not require further help |
| 1988-89 | 200/- | 200/- | Nil | Nil |
| 1988-89 | - | Could not be converted in money terms | - | Needs well and Indira Awas from Govt. |
| 1996-97 | - | -do- | - | Demand for canal irrigation |

*(Contd.)*

| S. N. | Name of the Tribal Block and village (in brackets) | Name of the Beneficiary | Age (yrs) | Amount of financial assistance provided (Rs) | Family income before available the subsidy and loan (Rs) | Family income after getting subsidy and the loan (Rs) |
|---|---|---|---|---|---|---|
| 29. | -Do- | Shri Virsa Oraon | 35 | 90,80/- | 10 Quintals Dhaan yearly | 15 Quintals Dhaan, 5 Man wheat, 2 Man Aalu |
| 30. | (Oramanjhi) Rukka | Shri Mogo Oraon | 25 | 90,80/- | 15 Man Dhaan | 20 Man Dhaan Potato |
| 31. | -Do- | Shri Binod Oraon | 45 | 5,500/- | 12,000/- | 12,500/- |
| 32. | -Do- | Shri Chandra Munda | 40 | 11,000/- | 5000/- | 5000/- |
| 33. | -Do- | Shri Mahavir Oraon | 42 | 15,500/- | 12,000/- | 18,000/- |
| 34. | -Do- | Shri Mukra Oraon | 45 | 22,000/- | 6 Man Dhaan | 8 Maan Dhaan, Potato, Onion, Vegetables etc. |
| 35. | -Do- | Shri Kamal Oraon | 28 | 14,000/- | 6 Man Dhaan | 12 Maan Dhaan, Potato, Onion etc |
| 36. | (Oramanjhi) | Shri Aaitwa Oraon | 48 | 9,800/- | 10 Man Dhaan | 15 Man Dhaan Potato, Onion |
| 37. | -Do- | Shri Madhu Oraon | 40 | 12,000/- | 10 Man Dhaan | 15 Man Dhaan |
| 38. | -Do- | ShriSakhichan Munda | 42 | 11,000/- | - | 300/- |
| 39. | -Do- | Shri Dhani Ram Munda | 35 | 10,500/- | - | 1,000/- |
| 40. | -Do- | Shri Birsa Pahan | 45 | 8,000/- | 833/- | 500/- |
| 41. | (Oramanjhi) Pahan Toli | Shri Jagnu Pahan | 31 | 10,000 | 12,000/- | 18,000/- |
| 42. | (Ormanjhi) Pahan Toli | Shri Bal Ram Pahan | 33 | 10,000/- | 6,000/- | 12,000/- |

| *Loan Sanction in the year* | *Increase in income* *Rs.* | *Monthly per capita income* *Rs.* | *Assets created by beneficiaries* | *Suggestions given by the beneficiaries* |
|---|---|---|---|---|
| 1986-87 | - | -do- | Desel Pump set | Electric Machine required |
| 1984-85 | - | -do- | Pump set | Electricity is required in the village |
| 1988-89 | 500/- | 500/- | Pump set, cycle purchased | Nil |
| 1985-86 | - | - | Rickshaw | No increase |
| 1988-89 | 6,000/- | 6,000/- | Cycle purchased | Needs a well and also Indira Awas |
| 1990-91<br>1997-98 | 2 Man Dhaan | - | Pump Set | Nil |
| 1991-92 | 6 Man Dhaan | - | Pump Set | Facility for irrigation should be made such as canal irrigation. |
| 1993-94<br>1996-97 | 5 Man Dhaan | - | Desel Pump set | Nil |
| 1989-90 | 5 Man | - | Desel Pump set<br>. | Electrical pump set alonhaan with subsidy should be Provided |
| 1986-87 | 300/- | 300/- | Rickshaw | Nil |
| 1988-89 | 1,000/- | 4.17/- | Water Pump set | Nil |
| 1988-89 | - | 500/- | Pump Set | Nil |
| 2002-03 | 6,000/- | 1,500/- | Seeds, fertilizer | Repair of road and bridge and Indira Awas |
| 2002-03 | 6,000/- | 1,000/- | Pump set | Suggessted that middle school (Upper Primary) should be opened in the village |

*(Contd.)*

| | | | | | | |
|---|---|---|---|---|---|---|
| 43. | (Oramanjhi) Rukka | Shri Suklal Munda | 65 | 28,660/- | 5,000/- | 24,960 /- |
| 44. | -Do- | Shri Lakhia Munda | 40 | 4,000/- | 5,000/- | 7,000/- |
| 45. | -Do- | Shri Jaleshwar Pahan | 45 | 6,300/- | 5,000/- | 7,000/- |
| 46. | -Do- | Shri Doman Pahan | 50 | 12,000/- | Nil | Nil |
| 47. | -Do- | Shri Sadhana Oraon | 23 | Nil | 1,000/- | 4,000/- |
| 48. | -Do- | Shri Somra Oraon | 48 | 12,000/- | 1,000/- | 4,000/- |
| 49. | (Ormanjhi) Suiyan Tola | Shri Shankar Oraon | 35 | 10,000/- | 500/- | 1,000/- |
| 50. | (Ormanjhi) Tungri Tola | Shri Mangru Oraon | 50 | 12,000/- | Nil | Nil |
| 51. | -Do- | Shri Ram Swarup | 28 | Nil | 2,000/- | - |

| | | | | |
|---|---|---|---|---|
| 2000-01 | 19,960/- | 2,080/- | House construction | Nil |
| 1987-88 | 2,000/- | 2,000/- | Pump set | Nil |
| 1988-89 | 2,000/- | 2,000/- | Cow | Nil |
| 1988-89 | - | - | Income could not be ascertained | Nil |
| 2002-2003 | 3,000/- | 250/- | - | Govt. programme should be properly implemented |
| 1992-93 | 3,000/- | 375/- | Pump Set | Processing units required |
| 1988-89 | 500/- | 500/- | Two cows | He wants to make 15 feet diameter well as the present well is only of 5' diameter |
| 1994-95 | Nil | Nil | Nil | Income could not be known |
| 1996-97 | - | - | He is not a beneficiary | Requires pump set |

**Table 3**

**Blockwise and Genderwise Sectoral (Primary, Secondary and Tertiary Sector)* Occupations of the 25 Beneficiaries of Village Guttigarha Block Murhu, Khunti subdivision, Ranchi and 26 Beneficiaries of village Rukka, Block Ormanjhi of Ranchi District**

| S.N. | Blocks | Villages | Occupations | | Male | Female | Total | Remarks |
|---|---|---|---|---|---|---|---|---|
| 1. | Murhu and Ormanjhi (The beneficiaries of these blocks are Scheduled Tribes) | (i) Guttigarha | (i) | Primary Sector | | | | |
| | | (ii) Rukka | | Agriculture | 47 | Nil | 47 | These two blocks of Ranchi district are representative of the two important tribes of Jharkhand namely Munda and Oraon. |
| | | | (ii) | Secondary | | | | |
| | | | | | Nil | Nil | Nil | |
| | | | (iii) | Tertiary Sector | | | | |
| | | | | Social worker | 1 | Nil | 2 | |
| | | | | Service | 2 | - | 4 | |
| | | | | Tractor Driver | 1 | - | | |
| | | Grand Total | | | 51 | Nil | 51 | |

* According to the classification of main workers by sectors (Primary, Secondary and (Tertiary).

The Primary Census Abstract (PCA) gives the classification of workers by nine fold industrial categories. For a more meaningful economic analysis, workers can be grouped into Primary, Secondary and Tertiary Sectors. Workers in Primary Sector would include all those who are working in industrial categories I,II, III and IV, i.e. all those who are classified as cultivators; agricultural labourers; workers in livestock, forestry, fishing, hunting and plantations and other activities alled to agriculture; and those working in mining and quarrying. Secondary sector would include workers who have been classified under industrial categories V and VI, i.e. manufacturing, processing etc. Servicing and repairs have been separately classified into those working in household industries and those working in non-household industries.

Tertiary Sector would include workers classified under industrial categories VII, VIII and IX, i.e. those working in trade and commerce; transport. storage and communications; and other services.

*Source* : Final population totals paper-2 of 1992 Census of India 1991, series 1, India.

**Table 3 (A)**

**Blockwise and Genderwise Sectoral (Primary, Secondary and Tertiary Sector) Occupations of the 25 Beneficiaries of theVillage Guttigarha, Block Murhu, Khunti subdivision, Ranchi District**

| *S.N.* | *Blocks* | *Villages* | *Occupations* | | *Male* | *Female* | *Total* | *Remarks* |
|---|---|---|---|---|---|---|---|---|
| 1. | Murhu | Guttigarha | (i) | Primary Sector | | | | Almost all the beneficiaries are engaged in Primary Sector |
| | | | | Agriculture | 24 | Nil | 24 | |
| | | | (ii) | Secondary | | | | No male and female beneficiary is engaged in Secondary Sector. |
| | | | | | Nil | Nil | Nil | |
| | | | (iii) | Tertiary Sector | | | | |
| | | | | Social workers | 1 | Nil | 1 | Only one beneficiary is engaged in the Tertiary Sector |
| | | | Grand Total | | 25 | Nil | 25 | |

**Table 3 (B)**

**Blockwise and Genderwise Sectoral (Primary, Secondary and Tertiary Sector) Occupations of the 26 Beneficiaries of the Village Rukka, Block Ormanjhi of Ranchi District, Ranchi District**

| *S.N.* | *Blocks* | *Villages* | *Occupations* | *Male* | *Female* | *Total* | *Remarks* |
|---|---|---|---|---|---|---|---|
| 1. | Ormanjhi | Rukka | (i) Primary Sector | | | | |
| | | | Agriculture | 23 | Nil | 23 | Most of the beneficiaries are engaged in Primary Sector only |
| | | | (ii) Secondary | | | | No male or female beneficiary is engaged in Secondary Sector. |
| | | | | Nil | Nil | Nil | |
| | | | (iii) Tertiary Sector | | | | |
| | | | Service | 2 | Nil | 3 | Very few are engaged in the Tertiary Sector |
| | | | Tractor Driver | 1 | | | |
| | | | Grand Total | 26 | Nil | 26 | |

**Table 4**

**Blockwise and Genderwise Literacy and Education Level in two Chosen Block (Murhu and Ormanjhi) of Ranchi, Jharkhand**

| *S.N.* | *Name of the Block and village* | *Name of the beneficiary* | *Details of Male Literacy* | | |
|---|---|---|---|---|---|
| | | | *Illiterate* | *Literate upto 5th Pass* | *VI and above* |
| 1. | Murhu (Gutigarha) | Sh. Ragunath Munda | - | 3rd pass | - |
| 2. | " | Sh. Sunil Munda | - | 3rd pass | - |
| 3. | " | Sh. Panda Munda | - | 3rd pass | - |
| 4. | " | Sh. Aitwa Munda | - | - | Non Matric |
| 5. | " | Sh. Prau Munda | - | - | 9th Pass |
| 6. | " | Sh. Bisa Munda | - | - | 9th Pass |
| 7. | " | Sh. Sainic Munda | Illiterate | - | - |
| 8. | " | Sh. Pulti Munda | - | - | 7th Pass |
| 9. | " | Sh. Hathi Ram Munda | Illiterate | - | - |
| 10. | " | Sh. Sama Munda | - | - | 8th Pass |
| 11. | " | Sh. Bodai Munda | - | 3rd pass | - |
| 12. | " | Sh. Parau Munda | Illiterate | - | - |
| 13. | " | Sh. Galu Munda | - | - | 7th Pass |
| 14. | " | Sh. Lomba Munda | Illiterate | - | - |
| 15. | " | Sh. Ram Munda | Illiterate | - | - |
| 16. | " | Sh. Kurchu Munda | Illiterate | - | - |
| 17 | " | Sh. Ramai Munda | | - | 9th Pass |

(Contd.)

*(Contd.)*

| S. N. | Name of the Block and village | Name of the beneficiary | Details of Male Literacy | | |
|---|---|---|---|---|---|
| | | | Illiterate | Literate upto 5th Pass | VI and above |
| 18 | " | Sh. Samu Munda | - | - | Non Matric |
| 19. | " | Sh. Panda Munda | - | - | Non Matric |
| 20. | " | Sh. Dayal Singh Munda | - | - | Matric |
| 21. | " | Sh. Ramai Munda | - | Literate | - |
| 22. | " | Sh. Mangan Munda | - | - | Inter Pass |
| 23. | " | Sh. Sagar Munda | - | 3rd Pass | - |
| 24. | " | Sh. Bhaiya Ram Munda | - | - | Upto 10th Std |
| 25. | " | Sh. Lodo Munda | - | Literate | - |
| 26. | Ormanjhi (Rukka) | Sh. Lodo Oraon | Illiterate | - | - |
| 27. | " | Sh. Udai Oraon | Illiterate | - | - |
| 28. | " | Sh. Suresh Oraon | Illiterate | - | - |
| 29. | " | Sh. Birsa Oraon | - | - | Matric |
| 30. | " | Sh. Mogo Oraon | - | 4th Pass | - |
| 31. | " | Sh. Binod Oraon | - | 5th Pass | - |
| 32. | " | Sh. Chanda Munda | Illiterate | - | - |
| 33. | " | Sh. Mahavir Oraon | - | - | Matric |
| 34 | " | Sh. Mukra Oraon | - | 5th Pass | - |
| 35 | " | Sh. Kamal Oraon | - | - | Matric |
| 36 | " | Sh. Aaitwa Oraon | - | - | 6th Pass |
| 37 | " | Sh. Madhu Oraon | - | 3rd Pass | - |

*(Contd.)*

*(Contd.)*

| *S..N.* | *Name of the Block and village* | *Name of the beneficiary* | *Details of Male Literacy* | | |
|---|---|---|---|---|---|
| | | | *Illiterate* | *Literate upto 5th Pass* | *VI and above* |
| 38 | " | Sh. Sakli Chan Munda | - | Primary Passed | - |
| 39. | " | Sh.Dani Ram Munda | - | Primary Passed | - |
| 40. | " | Sh. Birsa Munda | - | Primary Passed | - |
| 41. | " | Sh. Jagnu Pahan | Illiterate (Can write name) | - | - |
| 42. | " | Sh. Balram Pahan | - | - | Matric |
| 43. | " | Sh. Suklal Munda | - | - | 9th Pass |
| 44. | " | Sh. Lakhia Munda | - | 3rd Pass | - |
| 45. | " | Sh. Jaleshwar Pahan | - | 4th Pass | - |
| 46. | " | Sh. Doman Pahan | Illiterate | - | - |
| 47. | " | Sh. Sadhana Oraon | - | - | Matric Pass |
| 48. | " | Sh. Somra Oraon | - | - | Matric Pass |
| 49. | " | Sh. Shankar Oraon | - | - | Interrmediate Pass |
| 50. | " | Sh. Mangru Oraon | - | - | Middle Pass |
| 51. | " | Sh. Ram Swarup Oraon | - | - | Non Matric |
| Total | | | 12 | 16 | 23 |

**NB :** Among the persons interviewed, there were no female beneficiaries.

**Table 5**

**Blockwise and Genderwise Literacy Levels of ST Beneficiaries in Two Chosen Blocks (Murhu and Ormanjhi) of Ranchi District and their Occupational details**

| *Block (Murhu and* | *Illiterates* | | *-5* | | *+5* | | | | *Total* |
|---|---|---|---|---|---|---|---|---|---|
| *Ormanjhi)* | *M* | *F* | *M* | *F* | *M* | *F* | *M* | *F* | |
| Primary Sector | | | | | | | | | |
| Village : | 06 | Nil | 07 | Nil | 11 | Nil | 24 | Nil | |
| 1. Gutigarha | | | | | | | | | 47 |
| 2. Rukka | 06 | Nil | 07 | Nil | 10 | Nil | 23 | Nil | |
| Secondary Sector | Nil | Nii | Nil | Nil | Nil | Nil | Nil | Nil | |
| Tertiary Sector | Nil | Nil | 01 | Nil | 03 | Nil | 04 | Nil | 04 |
| Grand Total | 12 | Nil | 15 | Nil | 24 | Nil | 51 | Nil | 51 |

**Table 5 (A)**

**Blockwise and Genderwise Literacy Levels of ST Beneficiaries in the Blocks of Murhu of Ranchi District and their Occupational details**

| *Block Murhu* | *Illiterates* | | *-5* | | *+5* | | | | *Total* |
|---|---|---|---|---|---|---|---|---|---|
| | *M* | *F* | *M* | *F* | *M* | *F* | *M* | *F* | |
| Primary Sector | | | | | | | | | |
| Village : | 06 | Nil | 07 | Nil | 11 | Nil | 24 | Nil | 24 |
| 1. Guttigarha | | | | | | | | | |
| Secondary Sector | Nil | Nil | Nil | Nil | Nil | Nil | Nil | Nil | |
| Tertiary Sector | Nil | Nil | Nil | Nil | 01 | Nil | 01 | Nil | 01 |
| Grand Total | 06 | Nil | 07 | Nil | 12 | Nil | 25 | Nil | 25 |

**Table 5 (B)**

**Blockwise and Genderwise Literacy Levels of ST Beneficiaries in the Blocks of Ormanjhi of Ranchi District and their Occupational Details**

| *Block Chakrata and Kalsi* | *Illiterates* | | *-5* | | *–5* | | | | *Total* |
|---|---|---|---|---|---|---|---|---|---|
| | *M* | *F* | *M* | *F* | *M* | *F* | *M* | *F* | |
| Primary Sector | | | | | | | | | |
| Village : | 06 | Nil | 07 | Nil | 10 | Nil | 23 | Nil | 23 |
| 1. Rukka | | | | | | | | | |
| Secondry Sector | Nil | Nil | Nil | Nil | Nil | Nil | Nil | Nil | Nil |
| Tertiary Sector | Nil | Nil | 01 | Nil | 02 | Nil | 03 | Nil | 03 |
| Grand Total | 06 | Nil | 08 | Nil | 12 | Nil | 26 | Nil | 26 |

**Table 6**

**Blockwise and Genderwise Occupational Level of ST Beneficiaries in the two Blocks (Murhu and Ormanjhi) and their Occupational Details**

| *S.N.* | *Occupations* | *Male* | *Female* | *Total* | *Remarks* |
|---|---|---|---|---|---|
| 1. | Primary Sector | | | | |
| | Agriculture | 47 | Nil | 47 | No female beneficiary in Primary Sector |
| 2. | Secondary Sector | | | | |
| | Nil | Nil | Nil | Nil | No Male and Female beneficiary in Secondary Sector |
| 3. | Tertiary Sector | | | | No Female beneficiary in Tertiary Sector |
| | Social worker | 01 | Nil | | |
| | Service | 02 | Nil | 04 | |
| | Tractor Driver | 01 | Nil | | |
| | Total | 51 | Nil | 51 | No Female beneficiary in all the three sectors |

**Table 6 (A)**

**Occupations of the ST Beneficiaries (Genderwise) in Village Guttigarha of Murhu Block of Ranchi District, Jharkhand**

| *S.N.* | *Occupations* | *Male* | *Female* | *Total* | *Remarks* |
|---|---|---|---|---|---|
| 1. | Primary Sector | | | | |
| | Agriculture | 24 | Nil | 24 | No female beneficiary in Primary Sector |
| 2. | Secondary Sector | | | | |
| | Nil | Nil | Nil | Nil | No Male and Female beneficiary in Secondary Sector |
| 3. | Tertiary Sector | | | | |
| | Social worker | 01 | Nil | 01 | No Female beneficiary in Tertiary Sector |
| | Total | 25 | Nil | 25 | No Female beneficiary in all the three sectors |

**Table 6 (B)**

**Occupations of the ST Beneficiaries (Genderwise) in Village Rukka of Ormanjhi Block of District Ranchi, Jharkhand**

| *S.N.* | *Occupations* | *Male* | *Female* | *Total* | *Remarks* |
|---|---|---|---|---|---|
| 1. | Primary Sector | | | | |
| | Agriculture | 23 | Nil | 23 | No female beneficiary in Primary Sector |
| 2. | Secondary Sector | | | | |
| | Nil | Nil | Nil | Nil | No Male and Female beneficiary in Secondary Sector |
| 3. | Tertiary Sector | | | | |
| | Service | 02 | Nil | 03 | No Female beneficiary in Tertiary Sector |
| | Tractor Driver | 01 | Nil | | |
| | Total | 26 | Nil | 26 | No Female beneficiary in all the three sectors |

Table 7
**Sectorwise Classification of Main Workers of both the Blocks (Murhu and Ormanjhi)**

| *Sectors* | *Male Workers* | *Female workers* | *Total workers* |
|---|---|---|---|
| (i) Primary Sector | 47 (92.15%) | Nil (0 %) | 47 (92.15%) |
| (ii) Secondary Sector | Nil (0 %) | Nil (0 %) | Nil (0 %) |
| (iii) Tertiary Sector | 04 (8 %) | Nil (0 %) | 04 (8 %) |
| Total | 51 (100 %) | Nil (0 %) | 51 (100 %) |

**Table 7 (A)**
**Literacy Position of Surveyed Households**

| *Blocks* | *Illiterate* | *Literate* | *Total* |
|---|---|---|---|
| (i) Guttigarha village of Murhu Block is inhabited by Mundas (ST) exclusively. | 06 (12 %) | 19 (37.25 %) | 25 (49.01 %) |
| (ii) Ormanjhi Block is inhabited by Mundas, Oraon and Pahan | 06 (12 %) | 20 (39.21 %) | 26 (51 %) |
| Total | 12 (23.29 %) | 39 (76 .47 %) | 51( 100 %) |

**Table 7 (B)**
**Male and Female Position of Surveyed Households**

| *Blocks* | *Male* | *Female* | *Total* |
|---|---|---|---|
| (i) Murhu Block (Khunti Sub-division) | 25 | Nil (0 %) | 25 (49.01 %) |
| (ii) Ornanjhi Block (Ranchi Sub-division) | 26 | Nil (0 %) | 26 ( 51%) |
| Total | 51 (100 % ) | Nil (0 %) | 51 (100 % ) |

**Table 8 : Income Generated by the Beneficiaries in Murhu and Ormanjhi Blocks of Ranchi District**

| S. N. | Income of Different Categories of Beneficiaries | Amount (Rs.) |
|---|---|---|
| 1. | Average monthly income of an illiterate male beneficiary | 926.08 |
| 2. | Average yearly income of an illiterate male beneficiary | 11113.00 |
| 3. | Average monthly income of an illiterate female beneficiary | Nil |
| 4. | Average yearly income of an illiterate female beneficiary | Nil |
| 5. | Average monthly income of a literate male beneficiary | 1022.05 |
| 6. | Average yearly income of a literate male beneficiary | 12265.00 |
| 7. | Average monthly income of a literate female beneficiary | Nil |
| 8. | Average yearly income of a literate female beneficiary | Nil |
| 9. | Total monthly income of all the beneficiaries engaged in the Primary Sector | 51651.00 |
| 10. | Total monthly income of all the beneficiaries engaged in the Secondary Sector | Nil |
| 11. | Total monthly income of all the beneficiaries engaged in the Tertiary Sector | 1250.00 |
| 12. | Total monthly income generated by all the beneficiaries engaged in all the three sectors | 66025.00 |
| 13. | Average monthly income of a beneficiary engaged in Primary Sector | 1122.84 |
| 14. | Average monthly income of a beneficiary engaged in Secondary Sector | Nil |
| 15. | Average monthly income of a beneficiary engaged in Tertiary Sector | 312.50 |
| 16. | Average monthly income of a beneficiary combining all the three Sectors | 1435.00 |
| 17. | Average yearly income of a beneficiary combining in all the three Sectors | 17220.00 |

# Concentration of Tribal Population (1991)

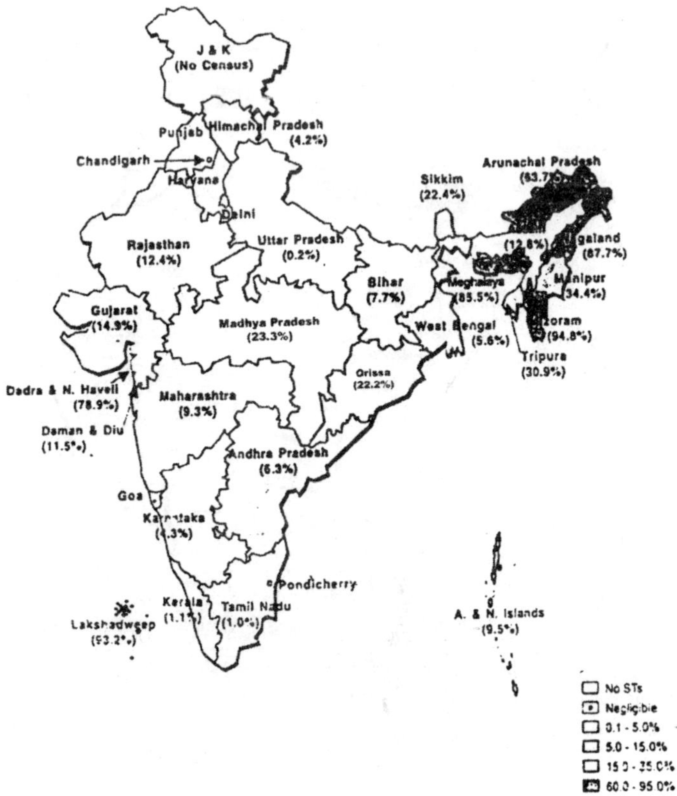

MAP OF
TEHSIL CHAKRATA
DIST. DEHRA DUN
RIVER TONS
TAROCH
JUBBAL
TEHRI-GARHWAL
RIVER JAMUNA
DEHRA DUN
DEVGHAR
BAWAR
PHANAR
VANADHAR
LAKHAU
SILGAON BAWAR
BHARAM
MASAU
JUNGLAT
KELO
DHANAU
BONDUR
MOHANA
DASAU
CHAKRATA
DWAR
BISLAD
UPARLI ATHGAON
CHHETAR
MALETHA
BANGAON
TAPLAD
ATHGAON CHANDO
BIRMAU
UDPALTA
SELI
SILGAON
SAMALTA
KORU
BISAHAL
BAHALAD
VANA
PAIGAON
FURTAD
LAKHWAR
REFERENCES
BOUNDARY LINE
KHAT BOUNDARY LINE
ROADS
SCHOOLS BOYS GIRLS
BUNGALOW
HOSPITAL
COMMUNITY-PROJECT-CENTRE
POST OFFICES
RIVERS

# Bibliography


1. Verrier Elwin – The Tribal World of Verrier Elwin: an autobiography, OUP, Delhi, 1964.
2. Sharma B.D. – Planning for tribal development, New Delhi, 1984.
3. Andre Beteille – "The definition of tribe": The Tribe, caste and Religion in India edited by Romesh Thapar, The Macmillan company of India Ltd, Meerut, 1977.
4. Sharma B.D. – The Fifth Schedule (Vols. I and II) Sahyog Pustak Kuteer Trust, New Delhi, 2000.
5. Dr. L.P. Vidyarthi (ed) – Tribal Development and its Administration, New Delhi, 1986.
6. Narayan, S. – Perspectives on Tribal Development, New Delhi, 1977.
7. Bhupinder Singh and Neeti Mahanti (ed) – Role of democratic decentralisation (Panchayati Raj in TSP Areas), Inter-India Publications, New Delhi, 1999.
8. Dube, S.C. – Antiquity to Modernity in Tribal India (Vol I) Tribal Studies of India Series, Inter-India Publications, New Delhi, 1998.
9. Kishore C. Padhy – Economic Development of Tribals – Approach, Method and Strategy, New Delhi, 1998.
10. Sharma, O.P. – Scheduled Tribes (Population and Literacy), New Delhi, 1991.
11. Sahay, K.N. – Dynamics and Dimensions of Tribal Societies, New Delhi, 1998.
12. Karmakar, K.G. – The Silenced Drums, New Delhi, 2002.
13. Gupta, Lalan P. – Tribal Development Administration, New Delhi, 1998.
14. Robin D. Tribhuwan – Studies in Tribal Rural and Urban Development, New Delhi, 2000.
15. Nadeem Hasnain – Bonded forever – A study of the Koltas, A CIC Himalayan tribe, Harnam Publications, New Delhi, 1982.
16. Dhyani, R.P. – A new approach to economic planning for the rural poor of Uttaranchal, Delhi, 2001.
17. Amir Hassan – Tribal Administration in India, B.R. Publishing Corporation, New Delhi, 1988.
18. L.N. Bhagat and U.K. Verma – Tribal Area Development, need

for alternate strategy, Ranchi University, Ranch, 2000.

19. Verrier Elwin – The Baiga, London, 1939.

20. J.P. Singh and N.N. Vyas (ed) – Tribal Development (Himanshu Publications, Udaipur, 1989).

21. Roy Burman, B.K. – Perspective for administration and development of Scheduled Tribes, NICD, Hyderabad, 1975.

22. Basu, Ashok R. – Tribal Development Programmes and administration in India, National Book Organisation, New Delhi, 1985.

23. Singh, Ajit Kumar – Tribal Development in India, New Delhi.

24. Majumdar, D.N. – Himalayan Polyandry – A study of Jaunsar – Bawar (Asia Publishing House, New Delhi, 1962).

25. Singh, K.S. – People of India, National Series Vol. III (The Scheduled Tribes), OUP, Delhi, 1994.

26. Biswas, S.K. (ed) – Central Himalayan Panorama (Vols. I & II), Institute of Social Research and Applied Anthropology, Calcutta, 1993.

27. Verrier Elwin – A philosophy for NEFA (2nd edition, Shillong, 1959).

28. Berreman, Gerald D. – Hindus of the Himalayas: ethnography and change (University of California Press 1972).

29. P.C. Pandey and others (ed) – Economy of Uttaranchal: Profile and Dynamics of change, New Delhi, 2001.

30. Guha, Ramchandra – Savaging the Civilised; Verrier Elwin, his tribals and India (OVP, New Delhi, 1999).

31. H.G. Walton – Gazetteer of Dehradun, 1911 (Reprinted in 1995 by Natraj Publishers, Dehradun).

32. Bhupinder Singh and Neeti Mahanti – Tribal Education in India, Inter-India publications, New Delhi, 1995

33. Singh, K.S. – India's Communities, People of India National Series Volumes IV to VI, OUP, New Delhi, 1998.

34. Singh, K.S. (ed.) – The tribal situation in India, Indian Institute of Advanced Study, simla, 1972.

35. Singh, K.S. (ed.) – Economics of the tribes and their transformation concept, New Delhi, 1982.

36. Singh, R.S. – changing occupational structure of scheduled tribes, Inter-India publications, New Delhi, 1986.

37. Sengupta, Nirmal (ed.) – Fourth World Dynamics: Jharkhand, Author Guild publications, Delhi, 1982.

38. Dubey, S.N. and Murdia, Ratna (eds.) 'Land Alienation and

Restoration in Tribal Communities in India', Himalaya Publishing House, Mumbai, 1977.

39. Fernandes, Walter, 'Forests, Environment and Tribal Economy, Indian Social Institute, New Delhi, 1988.

40. Lal, J.B., 'India's Forests, Myth and Reality' Natraj Publishers, Dehradun, 1989.

41. Paney, A.K. - Tribal Society in India Manak Publications Pvt. Ltd., New Delhi, 1977.

42. Bhatt, S.C. - The District Gazetteer of Jharkhand Gyan Publishing House, New Delhi, 2002.

43. Narayan, S. (ed.) - Jharkhand Movement, origin and Evolution, Inter-India Publications, New Delhi, 1992.

44. Sharat Kumar and Praveen Jha (eds.) - Development of Bihar and Jharkhand, Shipra Publications, Delhi, 2001.

45. Basu, Sajal - Jharkhand Movement, ethnicity and culture of silence, Indian Institute of Advanced Study, Simla, 1994.

## Reports

1. Report of the Scheduled Areas, and Scheduled Tribes Commission (1960-61) headedby Shri U.N. Dhebar, Publications Division, Government of India, New Delhi.

2. 28th and 29th Report (1987-89) of the Commissioner for SCs and STs.

3. Annual reports of the National Commission for SCs and STs (1996-97 and 1997-98).

4. Annual reports of the Ministry of Tribal Affairs, Government of India, New Delhi for the years 2000-2002.

5. Annual reports (2000-2002) of the Ministry of Rural Development, Government of India, New Delhi.

6. Annual report (2000-2001) of the Ministry of Agriculture and Cooperation, Government of India, New Delhi.

7. Annual report (2000-2001) of the Ministry of Environment and Forests, Government of India, New Delhi.

8. Working group reports of the Eighth, Ninth and Tenth Five Year Plans, Planning Commission, Government of India, New Delhi.

9. State of Forest report, Forest Survey of India, Dehradun, 1997.

10. Compendium of circulars and guidelines on Tribal Development, Tribal Development Division, Ministry of Welfare, Government of India, New Delhi, 1990.

11. District Gazetter of Dehradun District (1976).

12. District Census Handbook of Dehradun district, 1981.
13. Human Development Report, 2002 published by UNDP, OUP, 2002.
14. India Development Report, 2002 edited by Kirit S. Parikh and R. Radhakrishna, Indira Gandhi Institute of Development Research (OUP, New Delhi, 2002).
15. The Administrator, Spring 1975, Published by LBSNAA, Mussoorie.
16. The Administrator 38 (April – June 1993), Published by LBSNAA, Mussoorie.
17. National Family Health survey of Jharkhand (NFHS-2), 1998-99 published by the International Institute for Population Sciences, Mumbai (February 2002).
18. Tribals of Jharkhand: Victims of Development Indian Social Institute, New Delhi, 1995.
19. Report on Tribal and Forest question in Bihar prepared by Land Reforms Unit of Lal Bahadur Shastri National Academy of Administration, Mussoorie, 1991.
20. District Gazetteer of Ranchi district.

# Index